1 The apartment at
  Greifswalder Strasse 43
2 Hans Loewenstein's apartment
3 Ulrich's apartment house
4 Dudacy's apartment
5 Billiard Saal
6 Trudy's and Ilse's apartment house
7 Kitty's establishment
8 Opa's apartment
9 Eva's restaurant
10 The Vier Jahreszeiten and
   the Janowitz Bridge

SOARING UNDERGROUND

A Young Fugitive's Life in Nazi Berlin

SOARING UNDERGROUND

A Young Fugitive's Life in Nazi Berlin

by

Larry Orbach

and

Vivien Orbach-Smith

COMPASS PRESS
WASHINGTON, D.C.

Edited by Grammarians, Inc.
Cover designed by Janet West Garrett
Book and text designed by Anne Meagher-Cook and Gary Roush
Printed (alk paper) and bound by R.R. Donnelley

Published simultaneously in the U.K.

Library of Congress Cataloguing-in-Publication Data

Orbach, Larry, 1924–
    Soaring Underground : a young fugitive's life in Nazi Berlin
    by Larry Orbach and Vivien Orbach-Smith.
                                                        p. cm.
    ISBN 0-929590-15-5 (alk. paper)
    1. Orbach, Larry, 1924– 2. Jews–Persecutions–Germany–Berlin.
    3. Holocaust, Jewish (1939-1945)–Germany–Berlin–Personal
    narratives.   4. World War, 1939-1945–Underground movements,
    Jewish.   5. Berlin (Germany)–Ethnic relations.
    I. Orbach-Smith, Vivien, 1952- . II. Title.
DS135.G5073   1995
940.53' 18' 092–dc20
                                                [B]95-44274
                                                    CIP

The Compass Press
a Division of Howells House
Box 9546 Washington, DC 20016

I dedicate this book to
my beloved wife, Ruth Geier Orbach,
and to the memory of my dear parents,
Aaron and Nelly Orbach.

– L.O.

For the Third Generation: Tahlia Rebecca, Arielle
Johanna, and Jacob Alexander Orbach-Smith, and
Juliet Nelly Orbach. May their spirits be free to soar
in a peaceful and tolerant world.

– V.O-S.

"I sometimes ask myself: Would anyone, either Jew or
non-Jew, understand this about me, that I am simply a
young girl badly in need of some rollicking fun?"

– Anne Frank, *The Diary of a Young Girl*

Contents

Preface

When I was a young man, I spent nearly two years in the underground in Nazi Berlin, and then eight months in the hell of Auschwitz and Buchenwald. In those years, I learned to thrive where I happened to be and to take what pleasure I could in what I had. The lesson has been with me ever since; to this day, I have always viewed my glass as half full or better, never half empty.

The idea of this book sprang from those bumper stickers that appeared toward the end of the war in Vietnam declaring: "POWs Never Have a Nice Day." When I reflected on my own experience, this slogan struck me as an oversimplification, a misrepresentation of real life in a prison or concentration camp. There was nothing "nice" about a day as a prisoner in a Nazi concentration camp, to be sure, but one's definition of a nice day changes when survival is at stake. A day in which you aren't beaten could be considered "a nice day." It is certainly a lot nicer than the others. A day in which your gnawing hunger is eased by some food is, comparatively, "a nice day." A day in which you have a roof over your head, and freezing temperatures do not chill you to the bone, is another sort of "nice day."

I realized that my years of hiding from the Nazis in war-torn Berlin included quite a few "nice days." It may sound blasphemous to recall that time of darkness, and to remember also the flashes of light and warmth – to speak of romance, friendship, delight, and adventure in the midst of murderous oppression. But that is the way it was. As a teenaged "diver" who survived in the underground network of Jews and other fugitives in Berlin, long after the city had been officially declared *Judenrein,* free of Jews, I was aware that every day might be my last. I clung to life in that civilized city, my city, which had turned morally bankrupt, determined to savor whatever freedom and pleasures I could wrest from it. To improve my chances of survival, and my mother's, I did many things I would never have done in the circumstances in which I had been born and brought up. I am neither proud nor ashamed of them. I reveal them here because they illustrate, I think, what may be normal behavior in a world gone mad.

I realize, of course, that this memoir would have been quite different had I been even a few years older during the time called the Holocaust. As it was, I lost my father, my youth, and many good friends, including several relatives. Had I been older, I would have had a lot more to lose, perhaps a wife and children, everything, as did so many others. Or, had I spent those years trapped and starving in a ghetto or hidden in an attic, much less in a concentration camp, this would have been a totally different story, one without flashes of light or warmth, friendship or adventure, an altogether dark tale which might not have been told at all.

For years I thought about writing this memoir, but I was always too busy with concerns of the moment. That changed one day in November 1988, when I was walking in midtown Manhattan and began having crushing pains in my chest. I had suffered a mild heart attack several years earlier, but these pains were worse than anything I had ever felt. I staggered for blocks, gasping for air and foolishly telling no one, and managed to get myself on a bus back home to New Jersey. About a week later, a triple-bypass heart operation saved my life. But during that nightmarish trek through Times Square, I vowed that, if I were once again fortunate enough to survive, I would tell the story of the time when I found life in the underground.

This book is not an effort to describe the Holocaust, nor does it deal in detail with the months I spent in a concentration camp. I simply could not do justice to the unrelenting horror of Auschwitz, and have not tried to do so; that, I must leave to others. This is a story, then, not about the deaths of millions, but about the life of one young man at that time.

Studies of Holocaust survivors have identified some common traits – adaptability, tenacity, initiative, quick thinking, and the ability to disregard one's emotions and moral qualms by focusing single-mindedly on the goal of survival. I think I had all of them in some measure. I had another asset that has been shown to have been critical to survival – the knowledge that some of one's family still lived. And I had two others as important as any: dumb luck and a faith in my personal God, who seemed always to hover over my shoulder, albeit silently.

After writing this book, and reflecting on my life over the fifty years since I left Germany, I can say that hatred and vengeance have not motivated my life. Rather, it was the blossoming of my identity, commitment, and practice as a Jew, my wholehearted participation in Jewish life in America and in Israel, that was the legacy I took from those dark years from which God delivered me.

The dialogue herein has been recreated to the best of my memory and, while by no means verbatim, reflects the original intent and spirit. Several names and details have been changed to protect the privacy of those who are, or may be, still living. Otherwise, all that is written here is true.

– Larry Orbach
Union, New Jersey

Prologue

In the twilight of a spring evening, I stand unsteadily on a piano stool in the parlor of my parents' Berlin apartment, looking at myself in a gilt-edged mirror above the piano. The year is 1934, and I am ten years old. My mother, in the doorway, gazes at me with delight, though I have said nothing yet. My father sits expectantly in his old wing chair, his hands folded on top of the evening newspaper. Heinz and Manfred, my teenaged brothers, are sprawled on the floor, their expressions a mixture of amusement and envy.

I am about to rehearse an epic poem I have been asked to recite at the commencement exercises of my public school. Although I am only in the fourth grade, I have been selected for this honor because of my success in a schoolwide genealogy project. Through great diligence, not to mention a bit of help from my father, I have traced my German ancestors farther back than has any other student in the school – to the 1490s, when a Moses Auerbach (or Orbach or Urbach, since all three names are spelled alike in Hebrew) was a court Jew to the Bishop of Regensburg.

The school's rector, Herr Bothe, had assigned me the prized soliloquy earlier that day. "My heartiest congratulations, Lothar Orbach!" he had said, pumping my hand mightily. "And remember, you must speak loudly and forcefully, like a Senator!"

Loudly and forcefully, like a Senator. This, I know, will not be difficult for me, because the poem "Kaempfe, Blute!" is among my favorites. It was written by Hoffmann von Fallersleben who also wrote "Deutschland

Ueber Alles," our country's stirring anthem. And there is nothing, nothing in my whole life, I am prouder of than of being a German, a German descended from those who had served in the courts of Bishops. And, in fact, I have already fought and bled, if only a little, for Germany, having recently leapt off my bicycle to join my brother Heinz in a street brawl against some Communist youths who mistook us for members of a Nazi gang.

And so, turning to face my family, I declare in a voice filled with passion:

> *"Kaempfe, blute, werbe; siege oder sterbe,*
> *Deutsch sei bis ins Mark.*
> *Was dich auch bedrohe, eine heil'ge Lohe,*
> *bringt dir Sonnenkraft;*
> *Lass dich nimmer knechten,*
> *lass dich nie entrechten,*
> *Gott gibt den Gerechten*
> *wahre Heldenkraft!"*

(Fight, bleed, propagate; win or die,
be a German to your marrow.
Whatever threatens you,
a holy flame gives you the strength of the sun;
Ne'er let them enslave you,
ne'er forgo your rights,
God gives the righteous
true, heroic powers!)

Then I fold my wiry body into a low bow. Mama begins applauding. My brothers hoot loudly and call out sarcastic "bravos" as they race out the door to meet their friends. Papa rises wordlessly from his chair, and scoops me into a tight embrace. His eyes are filled with tears.

Although we are not a very religious family, I have been taught to pray the Shema Yisroel each night: "Hear,

O Israel, the Lord our God is One." I usually say it before drifting off to sleep. But that night, and for weeks thereafter, as I nestle into my bed I whisper, "Kaempfe, Blute! ..."

Several weeks pass. Just days before the commencement gathering, I am summoned to the rector's office. I am not nervous – in fact, I am exhilarated because I assume he wants to hear my oration, and I know that my delivery is flawless.

The rector smiles at me solicitously from behind his mahogany desk, and motions for me to sit. A portrait of the Fuehrer hangs on the wall facing me. In his usual polite tone, the rector tells me that the administration has decided that it would not be fitting for a Jew to represent the student body by reciting "Kaempfe, Blute!" Because I am a Jew, the indisputable fact that I won the genealogy competition is irrelevant. The second-place winner, a surly sixth grader whose German ancestors are all Aryan, will have the honor.

This cultured, intelligent gentleman, this respected pedagogue, relays this news to me in the most matter-of-fact way, as though he is pointing out some obvious anomaly that makes my participation in the commencement a logical impossibility: you have no legs, so you cannot run the race; you have no arms, so you cannot carry the torch; you are a Jew, so you cannot be a German.

I hold back the tears for what remains of the school day. But when I come home, I run sobbing to my mother. When I tell her what has happened, she is outraged that I, her youngest and most sensitive child, must endure such a disappointment. My father, possessed of a fierce temper, announces that he is going directly to the school to beat the hell out of the rector. My mother beseeches him not to cause trouble. "This racial hatred, you know, it comes and it goes," she reminds him. "In another six months, it

shall all pass." And my brothers – they are outright glee-
ful, because now they need not sit through the boring
commencement exercises, watching the pampered baby
of the family gather all the attention and applause.

That night, in bed, my throat sore, my eyes stinging,
I once again utter "Kaempfe, Blute!" It is my poem. They
cannot take it away from me.

In the days that follow, my mother notes my glum
face and tries to comfort me. "Every childhood has its
hurts, Lotharchen," she says soothingly. "And this one too
will soon stop hurting, though you will probably always
remember it." So this is the way we chose to view this
sorry episode; a lesson learned, a childhood hurt, a rite of
passage.

Today, a lifetime later, I look back and wonder if in
any way I could have sensed that my entire world, everything I trusted and believed in, was about to disintegrate.
That my education, to which I was so committed, would
end with the eighth grade, because no "gymnasium"
would accept me. That my schoolmates, those good-natured, jostling boys on the soccer field, would soon pledge
to destroy me. That my father, a staunch German patriot,
would be sent to die in a concentration camp by the
country he had served valiantly. That during my teens I
would be hunted like an animal and that, to survive, I
would have to cheat, steal, deceive, perhaps kill. Or that
in a dark and distant future, I would find myself repeating
the words "Kaempfe, Blute" as I stood, starving and
bereft, among my dying people in Auschwitz.

No, I didn't know then. I knew that something terribly wrong had happened, that this was not the way things
were supposed to be in my Germany. But I had no idea
of what was to come.

Chapter 1

Born in a Gathering Storm

By all accounts, I had fought vigorously against being born. Could I have had a premonition that I was about to be born in the wrong place at the wrong time?

My mother had delivered four babies before me – my brothers Heinz and Manfred, and two who died shortly after birth – but never had she had such trouble. For eight hours she pushed, and for eight hours the top of my head was visible, yet I remained lodged stubbornly inside her.

"Hold on, Frau Orbach, this may be your best heifer yet!" crooned the diminutive Dr. Schicke who, according to our housekeeper Minna, source of much of my earliest family lore, was sweating as profusely as his patient. Dr. Schicke was the only obstetrician in our small, eastern German village of Falkenburg, and also its only veterinarian. On many occasions he raced from one delivery to another, from a calf to a baby and then to a pony, treating all mothers and offspring with equal gentleness and respect.

My father stood nearby, eyes downcast and shoulders slumped. He looked constantly at his pocket watch, Minna later recounted with some amusement, grousing that it was time to open the store, that someone had to go to work to pay for all these children. The truth was Papa loathed the atmosphere of suffering; for all his bluster, he was the weaker and more tenderhearted of my parents, and could not bear to see his wife so helpless.

From his worn leather bag, Dr. Schicke took a set of huge, tarnished tongs, the same instrument he used to extract uncooperative baby lambs. "This is the only alternative," he whispered to my father, who stood frozen with fear. Panting and groaning, he pulled and squeezed and pulled with the forceps, prying me from my sanctuary into this world.

Alas, Dr. Schicke's ministrations also reshaped my head into a distinctly conical shape, a feature that proved permanent. For years to come my brothers and my schoolmates would call me *Eierkopf,* egghead. The nickname stung until my mother declared, and I leapt to believe, that the extrusion at the top of my head was in fact an extra piece of brain, a reserve of cunning and quick-wittedness that, as it turned out, would prove essential to my survival.

The date was May 22, 1924. Exactly eight days later, in the tradition of all the sons of Abraham, I was circumcised by an elderly mohel, nearsighted and trembling of hand, a specially trained rabbi who came to our town when summoned from the nearby capital of Stettin, for our own Jewish community was too small to afford a full-time circumciser. Afterwards he raised a goblet of sacramental wine, and declared my name before the community of which I was now a member: Eliezer ben Aaron Hacohen, Eliezer the son of my father Aaron, the same name as the son of the Biblical Aaron, and descended from that same lineage of High Priests of the Jewish faith. But exalted as my Hebrew name and its lineage was, it was used only in the synagogue at special times of year. I was, to myself and to one and all, Lothar Orbach. A German boy born of

German parents who happened to be Jewish. And so as Lothar, I embarked upon a carefree, unremarkable childhood in the lush Pomeranian countryside.

As the owners of the town's general store, my parents had many customers and a wide circle of friends, most of whom were not Jewish. People, women especially, were instantly drawn to my father, who exuded a rakish charm, and who was as handsome as an actor with his lustrous mane of mahogany hair and heavy-lidded hazel eyes. My mother was not as good-looking as her spouse, and she walked with a pronounced limp because of a childhood accident, but her keen dark eyes bespoke such forthrightness and intelligence that she commanded respect and admiration. My parents were sociable people, and our comfortable home was regularly the scene of noisy songfests and marathon card games.

My brothers and I were alternately spoiled and spanked by our adoring parents, who left us largely on our own while they worked long hours at the store. Schoolwork rarely interfered with playtime, for little value was placed on education or intellectual discourse by the simple farmers in this small village. In retrospect, it was a region rife with ignorance and superstition in which prejudice could easily take root.

My most vivid memory of my birthplace, ironically, is of the event that would trigger our family's departure. I was four years old, and my mother asked me to deliver a sandwich to my father at the local pub, a short walk from our store. Like so many of the other townsmen, he enjoyed spending an hour or two each day in the *Wirthaus*, Falkenburg's only pub and the site of every sort of gathering and celebration.

I found my father in his usual spot, drinking beer with his clique of friends, and holding forth as always on business or politics or local gossip. He also liked to brag a bit about his record in the German Army during World War I; as a Master Sergeant in the Medical Corps, he was awarded the Iron Cross, Second Class, for bravery after he caught and shot a knife-wielding French renegade in his barracks near Sedan.

I was sitting by my father's side when two bearded Orthodox Jews entered the pub, dressed in Hasidic garb – long black caftans, laced high boots, and large, fur-trimmed, black felt hats. Their clothing, though decidedly out of place, was finely cut and immaculate, for the two men were prosperous businessmen, well-known feed merchants who served all the local hamlets. While they did not socialize with their customers, they were highly regarded by the farming community because their prices, products, and general business dealings were considered fair.

A fellow named Wilhelm von Puttkammer reached across me to grab my father's arm. "Arnold, can you smell how all of a sudden it stinks in here?" he said in a loud voice. My father stared uncomprehendingly at Willi, who pressed on. "You mean to tell me you can't smell those two from over here?" he bellowed, holding his nose. "It reeks of garlic, it is terrible!"

Papa's face turned red and a vein in his neck began to pound. "You're right, Willi, I can smell it now," he said. "You probably shit in your pants, you son of a bitch, that's what stinks!"

Willi looked at my father with narrowing eyes. "What do you mean? Don't you see those Jews over there, those parasites? They are the ones who create all the problems in the world, they make the German folk suffer! You had better understand it now, my friend, before it is too late!"

"Well I am one of those parasites," said my father in an even tone. "And I will show you where it really smells, where you belong!" With those words, my father rose to his feet. He was a powerfully built man, and the elfin Willi was no match for him. I watched him pick up his stunned tablemate like a toy, carry him yowling into the pub's back room, and throw him through the open window onto a pile of fresh manure.

What was I, a young child, to make of all this? I was shaken by the menacing tones I heard around me, but it was thrilling to witness my own father transformed into a real-life "Superman" who tossed his adversaries out of windows. What I didn't understand was why my father had assaulted one of his own comrades in defense of them, the foreign-looking men in the funny clothing. The everyday rhythms of our family's life were more akin to those of a Willi von Puttkammer than to the bearded men who had fled the pub. It was clear that those men were aliens and outcasts. I viewed them that way myself, and did not understand how my father or I could be connected to them.

Papa took my hand, and we exited the pub. I sprinted ahead to the general store because I couldn't wait to tell Mama about his heroic display of brute force, an event far more exciting than the fumbling fights in which we youngsters routinely engaged. But Mama didn't seem excited at all. "You're all right, Arnold?" she asked quietly. He nodded and looked at Mama with a sorrowful, clouded expression I had never seen before, an expression I realized much later was fear.

Wilhelm von Puttkammer became the most outspoken Jew-hater in Falkenburg, and he and his cronies made life miserable for its few Jewish families. Years later, we would learn that he had been appointed one of the *Gauleiters*, or vice governors, of Pomerania, overseeing the mass deportations of Jewish citizens and seizing their property.

As brown shirts and Nazi uniforms became common in the village, many of the townspeople boycotted our store. Its front windows were smashed on several occasions, and we knew very well by whom, but we had no proof and no recourse. Papa stopped going to the Wirthaus, and few neighbors greeted us as usual. We children continued our rough and tumble play, but it was laced with a new antagonism.

Less than a year after my father's confrontation with Willi von Puttkammer, he and my mother sold their store and all its contents. They received only a small fraction of the business's worth, but it was better than going bankrupt, being further vandalized, or worse. With this modest nest egg, our parents announced, we would make a new start where there were more of our own kind, a cosmopolitan city populated by people of learning and culture, where diversity was better tolerated, and where bright youngsters like us would have greater opportunities.

And so, within weeks, the Orbach family boarded a train bound for Berlin. As the train snaked through the verdant countryside, the five of us sat silently, eating oranges my mother had packed for the trip. The serene landscape outside the window looked like a picture postcard; how beautiful and sedate was this homeland of ours, how incongruous with the ugliness that had led to our departure.

We moved in with my grandmother, Fanny, who was alone after the recent death of my grandfather. She lived in a spacious second-floor apartment on Greifswalder Strasse, a middle-class neighborhood in the eastern part of the city. There were four medium-sized buildings in our complex, with an inner courtyard that was an ideal place to run and play. My mother's mother was a dour woman who kept largely to herself. My parents always treated her with respect, as did we boys, but she did not seem interested in any kind of relationship with us. Papa put his experience as a merchant to good use, and landed a job as a salesman for a large textile manufacturer. Mama threw herself into her role as Hausfrau, a relatively new experience, for she had been co-owner and bookkeeper of the general store and, in the years before her marriage, the executive secretary to the president of a large corporation. Yet she was equally talented at cooking and baking, and quickly became known throughout the neighborhood for her delicately seasoned whitefish, savory lamb shanks with potatoes and green beans, and her moist, fragrant plumcake.

In September, like every other German child about to enter kindergarten, a picture was taken of me holding my enormous *Zuckertuete*, a funnel-shaped cardboard container stuffed at the bottom with paper and brimming at the top with colorfully wrapped candies. Learning came easily to me, and I relished every minute in the classroom. My teacher for the first three years was a middle-aged woman with the most gentle, soothing voice. I could hardly wait to see her each day. Clearly, school would be a place where I would thrive, even excel.

I got along well with the other boys, and had many friends. Of my class of twenty-four children, four of us were Jews. Coincidentally, three of the four, myself included, were the best students in the class and we were well liked since we readily gave our time to anyone who needed help with his schoolwork. After school, I would return to the apartment, quickly complete my homework, and then run back outside until after dark. Although we had few store-bought toys, boredom was unknown to us. When the weather was good, we played soccer for hours on end, breaking many windows and occasionally losing our ball to some enraged apartment dweller. Even in the pouring rain, there was fun to be had: my friends and I, drenched to the bone, would throw matchsticks into the gutter, assign each match the name of a famous race-car driver – mine was always the Italian champion Nuvolari – and cheer them on as they streamed downhill in the surging rainwater. The first match to reach the next street corner was the winner. I stayed indoors only when I was being punished.

Our large veranda, which held a table that could seat a dozen, was also the site of many birthday parties and holiday gatherings. Late into the night, we joined Mama and Papa and their friends as they ate and drank and serenaded passersby with *Deutsche Lieder*, the lively and often touching German folksongs. The Orbach home, as in Falkenburg, was once again a social hub. Only now, most of my parents' friends were Jewish.

Jewish, yes; but, like us, not "too" Jewish. My mother, while she believed in God and prayed to Him fervently each night, had received little religious training from her own parents. My father enjoyed Jewish ritual and liturgy, and took me to synagogue with some regularity. He particularly loved presiding over the Passover table each year and conducting the family's Seder. But deeply devout Jews, like the ones we and Willi von Puttkammer had seen in the pub in Falkenburg, remained alien to us. We were Germans first, and Jews second, and disdained anyone for whom religion superseded national identity. My father rose through the ranks to become president of the local chapter of the Reichsbund Juedischer Frontsoldaten, an elite Jewish veteran's organization. He never went out without wearing his veteran's insignia, a black, red, and gold ribbon, pinned to his lapel. Mama once showed me one of his letters from army training camp in 1916, just after they were married: "Kaiser Wilhelm has said that we must persist as long as the Fatherland is in peril," he had written. "No German man shall be missing who is healthy and strong enough to defend his Fatherland!"

My brothers and I were members of the Bund Deutsch Juedisher Jugend, an umbrella organization for Jewish youth that included political groups, and scouting and sports clubs. We were proud to march behind its banner at the annual Jewish Sportfest held at the Grunewald Sportsplatz, a large Berlin stadium, where we competed in track and field, soccer, and other sports against other Jewish groups. Some of them were Zionists, with the left-wing ideology of Hashomer-Hatzair or the militantly right-wing Betar. We regularly got into fist-fights and shouting matches with those opponents because, to many of us, Zionism was a traitorous ideology; the Holy Land was an ancient artifact revered by those bearded rabbis and their narrow-minded flocks, old-fashioned types who were sadly ignorant of the blessings of German culture and civilization.

During those early years, our new life in Berlin was so happy and rewarding that my parents regularly congratulated themselves for their wisdom in fleeing Pomerania. They did not anticipate that, with the election of Adolf Hitler as chancellor, a murderous hatred would begin to poison Germany's elite as readily as it had consumed the simple farm folk we had left behind. In February 1933, barely a month after Hitler's election, Berlin's parliamentary building was set ablaze, and the Communists were blamed. The arsonist was said to be a Dutchman named Van der Lubbe, who was scapegoated in an absurd trial and executed amidst great fanfare, as a warning to all supposed enemies of the state. This episode launched the enactment of race laws by the new masters of Germany who sought protection for the good German folk from Hitler's so-called "undesirables," the Jews and their Communist friends.

It so happened that our block was the unofficial border between the Christburger Strasse neighborhood, home of many of the Communist street gangs, and a large Nazi enclave in the Pasteurstrasse district. Street fights between ruffians on both sides became a common occurrence on Greifswalder Strasse, right outside our window. I once ran to assist my brother Heinz when he got caught in the middle of a melee. As he wildly swung his bicycle pump against the Communist punks, a group of young Nazis mistook him for one of their comrades, and helped him escape. One of his defenders called after him to be sure to attend the next Party meeting at the local headquarters.

At ten years old, I was immersed in my studies and sports and secure in my many friendships; the racist headlines and growing unrest in the adult world seemed distant and unreal until … until I was barred from reciting "Kaempfe, Blute!" at the commencement exercises. Even then, our Aryan classmates seemed to want to keep their Jewish friends as long as they could. It was only when their parents began punishing them for associating with us that they turned away, and then reluctantly at first.

Most of the boys and girls I knew ended up joining the Hitler Jugend, as membership became mandatory for all school students. Dressed in perfectly pressed uniforms with ribbons and badges, they marched in big parades far grander than those of my sports club. Some of my classmates were given the honor of carrying the flags and banners; a few even brandished drill weapons. I watched them go, these classmates and teammates and neighborhood friends of mine, withdrawing into their own circle and leaving me outside. I was captivated by the pageantry of the Hitler Jugend, jealous of the camaraderie, and would have joined in a minute. It never occurred to me that I would be an enemy against whom they were joining forces.

In September 1935, the Nuremberg Laws were passed, and the hostile atmosphere became official policy and now pervaded our school. We, the four eleven-year-old Jewish boys of the 228 Volksschule of Berlin, became second-class citizens, our long-standing friendships declared null and void. We were separated from the other pupils, and made to sit in a back corner of the room. The Aryan children were told not to fraternize with us unless absolutely necessary, which was a bitter blow for us as well as for those who had grown dependent on our tutorial services. But I was always an entrepreneur; instead of helping my classmates with their schoolwork for free, I now began selling my answers for ice cream and other treats that were increasingly hard to come by. My parents were clearly unhappy about our treatment at school, but they said nothing; it was the law and, after all, we were Germans, we obeyed.

Even though my grades were excellent, my early application to a topflight Berlin gymnasium was rejected. My three Jewish classmates and I then decided to apply for admission to the Jewish Middle School on the Grosse Hamburger Strasse, for the public school atmosphere was becoming unbearable. One of the boys was a mediocre student whom we had always helped through school, and he was terrified he might fail the entrance examination and be forced to return to the public school class as the only Jew. I promised him I would show him my answers during the test, despite the proctor's lecture about Germany's age-old "honor system." I kept my promise.

I was proud to have helped a friend, but it was a disastrous decision for me – the proctor caught us cheating and ejected us both on the spot. I had blown my chance to enter the only Jewish high school in Berlin, and I was excluded by law from any other public high school. I finished my grammar school days in the back row of the classroom; I buried my head in my books and tried to hear only the voices of the poets, tuning out the taunts of my classmates, and the ominous, raging threats of Adolf Hitler.

In May of 1937, I had my Bar Mitzvah, a subdued celebration that was a far cry from the elaborate, catered affairs that had marked my brothers' comings of age. By then, it was forbidden to gather in a synagogue, so I chanted from the Torah and led a small congregation in the auditorium of the Jewish Orphanage of Berlin, founded in 1833 by a Baruch Auerbach. That Sabbath's reading from the Book of Numbers spoke of the special honor given to the High Priest Aaron and his sons to kindle the lamps of the Tabernacle. The rabbi, in his sermon, said that God had given the Jewish people the mission to be the gentle agency of light unto the world. "And, from this day forward, you, young Lothar, Eliezer son of Aaron the Priest," he declared, "must strive to become a light unto the Jewish people, as God had commanded the 'Kohanim,' the priests from whom you are descended!"

I loved chanting the Trope, the ancient, singsong melody prescribed by the symbols adjacent to the Hebrew characters in the Torah. But I did not feel like a "light" unto the Jewish people. In fact, I felt quite downhearted. My Bar Mitzvah was the last celebration the Orbachs would share as a family, because in a few days my brother Heinz was scheduled to leave the country. Heinz had just been released from the Alexanderplatz Prison after being falsely accused of organizing a Socialist gathering. But he was given an ultimatum: unless he made plans to emigrate immediately, he would face further jail time, or "worse" – meaning deportation to one of those still little-known concentration camps. Fortunately, my family had arranged to receive an emergency affidavit from our cousin Egon Orbach, who owned a small fleet of taxis in New York. Because of the ultimatum to leave or perish, Heinz qualified as a political refugee, and the U.S. Consul gave his application priority.

I longed to go with my brother to America. But as the youngest child, my name was included in my parents' affidavit, which meant I could not emigrate until they did. "You will see, my boy," said Mama, as she hugged my brother goodbye, "this will all be over in six months."

"And soon you will join me in America!" said Heinz, his voice catching. Papa gave him a skeptical look, and repeated his standard line: "Look here, children, if I ever leave the Fatherland, it will be on the very last train."

And then he embraced his eldest son, whom he would never see again.

Chapter 2

The Institute Orbach

With all doors to a high-school education closed to me, I went to work as an apprentice in one of the retail outlets of the textile firm for which my father worked. My new boss was a huge man, weighing at least four hundred pounds, who farted and snorted and spat all day long with no regard for anyone around him. I wanted to quit after the first day, but feared jeopardizing my father's already tenuous position in the sales department. One day, about three weeks into my employment, my boss demanded a glass of water in his usual obnoxious manner. I ran to fetch it, and brought it to him in his cubicle, where he sat in a custom-designed rattan chair, his massive body hanging over the sides. Suddenly he emitted a tremendous fart, which caught me so off guard that I jumped and spilled the water all over him. Mercifully, he fired me on the spot.

After that I went from one menial job to another – handyman, street cleaner, snow shoveler, cart puller, sandblaster – trying to earn what I could to supplement my parents' meager income. While at work, I fantasized about getting my life back, about school and my friends, about being a normal teenager. But events did not support my hopes; in November 1938, came the first official Nazi pogrom, Kristallnacht, the night of broken glass, of broken people, of broken dreams.

From our veranda overlooking the Greifswalder Strasse, I could see a caravan of open military trucks filled with brown-shirted troopers, yelling at the top of their lungs, *"Jude verrecke, Juden raus!"* (Jews should rot, out with the Jews!) I watched the troopers leap off one such vehicle in front of Sochachever's millinery and smash all its windows. They paraded the terrified owners through the streets, wearing placards that read, *Deutsche kauft nicht bei Juden!* (Germans don't buy from Jews!) But they did loot: the good Germans, many of them parents of my schoolmates, swarmed into the store and came out smiling, wearing elegant new hats. When Friedlaender's Chocolatier was destroyed by the Nazis, the neighborhood children grabbed bags of candy, and came out with chocolate all over their faces. There was no shame or protest, only self-satisfied grins and a good deal of backslapping.

The violence of Kristallnacht was shocking but, looking back on it, I realize now that we were all in a state of denial. The morning after Kristallnacht, we learned that many Jewish men had been picked up and sent to destinations unknown — camps of some kind. But a rumor that spread rapidly through our community was that nearly all those arrested were Jews of Polish origin, and it supported the vain notion among families like ours that we Jews who were "true" sons and daughters of Germany would have special status. In the days after Kristallnacht, hundreds of traumatized Jewish families showed up on the steps of the American Consulate at Unter den Linden to seek visas from the then very anti-Semitic U.S. Consul in Berlin, named Rose, or to have existing papers stamped and readied for an immediate exit. But not the Orbachs. We would leave only on the very last train.

In early 1939, I finally found a job I enjoyed, in the French Tourist Office in the beautiful Unter den Linden section. Although as a Jew I could not be called anything other than a messenger, my work was interesting and I became a full member of the staff. All that came to an end, however, with the German invasion of Poland on September 1, and, for us, the beginning of World War II.

When the War Effort Authority decreed that all able-bodied persons must work for the war effort, I was assigned to the German Weapons and Munitions Factories in Borsigwalde, on the outskirts of the city. I worked at least six days a week, sometimes even on Sundays, and twelve hours a day, leaving home around seven and returning at eight. For seventeen pfennig an hour, I polished 88-millimeter howitzer shell casings. We were shown how to polish the insides of the casings with a smoothing sandpaper drill, and were told that any departures from the specifications would make the shells more likely to explode inside the gun or before they arrived on target. This was not considered difficult work because we Germans were renowned for our precision in everything, especially manufacturing. In this case, however, I tried to be an exception; the image of my shells exploding in Nazi gunners' faces simply transported me, and I found I could polish the shells thinner than required without being detected and while looking conscientious. This made for more job satisfaction than I would have had otherwise, but I doubt that my sabotage affected the outcome of the war.

In the factory I met Taddeus Vronski. He was several years older than I was, and strikingly handsome with blond, curly hair, turquoise eyes, and high Slavic cheekbones. He and I were the only two younger men in the galvanizing department, and we attracted a great deal of attention. The ladies, who had a nickname for everyone, christened him "Goldilocks," and me they called the "Wunderkind."

I was a sixteen-year-old virgin, and was uncomfortable – but also aroused – by the blatant sexual advances these women made, including fondling our behinds as we walked by. The *Rassenschande* (race mixing) laws that forbade liaisons between Jews and Aryans were strictly enforced; even a hint of fraternization could cost me my job, or even land me in prison. Much of the time I skulked around with an anxious expression on my face, and I kept largely to myself.

Tad's classic Aryan appearance, however, was an excellent disguise for a young man with a few secrets of his own. One day he whispered to me: "Don't look so gloomy, Lothar! At least we don't have to shoot these things. At least we can say someday that we were on the right side of this shitty war."

I was stunned at his forthrightness, and shyly nodded my approval. Tad told me that he was born in Krakow to a German mother and a Polish father. He and his mother moved to Berlin when he was a boy, after his father was killed in a mining accident. He had been drafted into the German Army, but chose to keep his Polish citizenship. The War Effort Authority had designated him a foreign laborer and remanded him to the factory.

Tad's decision puzzled me. "I'm a Jew so I have to take all this crap," I said, "but you have a chance to live a normal life. You could be in the army, or go to college. I don't get it."

"I don't get *you!*" he countered. "Why should I sell my soul to the devil and fight for these bastards? Shooting at the Poles, the British, the French – for what? This is not *my* war!" His face flushed, and I thought it better to end the exchange before we drew too much attention. But I could not stop thinking about what my new friend had said. Maybe there were others like him, maybe this madness could be stopped by people who believed the way he did.

I was, most of all, preoccupied with my adolescent fantasies about the brazen women who rubbed up against me in the munitions plant, about the great poetry I would write someday, about touring New York in one of Cousin Egon's yellow cabs. I still mooned a bit over Erika Weissmann, a beautiful, haughty girl who attended the Jewish Middle School, and who had stood me up for a movie date some months earlier. In fact, at that point, what distressed me above all was to be barred from public places and entertainment, movie houses, theaters, concert halls, museums, restaurants, and even public bathrooms – to be barred from sitting on a park bench unless it was painted yellow. Here I was, finally old enough to go out on my own, to go on dates and have adventures like my older brothers, and this beautiful, fascinating city, my city, slammed its door in my face.

My parents did what they could to maintain some sense of normalcy. My father organized a bridge club, and every Saturday night our apartment was crowded with people, laughing nervously and smoking and playing cards with an almost frenetic intensity. Sometimes it seemed that all the Jews still in Berlin were inside that apartment, huddled together for warmth and safety.

Increasingly, money became our most pressing problem. My father suffered from diabetes, prostate problems, and gallbladder disease. His health had plummeted after a horribly botched surgery, during which doctors left a sharp instrument lodged inside his bladder. After several lengthy hospitalizations, he was fired from his job, and there was no chance, as a disabled Jew, for him to get another. Despite his flagging energy, he could still trade on his charm and good looks. Olga Schreiner, the daughter of one of our gentile neighbors, had been married to a butcher with a wholesale business in the Hallen, Berlin's central open-air market. She had run the business single-handedly since her husband's death. My father would visit her several times a month, and, though officially Jews were rationed no meat whatsoever, she supplied us with chickens, duck, and even geese. Sometimes my father came home laden with so much food, much more than he had paid for, that we were able to offer some of it to our friends.

I never knew if he had something going with the meat lady, or if it was just his dashing smile – everyone said he resembled the actor Robert Taylor – that persuaded her to throw in all those additional chickens and chops. I was curious, but too loyal a son to dissect my father's behavior or to judge him, for he was unquestionably devoted to my mother and my brothers and me, and I considered us a very happy family.

In the final months of 1940, it seemed as though our troubles might be over. As a contingency measure, my father had reluctantly applied for affidavits when the war had begun with the invasion of Poland. Now the affidavits from cousin Egon arrived, bearing the court stamp of Bronx, New York, with an accompanying letter declaring that cousin Egon awaited our arrival. By 1942, after several operations, my father would recover so well that he was made to work as a forced laborer, but at this time he was still too ill to travel. My mother could not leave because there was no way he could manage without her, and I was legally bound to stay with the two of them. The anti-Semitic U.S. Consul refused to grant us extensions, which meant we would have to apply all over again, a process that already took over a year and was becoming longer with each exodus. But my brother Manfred booked his passage to America.

Then one June morning, in 1941, my grandmother died. With her gone, Heinz already in America, and Manfred about to leave, our apartment seemed vast and empty. Soon thereafter, a friend of Mama's approached us with an idea to help keep the family afloat. She was a social worker with the Juedische Gemeinde, the so-called self-governing body of the Berlin Jews, a well-meaning organization used by the Nazis to monitor the Jewish population. She said that the government had instructed her to set up several state-subsidized halfway houses for female Jewish mental patients considered nonviolent and ready to be released, in order to make more room for Germans in the overcrowded public sanitariums. She admired my mother's organizational and homemaking abilities, and asked if we would consider converting our apartment into such a residence.

After being assured that these women were not dangerous, my mother nervously agreed to take on the new venture. Our apartment had two bedrooms, a sprawling parlor-dining room with an additional triangular alcove (known as a *Berliner Zimmer*), a *Kontor*, home office, a tiny maid's room, a well-appointed kitchen, and one bathroom. We bought eight used beds to accommodate four tenants in each of the two bedrooms. My parents would now sleep in the parlor, and my brother Manfred, until his departure, would share the kontor with me.

The first of our new tenants was Fraeulein Grczimisch, a stooped-over woman of about sixty who seemed to be scared of her own shadow. She was accompanied, like the others who would soon follow, by a social worker who discreetly explained to my parents the peculiarities of her case, and then handed over the patient's documents and meager possessions. Dressed in an expensive black wool coat with a fox collar, Fraeulein Grczimisch appeared to come from a well-to-do home, but her dour, wrinkled face suggested that she hadn't had much love or tenderness in her life. She picked a bed in the largest bedroom, next to the veranda that overlooked the Greifswalder Strasse's gracious, tree-lined promenade. The Fraeulein kept mostly to herself at first, though her occasional utterances were always on the morbid side. "May you die today, you worthless scum, and may your bones rot in hell for eternity!" she would screech at anyone she believed was giving her a hard time. And, as she was thoroughly paranoid, she always assumed that everyone was giving her a hard time.

After Fraeulein Grczimisch got settled in, three more new arrivals came all at once: Kaethe Levy, Nora Wander, and Gretchen Oppner. All four women shared the same room, but it was soon apparent that the trio of animated newcomers disliked Grczimisch, believing her to be a snob. This was really not the case; she simply had no idea how to make friends or interact with people.

Kaethe, the most normal of the lot, was about sixty-five, and the good-natured peacemaker of the group. She had no family whatsoever and was thrilled to be with us. Kaethe was a big help to Mother in the kitchen, cleaning vegetables, peeling potatoes, and occasionally doing some simple cooking.

Nora, who was a few years younger, took the role of laundress. She babbled on incessantly, making absolutely no sense. Fraeulein Grczimisch stuffed cotton in her ears so as not to be plagued by Nora's prattle, removing it only when Nora was upstairs in the laundry room doing the wash or hanging it out to dry on the rooftop clothesline. Later, with more than a dozen people living in our apartment, there was always a lot of laundry, and Nora would spend hour after hour up on the roof. Sometimes I would go up there to see if she was all right, and invariably she would be muttering to herself how bad all men were, and that she would never give one the time of day. In my opinion, Nora had nothing to worry about.

Gretchen was by far the cutest one of the bunch. In her thirties and only a few inches over four feet tall, she looked as if she were fresh out of the circus, a cross between a monkey and a clown. Everywhere, she was a ruddy color: her hair, her face, her arms, her legs, her stubby little fingers, and her disproportionately big bosom. Her assigned task was to scour all the floors, sinks, and toilets, and she did it with great enthusiasm. She was usually splayed on all fours, scrubbing and buffing the parquet floors.

Hard-working Gretchen was constantly sweaty and flushed, and wore as little as possible. Her sleeveless, scoop-necked housedress was usually unbuttoned at the top, and her rosy breasts were more out than in. Gretchen was retarded and as innocent as a little child. Whenever I walked past her, she would look up at me and grin from ear to ear, raising her tiny hand with the stubby fingers high in the air. "Hallo, Mr. Lotharchen, I will be finished right away, only a few more minutes, then I will start in the next room!"

Her breasts often popped out when she lifted her arm to greet me. She was my newest fantasy, and when I walked past her I would try to brush up against her. She never objected to me getting my teenaged thrills that way, and even seemed to enjoy the attention. She had spent most of her life in one institution or another, and kept telling everybody how happy she was in Mama Nelly's house.

We soon saw that our initial apprehension about bringing these people into our home was unfounded. It was remarkably easy adjusting to their presence, and, I confess, they gave us more laughs than problems. They were responsible for making their own beds and keeping the bedrooms clean, which eliminated any additional housekeeping expenses. And each had a nightstand upon which stood a washbasin and pitcher, which were to be cleaned and dried after every use. Under every bed was a chamber pot that was to be used only at night, when absolutely necessary, and then only for urination. But, to our distress, many times during the two and a half years in which we operated the "Orbach Nut Institute," as my brother and I called it, the inmates used the chamber pots for all kinds of relief; the smell was awful, but there was nothing we could do about it.

We had our meals cafeteria-style in the big dining room. Father once showed us an excerpt from an official government report in the newspaper stating that the Germans got 2,310 daily calories on their food ration cards, the Poles only 934, and the Jews 183. But with the rental and pension money from our tenants beginning to pour in, and all of their ration cards at our disposal, Mother was able to provide for us well. Potatoes, flour, and vegetables were in good supply, and were added to tasty, nutritious specialties – chicken stomachs, lung stew, and stuffed spleen, items rarely seen on menus in normal times, but which were saved by generous butchers for those who, like Jews, had no ration cards for meat. We also bought food on the black market. The kontor where Manfred and I slept became so loaded with food that we had to get a secondhand icebox, and it became my job to go out and get fresh ice every day.

Soon we were notified by the officials that all the residences for released patients would be required to accept men as well. Mother protested but, with several beds still vacant, she had no choice. We gaped at our first male tenant, Franz Steiner, who must have approached six-and-a-half feet in height. He wore a stunned expression, as though he couldn't believe he was actually outside an institution. He sat woodenly on his new bed, rocking and clinging to it for dear life, dumbfounded that the Nazis had released him. The social workers told us he was originally from Stettin, the city near my birthplace. Through them, we learned that the Jews of that region, as we had feared, had not fared well. By February of 1940, they had been deported to the ghetto of Lublin in Poland, most of them never to be seen again. Franz lost his entire family. He claimed that his only living relative was a sister in Santa Domingo, which was par for the course; most Jewish families, fleeing for their lives, had scattered to the four corners of the earth. Once he got over the shock of his transfer, *Lange Franz* (tall Franz), as we nicknamed him, fit right in. He was a gentle giant, and pitched in happily with the household duties.

Then came Georg Benas, the hunchback. He was extremely friendly, always grinning and helpful, and fast – so fast, that when he dashed around the apartment, he was always banging into everyone with his hump. I was terrified of his hard-hitting backpack, and would leap out of his way when I saw him coming. Georg wore a jacket and tie at all times and, like a few of the others, appeared to come from an upper-class background. Occasionally, I would quiz Mother about our tenants' personal histories, but in most instances she did not think it was my place to know. My parents tried not to get too intimate with any one of them, and remained as neutral as possible in their disagreements. The bickering seldom got out of hand because these poor souls were so out of touch with the world around them that events were quickly forgotten, which was a blessing for us.

Karl Gold, the next man, was as strong as an ox and about as bright. He needed to be told everything three times before understanding it. But when it came to hard work, like moving furniture or carrying piles of laundry up and down three flights of stairs, Karl was our man. He, too, was eager to please, and only wanted a chance to contribute to the household.

And after Karl came Kurt Rosenberg. He was the most intelligent, and also the most difficult, of the whole lot. Kurt looked like an elected official, wearing the same brown-flecked suit day in and day out, and carrying himself extremely erect so as to appear better than his constituents. The three buttons of his snug jacket were always closed; it was as though this jacket held him together and if he opened up the buttons he would come apart. He walked with the stiff gait of a robot when he passed you by, and stared in a sly and malevolent manner. He really gave me the creeps, and I am sure that he affected everyone else the same way.

Completing the quintet in the men's quarters was the inimitable Botho Rothenberg. He arrived with two pieces of luggage, which was very unusual, for most of the others had come with just the clothes on their backs, and maybe a couple of extra sets of underwear. It fell to us to scrounge up additional clothing for them from the Juedische Kleiderkammer, the Goodwill depot for poor Jews, which was by now the only source of clothes for the entire Jewish population of Berlin. I thought Botho resembled my favorite comedian Grock the Clown, or the American funnyman Ed Wynn. A very strange-looking fellow, indeed; you could not help but laugh when you studied him. His cheeks were furrowed with horizontal lines so deep that dust or water could settle into each little trough. There was perpetual animation and movement in this very comical facial terrain.

Botho showed up wearing an oversized plaid coat that would have made Chaplin proud, canary-yellow slacks, white tennis shoes, and, to top it all off, a big old Borsalino hat worn at a tilt. He carried a wooden trunk and a small, round instrument case that appeared to contain some sort of accordion. As I inspected our latest arrival, it occurred to me that if Botho really were a musician he would be a godsend. We sorely needed some new entertainment in this madhouse of ours. By then there were already bridge parties and Kaffee-Klatsches almost every night, but a vaudeville act might replace the amusements no longer open to Jews, the much-missed movies and musicales. I was right, as it turned out, and Botho's antics turned out to be wonderful diversions during an otherwise very bleak time.

Kurt the outsider, the perennially angry one, glowered at Botho and refused to say hello to him, but all the others seemed to take an instant liking to this striking figure. I sneaked a look at Botho's papers and learned that he had been castrated several years earlier, after a German woman had accused him of rape. I didn't know the circumstances, of course, but Botho seemed incapable of harming a fly. Nonetheless, Father ruled with an iron hand, always on guard against any hint of violence. At the slightest flare-up, he would threaten the warring parties with a return to their sanitariums, which immediately stopped any further conflict.

The only one who regularly disturbed the peace was Kurt Rosenberg, who grew more hostile and menacing by the day. He complained of excruciating abdominal pains and we took him to our family physician, Dr. Jacoby, but he could find no physical problem. Kurt stalked through the apartment like a zombie, shoving everyone aside in his savage hunt for imaginary moths. Enraged, he would snarl over and over: *"Schon wieder eine Motte! Schon wieder hab' ich eine Motte gefangen!"* (Once again a moth! Again, I have captured a moth!). And then he would smack his palms together malevolently, squashing his prey to death. Everyone was becoming quite frightened of Kurt, and feared that a violent incident loomed ahead. Fraeulein Grczimisch would burst into tears merely at the sight of him, for he had once shoved her so forcefully that she had fallen to the floor and injured her arm. Father declared that Kurt's days in our home were numbered, and that he would see to it that this disruptive character be sent back to the Wittenau Sanitarium as soon as the arrangements could be made.

Meanwhile, little Gretchen's spirits had taken a turn for the worse. She went sobbing to Mama that her roommate, the sourpuss Fraeulein Grczimisch, was being mean to her and punching her. She begged Mother to let her move to the minuscule maid's room in the back of the apartment, and Mama agreed. Gretchen cheered up immediately, and scurried to gather her things.

Many evenings it had been my habit to sneak from the maid's room into the adjacent pantry, where I'd have some of Mother's homemade pastries, but now I had a good reason to work in reverse: I'd enter the pantry via the kitchen, and peer from there into the maid's room. Now I could watch Gretchen asleep; she was half-naked most of the time, her breasts pointing up at the ceiling. I made sure never to stay for more than a few moments, for if my father had caught me there would have been hell to pay.

Being released from their respective sanitariums seemed to have had a positive effect on all our inmates. Because of the wartime shortage of civil service workers, Karl and Franz were able to get jobs shoveling snow, and later, in the summer, digging excavations for the municipality. The pay was practically slave wages, most of it going directly to the Juedische Gemeinde, with only a small portion returned to the two of them as pocket change. This didn't matter to them in the least, for they had little use for money; they were proud and excited to have found an occupation. From our point of view, their work got them out of the house for much of the day, giving the rest of its inhabitants some breathing room.

In the evenings, both men returned home with their clothes smelling like a dungheap, and it took them quite a while to clean up. Karl had always given off an unpleasant body odor, but now that he was doing physical labor, it was far worse. With Franz monopolizing our only bathroom, Father would send Karl upstairs to the laundry sink to scrub himself clean. He loved being up there with Nora, who spent half her day among the soapsuds and clothespins, and it seemed that her hatred of men had begun to relax a bit. The two of them would have extended, urgent-sounding conversations that made not a lick of sense. I think they were falling in love.

At times it seemed as though the entire Jewish population of Berlin, a sorry and dwindling number, banded together around our piano, drinking cup after cup of steaming *ersatz Kaffee* brewed from chicory, and munching generous hunks of Mother's bund cake. The regulars included Uncle Isidor and Aunt Ella Orbach, Uncle James Loewenstein, the Goldsteins, the Gersons, the Joachimthals, and many other friends, all of whom would perish in concentration camps.

The dining table was outfitted with a net for Ping-Pong, Father presided over nonstop card games, and now there was Botho. I acted as the master of ceremonies, presenting him with much ado as "Botho, the world's greatest singer and accordion player!" Botho's eyes fluttered open and shut with every heartfelt note. He did, in fact, play his miniature octagonal accordion like a master, accompanying the music with his passionate renditions of old German folk songs. Karl was jealous and usually pleaded to sing a few numbers with him; Karl's terrible voice was a perfect match for Botho's kooky presentation, and added up to a hilarious performance. The crowd cheered and applauded Botho, bringing him back for several encores. We passed the hat to reward him for putting on the best show, possibly the only show for the Jews, in town.

Printing was another one of Botho's prized hobbies. He had a little printing set stocked with insignias and letters in different typefaces and sizes. His collection of stencils included many different kinds of symbols, pictures, and animals, and he used inks in red, blue, and black. He liked to create elaborate calling cards and business letterheads for all of us, some of them actually usable. Once he presented me with a funny card that said, *Komme gleich wieder: G. Pullen.* It loses something in the translation, but the message was: I'll be right back – (signed) I.M. Pissing.

Botho was such a buffoon that we couldn't resist playing practical jokes on him. One time my friend Heinz Jacobowitz and I wrote him a letter, signing the name of his former girlfriend Lotte Volkner (he had once told us about her), in which she informed him that she was carrying his child via "tele-floration," a sort of long-distance insemination by telepathy. A few months later we followed up with a birth announcement notifying him that he was now the proud father of a healthy baby boy. Botho believed every word of it. He puffed out his chest and strutted around the apartment, as giddy as if he'd won the lottery, crowing about the glories of fatherhood. He even printed up his own birth announcements, handed them out to everybody who walked into the house, and beamed at all the backslapping and congratulations. Even Georg, the hunchback, knew better, and joined in the joke. There was never a dull moment.

One night I awoke to blood-curdling screams coming from the men's quarters. The angry Kurt Rosenberg was finally losing his mind. Father and I rushed in to find him frothing at the mouth in the midst of some sort of seizure, his arms flailing out of control, his torso rigid, his eyes rolling in their sockets. A while back I had already wheedled out of my parents Rosenberg's tale of woe: he had contracted syphilis from a prostitute many years earlier, and had let it go untreated for too long. Now the infection had spread through every part of his body and brain.

The poor man was swinging wildly, but Father and I managed to subdue him and tie him up with some cord. We called an ambulance, and when the medics arrived, they put Rosenberg in a straitjacket and whisked him back to the sanitarium. It would take me a long time to erase the memory of the white foam that bubbled from the madman's lips, or the weird, raging look in his eyes as I held him down. But fortunately, that was the only frightening incident in the history of the Institute Orbach.

As 1941 wore on, Goebbels would remind us daily over the radio that the great German nation was undefeatable, and he declared victory after victory, on land, at sea, and in the air. The U-boats sank everything in sight, the Luftwaffe devastated England, and the brave German soldiers were taking all of Europe by storm. The good citizens of Germany appeared to be gleefully united behind their leaders, and there was not a peep of opposition to be heard. Manfred left Germany in September 1941, riding by blackened train through occupied Vichy France to Lisbon, where he boarded what was virtually the last boat of refugees to leave successfully. My parents were heartbroken; the last train, it appeared, had now gone. Now, my father's health was better and he could have traveled and all of us could have left, but our affidavits were no longer valid; only Manfred was still in line. Sometimes, survival is as random as roulette.

Now every Jewish citizen was issued a yellow swatch of fabric bearing the label "Jude" inside a Star of David. The Nazi authorities decreed that this emblem was to be sewn on all outerwear, and anyone caught without it would immediately be deported. With the cockiness of youth, I didn't believe that anything could ever happen to me, so I was selective about wearing the yellow star. I pinned it on only at work, or when I was visiting some kind of public institution. To hide my identity during some of my forays around town without the star, I would sometimes resort to a "Heil Hitler!" salute to an officer in uniform, or in the direction of some banner with a swastika. At first the hypocrisy made me gag, but then I began to hiss to myself as I shot out my right arm: "The shit in Germany stands ... *this high!*"

One afternoon after I returned home from the munitions plant, my mother asked me to come into the parlor. There, with hands demurely folded, sat a woman of about thirty, a strikingly elegant beauty who resembled the German film star Magda Schneider. She was our newest tenant. "This is my son, Lothar," said my mother, ushering me closer. "And here, my boy, is Frau Ilona Anker."

"I am pleased to meet you, Frau Anker," I responded, bowing slightly, but the lady did not reply. She just stared into space, with a faint smile on her lips. My mother had never before introduced me so formally to any of our newcomers. I suspect that she, too, was taken aback by Frau Anker's extraordinary looks and graceful carriage. Since she didn't seem to see me, I stared at the gleaming, jet-black hair that fell to her shoulders and covered part of her cheek, the alabaster skin of her slender neck, her trim figure in an expensively cut, cream-colored dress, her legs, long and shapely, and her black-brown eyes, so very far away. I wondered what her story was, what twist of fate had brought her to us.

By now, many of our relatives and friends had been picked up by the Gestapo. The Nazis assembled them first in a collection depot at the Levetzowstrasse Synagogue in Moabit, and then sent them on to the Schlesische or Goerlitzer train station. From there they were shipped in cattle cars to various ghettos and concentration camps in Poland and Germany, and nobody ever saw them again. They disappeared as though the earth had swallowed them.

Several of our tenants, too, had already been picked up from the apartment, and whenever one bed became vacant, the Juedische Gemeinde would immediately send us a replacement. Finally, it dawned on me that our house was only a fleeting stopover for these wretched souls. Why did the authorities even bother? Coming at irregular intervals, a Gestapo officer and a Jewish *Ordner*, or helper, would ring our bell at dinnertime to do their dirty work. The Ordner, a corpulent, middle-aged man named Behrend, stood stiffly in the doorway, hat in one hand and thick sheaf of papers in the other. Papers, there were always papers. And yet, with all the meticulous records they kept, no one professed to have known a thing.

Behrend would lead off with a comforting smile and a smarmy speech about only doing his duty. "Wherever you'll be taken it's for your own protection, and your own good," he would intone reassuringly. "Our government will surely take good care of you and will guarantee your well-being." Behrend once whispered his own story to my father while the officer who accompanied him was in the bathroom. He claimed he had had sex with his Aryan ex-wife, after having been forced to divorce her. Their oldest son, a Nazi sympathizer, was the one who put the Gestapo on their tails. Behrend was threatened with deportation, or worse, if he ever saw his ex-wife again, and was commanded by the Gestapo to assist in the loathsome capacity of Ordner. He moaned that he still loved this woman, that he was cursed to be a pawn in the hands of such murderers. We did not overflow with sympathy.

The worst time was the evening in early 1942 when they came for Karl. He was so grateful to be with us, and he loved his job digging excavations for the city; to him it was the most prestigious position anyone could hold. He felt important, he liked everybody, he loved our food. Though he was nearly my parents' age he referred to them reverently as "Mama" and "Papa," as if they were his own.

I went to answer the doorbell, and Behrend greeted me in his usual cordial manner, confiding in a low voice: "Please, young Herr Orbach, I need Karl Gold. Have him get ready, orders, you know." I left him and his Gestapo sidekick standing in the foyer, as Father usually did. There was no room for them in the dining room where we were all seated, and I wasn't about to offer them any special courtesy. I didn't think it was my place to inform the victim, so I quickly alerted my father. It was he who always tried to allay their fears with a few reassuring words, as though they were his own children; indeed, for the brief time they lived under his roof, that was what they were.

But this time, when Father told Karl why the officials had come, the poor man became transformed. His eyes darted back and forth, his breath came in gasps, his body writhed in agony. His voice began as a low moan: "I'm not going with anybody, Papa Arnold – I'm staying right here by my Mama and Papa!" Silence. His voice rose to an assertive wail: "I'm safe here, this is my home, there is no reason for me to go away! I have a job and I like it here." Again there was no answer, and his voice became a hoarse scream: "I am not going, I don't need anybody else to take care of me ... *I don't want to go away!*" Then, subsiding to an anguished plea, "Please, Papa, please don't let them take me ... *please* ..." until his voice choked and he collapsed sobbing at my father's feet. Even today, I hear the fear, agony, despair – his aloneness, as if he were crying out to us from the bottom of a well. But there was nothing we could do.

Behrend and the Gestapo man heard the commotion and came running into the dining room to subdue the hysterical man, but now Karl, terrified, rose and fought in desperation, swinging wildly and knocking them both down. Behrend was hurled against the ornate Bleichroeder buffet and bloodied his nose. Once again, Karl shouted out at the top of his lungs, *"No, no, I want to stay home, here by Mama and Papa Orbach, I will not go, I will not go!"*

I had made plenty of jokes about Karl's stupidity in the past, but at that moment I saw a brave man, a true lion of Judah, defending himself against the barbarians the way we all should have. He was so powerful they had to call two additional policemen from downstairs to subdue him. Two of them grabbed Karl from behind, and then one hit him over the head with the butt of a revolver.

When he fell, they strapped him into a straitjacket. Then, without a word, they carried him out.

When they had gone, we remained for a moment frozen, shattered. My father went silently to close the door, my mother sobbed softly, her eyes closed. I was drained. I had never felt such empathy, such pity, such sorrow for anyone in my life. But I was also proud that he had put up a good fight. Karl seemed to have had a keener sense of what was coming than did those of us still in denial.

While most of the residents scurried to their bedrooms during these deportations, fearing their own time had come, Ilona Anker would remain seated at the dinner table, staring straight ahead without so much as moving a muscle. I had badgered my parents to tell me what the social worker from the Juedische Gemeinde had revealed about her past. Ilona had married a prominent young doctor, and they were deeply in love. After a lavish wedding, the couple went to Karlsbad, one of the world's most luxurious spas, for an extended honeymoon. It was in 1938, when the German Army was marching into Czechoslovakia, so the young lovers were forced to share their vacation idyll with a large contingent of Nazi officers. Apparently the doctor had a run-in with an officer who was drunk and insulting. The others swooped down on Ilona's new husband, and beat him viciously. When Ilona tried to intervene, she was gang-raped by the entire horde. Her husband, trying to protect her, was arrested and carted away. She never saw him again, and assumed he was killed. Afterwards, Ilona's mind became completely encased in darkness. She was well-behaved, always neat and clean, and even smiled from time to time, but she was catatonic, her agony alive and buried inside her.

Georg, the hunchback, had now taken over the pursuit of the imaginary moths from Kurt Rosenberg. When he got especially nervous, he would bat at them nonstop. Botho remained happily oblivious to all the dangers that surrounded us. He continued singing and playing his heart out, and nothing could get him down. He could hardly wait for evening to come, and for the show to begin. Neither could the rest of us for, as time went on, Botho's act became the manifestation of the survival and collective well-being of the Orbach family and friends.

In those days, my youth was my shield. I did not dwell on the evil that surrounded us, for my restless brain needed other things to think about – like Ilona Anker's Mona-Lisa smile, her voluptuous body. I continued to sneak through the pantry to peek at Gretchen's breasts, and sometimes had dreams about her. But Frau Anker's tale haunted me so that I felt guilty for even a single lustful thought about her.

At the factory, the lonely ladies kept hanging around me during the lunch break. All of their husbands were off fighting the war, and the sight of young fellows like Tad and me – especially Tad, I had to admit – seemed to stir them up. One day, I was eating my lunch and reading a book in a narrow storage alcove when one of the women, rather plain looking but with a friendly smile, sidled up to me and handed me a sandwich. "Here, kid," she said, "I know you Jews don't get any meat, so have some good salami. It will give you strength."

"Thanks, ma'am," I responded nervously. "I love salami, but I really shouldn't be talking to you."

"Ach, come here, kid, you worry too much!" And with that she grabbed my elbow and guided me down the corridor. "Check out the motor room, right around the corner; the motors are not running during lunch time and it's quiet. The door locks from the inside."

"I don't think I should," I stammered. "Thank you, but I'd really better not."

"Come on, trust me, you'll see it's nice to chat with me and you can eat your sandwich in peace. You know, my upstairs neighbor was a Jew, too. He left for America, but he used to give me and the kids the nicest presents for Christmas."

She pulled me by the string of my work apron through the dark gangway, made a short right turn, and opened a heavy metal door marked "Motor Room: Entry Forbidden." I followed.

"Nobody ever comes in here, except in an emergency," she reassured me. "Now, what's your name? I'm Paula."

"I am Lothar," I told her. "You know we can't talk for long …"

"Who wants to talk?" she said impatiently. "Come over here and let's have some fun!"

She opened the top two buttons of her smock and lifted out two flabby breasts. I had the sandwich in my right hand, and she put her right breast in my left. My hands were full. Her hands went under my apron, unbuttoning my pants, and began to fondle me. I was very excited but also scared to death. It was all over in a minute.

"Uh-oh, there you go. Well, we didn't have much time anyway," she sighed, breaking away from me and wiping her hand on my apron. The bell rang and we went back to work as though nothing had happened. But something had happened, and with Germany's Rassenschande laws, it was dangerous as hell. And I loved every minute of it.

Paula and I reenacted our little lunch-time tryst on several more occasions. Luckily, this limited act seemed to amuse her; I would have been too afraid to have tried

anything more serious with her. It could have been ex-
ceedingly dangerous and I was still, after all, a virgin. I
found out from Tad that I was far from the first guy Paula
had lured into the motor room and she had done the same
thing with him. He told me that Paula was constantly
propositioning him, but he had no interest in her; he had
his pick of the women, and she wasn't on his list.

Tad's deep-blue eyes drew in women like magnets.
Around them he adopted a sophisticated manner and a
throaty, sensuous voice that appeared to make them weak
in the knees. With such lady-killing techniques not in my
own repertoire, I was flattered by Paula's attentions. I
began to think that, in these lousy times, I should take
whatever I could get. Even in a dank and filthy motor
room.

As winter gave way to spring, I had to be conscientious about replenishing the ice every day to keep our food
cold, or my room would begin to smell like a slaughterhouse. Despite everything, I always managed to sleep like
a baby. To be able to summon sleep, even when the world
was collapsing around me, was the gift of my youth, and
of my nature, too, I suppose. When I awoke in the
morning, I tried to savor my dreams, to revisit the happy
childhood not so far behind, a congenial world in which
the words Hitler and Nazis meant absolutely nothing.

One morning, just before dawn, I was in the midst
of such a dream, a lively fantasy of a big snowball fight
in the schoolyard. As usual, my fingers were numb with
frost when one of the girls from the neighboring school
coyly threw a load of soft snow in my face, and I was
jolted awake. My alarm clock showed four-thirty. I was
groggy, but I could have sworn I heard bare feet shuffle
past my bedroom into the large parlor. And then I was
sure: somebody was shutting the parlor doors ever so

gently. By now, all our male boarders had been deported and my parents had moved into a bedroom of their own, leaving the parlor empty at night. Slowly I staggered to my feet and opened my door to see who was moving about before sunrise.

Now I could hear someone playing the piano. It was Beethoven's "Fuer Elise," one of Mother's favorites, but surely it couldn't be her at such an ungodly hour. Yet who else in our "cuckoo's nest" could play the piano so expertly, with such feeling and grace? I opened the parlor door quietly and peeked inside. Was I still dreaming? There sat Frau Anker, her shiny black hair streaming down her back, her eyes half closed as if in a trance, her moist, full lips humming the melody, and her head swaying from side to side, keeping the beat like a metronome. She was stark naked.

My adolescent heart began to hammer. My breath came fast. Never before had I seen a woman nude. I had seen the massive portraits hung in the Berlin Museum, and the nudes in the heavy art books my mother loved to leaf through at the public library, but never before a real, naked woman. And this one lifted on a cloud of music. I gazed in awe and mounting emotion at the curve of her shoulders, the fullness of her breasts. Her lower half was hidden by the piano, a wall of ebony that suddenly seemed quite massive, blocking her from me.

Slowly, silently, I lowered myself onto the Persian carpet and crept on all fours into the parlor. I was having trouble crawling along in my long nightshirt, so I yanked it up to my waist, fully exposing my behind. I moved stealthily forward, trying not to make a sound. Finally I was there, and I sat, motionless, riveted beneath the piano.

Now she launched into "Dream of Love" by Schumann. I fantasized that she knew exactly what I was up to, and with full approval, was serenading me. And then my eyes fell on a place I had never seen before; for the first time in my life, I peered between a woman's legs, my eyes staring with wonder, without shame. I was fascinated by every inch of her, and longed to touch her, but I knew that it might quickly, perhaps disastrously, draw this adventure to a close. Next, she played Beethoven's "Ode to Joy," the music stoking the fire inside me. Only inches away, I watched her finely veined feet pump the pedals. The music showered around us, making us one.

I wrapped my erection in my nightshirt. Then, with no warning, a great rush came over me, the release of a volcanic eruption, and I was soaring, soaring through space at the speed of light – then suspended, breathless, in silent infinity until I landed slowly, softly back in my nest under the piano. It took me several moments to regain full consciousness. How could I have suspected that such wondrous sensations were stored in my body, and that they would spring forth in honor of Frau Anker?

I had tried not to make a sound, but she must have heard my heavy breathing, because she leaned down and trained her vacant stare on me. I was ready to bolt, but all she did was give me a smile; she did not say a word, and I remembered then that I had never heard her speak. Before making a hasty retreat, I gently kissed the little toe on her left foot to thank her for her silent collusion in the greatest thrill of my life.

I hastened to my room and slid into bed, wet gown and all. Now I could hear her playing Tchaikovsky's "1812 Overture," a finale for my fantastic trip. There were some heavy footsteps, and then the sound of my father's loud baritone: "Listen here, Frau Anker, you can't run around like that here. And you'll wake the whole neighborhood. Now get back to your room, quick!" No question about it, there was a trace of humor in his gruff voice. He, too, must have appreciated the sight of this exquisite woman at his piano, wearing only a smile. I fell quickly into a deep, blissful sleep.

Although my encounters with older women had been exciting, I yearned for a girl my own age. I enjoyed dancing with Inge Baruch, a busty little girl who pushed her thighs between my legs and pressed her breasts against me, but she also chattered incessantly and left me with nothing to say. Eventually I started going steady with Ruth Goldschmit, a pretty and vivacious girl who had been a friend since childhood. I spent many evenings with her and her family in their apartment on the Christburger Strasse, where we danced to records by Jack Hilton and Count Basie. Occasionally we listened to classical music. Ruth's favorite was Grieg's "Peer Gynt," and she would often rise, dreamily, to dance Anitra's dance.

Before the war, Ruth had spent many years training in gymnastics, and I loved watching her do somersaults and splits, tumbling and reeling the entire length of the apartment. She worked as a secretary for a food wholesaler, and was able to bring home some extra provisions, which her warm-hearted parents were kind enough to share with me. She was my first love but, though we spent hours kissing in the hallway of her apartment building, I would never have gone any further. I was still a kid, really, and naive in my own way. More important, I could not think of intercourse with a good girl like Ruth before we were married. This remained an unwritten law in our ever-shrinking Jewish community.

Ruth and I talked about a future together, but knew that we were living from day to day in turbulent times. Whenever we fiddled with my makeshift radio to hear the war news, our faces turned grim. It was now 1942, and there was no end in sight. Allied air raids were getting ever more frequent and cities were blacked out at night, and yet Hitler would harangue us with his insane posturing, and Goebbels would bluster such inanities as "the Fuehrer has been selected by God to lead the Reich and all other nations in united victory over the Jewish, Imperialist, Bolshevik aggressors!" I was no geopolitical genius, but I knew the walls were closing in on us. Sometimes I looked around that noisy parlor, pulsing with life and imbued with the decency, culture, and intelligence of my parents and their friends, and wondered silently: Which of them – of us – will be here in a year? In a month? Whose turn is next? The future would have to wait.

There was a curfew for Jews after dark, so our friends either unpinned the yellow star from their coats before venturing homeward, or they stayed around until day-break, curling up on the rug for a few hours of sleep. By now Jews were forbidden to use any public transportation, and emigration was completely out of the question. We were trapped, like bugs under glass. Now, when he called, Behrend the Ordner was no longer so solicitous; he appeared haggard and much more frightened of his Nazi companions than before. Different Gestapo men accom-panied him each time, and most of these hulking young officers treated him, the veteran of so many deportations, like dirt. I saw the growing terror in Behrend's rheumy eyes. But he had made his choice.

One by one they went. Georg and Botho had been taken, the last of the men, and now it was time for Frau Anker and finally Gretchen. None of them went happily, but none fought like Karl. Because I came home late from the ammunition factory, I was usually not home when Behrend and his thugs came, so I was spared most of the partings. True to Hitler's declaration, even our little haven was steadily becoming Judenrein. But who were the real lunatics – the hapless, gentle residents of the Orbach Nut Institute, or the murderers who thought they would rule the world?

Chapter 3

We Are Going Under

In May of 1942, I turned eighteen, a birthday considered a milestone on the road to adulthood. Yet for me, there was just a tedious sameness, waiting for the nightmare to be over, and for my life to begin.

My father and I had been arguing, the way teenagers and their parents do. He was annoyed by how loudly my friends and I played our music. For several days we did not speak. On my birthday, he handed me a package, still not saying a word. I opened it to find a blue shirt, made of a rich cotton. I knew it must have cost him a fortune on the black market, for clothing was hard to come by. I knew it was his way of making peace with me.

Papa and I threw our arms around each other. "Ach, Lotharchen, mein Junge," he murmured into my neck in an hoarse voice. He was a shaken man, I think, wondering in his heart if he had signed our death warrants with his determination to stay home and ride out the storm. I was happy to be back on good terms with him, and could not wait to visit Ruth in a shirt that was neither threadbare nor too small.

The Juedische Gemeinde had stopped sending us replacements for the tenants who had been picked up. To bolster our income, we retained several private lodgers, and some people who came just for supper. Mr. Pieck, one of our tenants, had a daughter who was married to a gentile. Through her, the elderly Mr. Pieck had developed a friendship with an Aryan family, the Dudacys. Anne Dudacy and her older sister Hedel, who was nearly Mr. Pieck's age, came to visit him at our home almost every week. The Dudacys were fiercely Communist; Anne's husband, a dues-paying member of the Communist party, had been arrested by the Nazis in 1934 and had spent two years in one of the first concentration camps, Esterwege, in Friesland. He was freed during a general amnesty on Hitler's birthday. In 1940, to clear his family name of the political stigma, he volunteered for army service, but privately he remained a devout Communist.

Anne was a striking brunette in her early forties, with a daughter about my age, and a son slightly younger. Both she and her sister denounced the Nazis, and professed sympathy for us. Hedel asked me to call her *Tante*, and urged us to call on her if we needed anything. But I always had the feeling there might be something else behind Anne's frequent visits. She couldn't take her eyes off my father, and called him "Arnoldchen." I wondered if she could be trusted. But friends were hard to come by, especially Aryans. So I swallowed my misgivings about Anne Dudacy, and treated her like a member of the family. This would prove a very wise decision.

Late in the afternoon of May 27, five days after my birthday, there was a knock at the door. When I answered it, there stood two Berlin policemen, in black uniforms and star-studded helmets.

"Herr Orbach, Herr Arnold Orbach?" they said, smiling and polite.

"That's my father. What do you want with him?"

"We are under orders to bring him to the station for interrogation." Somehow I was not frightened. It was Behrend who made my skin crawl, Behrend and his thugs who snatched away people who never returned.

My father and mother were in the kitchen together. He had heard the knock, too, and came to the door with his shirtsleeves rolled up. "Yes, officers, may I help you?"

"Please, sir," said one of them. "Routine questioning, we don't know the details."

"Well," said Papa, "I hope it won't take too long. We are about to have supper."

"We'll do our best, sir," said the other one.

With that my father rolled down his sleeves and put on his brown tweed jacket, with the leather patches on the elbows. He and I went to the kitchen, where Mama was working and he told her he would be right back. He kissed her, which was unusual, because he was not particularly demonstrative to her in front of us. He looked at me and smiled. He patted me on the shoulder and gave me a wink, as if we shared a secret, a treasure, and in that moment I felt he saw me as a man.

And then he was gone.

At first we were not very concerned because we believed that all deportations were handled strictly by the Gestapo, never the police. But when Papa had still not returned by nine o'clock, we began to worry. "Do you think his jacket is warm enough in the night air?" Mother said anxiously. "What if he must stay the night without pajamas, no toothbrush?"

The two of us decided to walk to the police station, which was several blocks away. When we approached the building, we saw that a large crowd had gathered, mostly women and children. I could hear screaming and crying. Fear mounted in my chest. We tried to push through the crowd to enter the building. Suddenly an armed guard stood before us, and shouted, "Halt! Where do you think you're going?"

"I am looking for my husband," Mother answered. "He went off with two policemen this evening for investigation."

"Are you Jewish?"

"Yes," my mother answered in a small voice.

"They are all gone, the whole lot of them," the man barked. "To Sachsenhausen. You'll be notified by mail." I could feel my mother slump alongside me. She, my pillar of strength, began making soft, whimpering sounds. All my life I had been the baby of the family. In that moment, I became the man.

We returned home, numb and wordless in shock. We had never expected this to happen to us. We had assumed that running the convalescent home somehow had given us a preferred status. Now we knew better; there were no exceptions. They wanted to be rid of us, one by one. Like crazy Karl, who had kicked and screamed and fought when they dragged him from our doorstep, like my father, who had buttoned his jacket and flashed a smile, we were all doomed.

We learned that my father was one of a thousand Jewish men rounded up that evening in retaliation for a bomb planted by the only Jewish resistance fighters in Berlin, the Herbert Baum group, at a Nazi anti-Communist exposition called "Das Sowjet Paradies." At the time, I was angry with those Jews who had taken actions for which my father had been arrested; later, I came to know some of them, and I recognized their courage and foresight.

For one month, we heard nothing from him. Mother and I tried to be strong for each other, but the pain was evident on both our faces. Finally we received a letter from him from the Sachsenhausen concentration camp. He wrote that he was fine and in good spirits, that he was working hard and being well treated. He said that he hoped to be home soon. We knew that was all he was permitted to write; we could not know what the truth was, but we were sure it would never have gotten to us.

Just a week after that letter, a man came to the door. He was haggard and thin, dressed in old clothing; his eyes darted nervously from side to side. He gave us a note in my father's handwriting. Again, the caution was evident; he said that father was working and was fine, that he could buy a few things, and asked us to send some money. The man told us that he was a civilian worker in a plant that drew its labor from Sachsenhausen. He said that he had befriended my father there. In a very secretive manner, he produced my father's pocket watch.

"Your father asked me to give you this," he said in a confidential tone. "He needs about five hundred marks for extra food and clothing. I travel to Berlin every second week to visit my family. I will bring you a receipt and more letters from him." We doubted the man's story, of course, but we were so grateful for any news from Father that we gave him the money, no questions asked.

"What is your name, sir, so that after my husband comes home we can thank you properly for your kindness?" asked my mother.

"It's better you do not know," said the man. "I want no trouble in the plant, you understand." We did understand. In these times, even a swindler and a liar could be an angel of hope. We knew we would never see the man again. After he left, I examined the pocket watch. It was definitely my father's, and it was still ticking. I imagined I was listening to his heart, still strong, still beating.

Another month passed with no word from my father. The atmosphere in the apartment was oppressive. Although friends still congregated at our place, the days of dancing and boisterous fun were over. We all knew now that we were living on borrowed time, and spent hours trying to come up with strategies to save ourselves. I didn't spend much time at Ruth's apartment, either. I felt my mother needed me, and I had promised myself I would not let her down.

On July 27, 1942, exactly two months from the day my father was picked up, a policeman once again came to our door. Under his arm he carried what appeared to be a vase, striped vertically in black and white.

"You are young Orbach, yes?" he asked. I nodded, unable to speak. He handed me the vase and said briskly, "One hundred and forty-four marks, please."

"I don't understand," I said.

"Well, this is your father's urn."

"My father never had an urn like this," I replied, staring at it in my hands.

The policeman's voice was devoid of any emotion. "Young fellow, this is from Sachsenhausen. It contains your father's ashes. He died of natural causes, heart failure. I have an envelope containing his death certificate, and a bill for the urn."

I thought I had stumbled into a nightmare. How could I break the news to Mother, who stood, unsuspectingly, peeling potatoes in the kitchen? How could I tell her that these barbarians had not only taken my father to his death, but also now wanted to be paid for it? I wanted to tell her gently and slowly, but first I needed the money to get rid of the policeman. I put the urn down on the Bleichroeder buffet in the parlor and went to the kitchen. Trying to control my voice, I put my arm around her shoulder and said quietly, "Mameshi, there is someone at the door who must get 144 marks. Please, don't ask any questions."

She looked at me disapprovingly. "Lotharchen, what is the secrecy? Have you been gambling? You know we have no money to squander!"

"Mama, please, it's much more serious than gambling. There's a policeman out there."

"What has happened?" she said slowly, as though she already suspected the worst, but was trying to make herself believe otherwise. I watched the color leave her face.

"Papa's urn."

"What urn?"

I could not hold back any longer. "Mama, he's dead!" I shouted out. "They killed him! And now we have to buy his ashes from them!" Her mouth opened wide but no sound emerged. She slid to the floor, unconscious. I shook her, but could not rouse her. I could hear her shallow breathing.

I ran back to the buffet where I knew she kept some cash, and broke into the locked drawer. I handed the policeman the money without looking at him, slammed the door in his face, and immediately called Dr. Jacoby.

Then I picked up the urn and stared at it. It was simply impossible that I would never see my father again, that all that was left of him was in a container in my hand. That my father was dead was bad enough; that he had been cremated, strictly forbidden by Jewish law, made it an abomination.

"I love you, Papa," I sobbed, pressing the urn to my face. "See, I am holding you in my arms." Yes, like any grieving child I cried. But strangely, even through my tears, I began to feel I was growing stronger, not weaker. It was as though my father's death at Nazi hands, the unnecessary, unjustified death of Arnold Orbach, Aaron Ha-Cohen, proud son of Germany, had prepared me to fight. Whatever lay ahead, whatever it would take, my Mother and I would survive.

Doctor Jacoby said my mother was in shock, and that she had suffered a mild stroke. He gave her an injection and prescribed some sedatives. He gave me a letter so that I could take a week off from my job to care for her. She recuperated rapidly, and the only sign of her ordeal, a slight crookedness of the mouth, was gone after a few months.

We buried Papa's urn on top of my grandfather's grave, because we could not afford another plot. I said the Kaddish, the mourner's prayer, over the ashes, well aware that we would never know if they were really his ashes. This was the only time, other than at work, that I wore the yellow star, because we had to have official permission to gather at the Jewish cemetery.

It was a hell of a time to become the man in the family. Wherever I walked in Berlin, newsstands displayed the Nazi tabloid *Der Stuermer* (The Stormtrooper), whose covers frequently featured elaborate cartoons of stereotypically Jewish faces – repulsive, malevolent-looking men and women with huge, hooked noses, beady eyes, and big, rubbery lips. The newspaper also featured caricatures of other groups that had fallen into the Nazi's subhuman category: gypsies portrayed as stupid and filthy, covered with cheap jewelry and veils, and homosexuals as slender dandies who batted long eyelashes while they groped after terrified young boys.

One Friday evening in November 1942, my girlfriend Ruth invited me for Sabbath dinner with her family. After Papa's death I had seen less of her because I felt I should be with my mother when I wasn't working. That made the time Ruth and I spent together even more precious.

The evening air was crisp and clear as I approached her building. I saw a Gestapo vehicle parked in front, the same type of car that Behrend and company had so often driven up to our apartment complex. I hid alongside the building next door, and waited to see who would emerge. There were several Jewish families living in Ruth's building. I prayed to God, whom I had begun addressing with some regularity, "Please, don't let it be them! Don't let it be my Ruthchen!"

But my prayer was not answered. I watched Ruth, her mother, and her sister, each carrying a suitcase, being bullied down the stairs by two soldiers. The swine pushed them into the back seat of the wagon, and drove off. They did not make a sound.

The sweetness, the exuberance, of this innocent girl, her family, generous and warm hearted and law abiding – why had this happened to them? I stood there, filled with panic, but unable to move. Should I have tried to intervene? Should I have gone with them? Had I arrived five minutes earlier, I would have been taken with them. Could I have helped? I felt, at that moment, as though the last vestige of my childhood had been erased.

"Why, God, why?" I asked over and over. But there was no answer; my God did not give answers. And yet, believing in Him was better than not believing; then there would have been no faith and therefore no hope.

My world got smaller by the day. People simply disappeared. We seldom knew the details, and never the destination. Not long after Ruth was picked up, they took my friend Heinz Jacobowitz, the fun-loving kid who had helped me convince Botho of his paternity by "tele-floration." This time I was standing barely twenty meters away from Jaco's house on the Elbinger Strasse when I saw him try to escape from the moving vehicle and break his foot.

As he writhed and cried in pain, the Nazis collected him from the street and threw him back inside the car. Once again, churning with guilt and fear, I stood by in silence.

Mother and I knew our own days were numbered, but we did not just sit and wait. Father's death had finally opened our eyes. There was no more self-deception, no delusions of preferred status or other pipe dreams. Yes, we continued to pray for a miracle that would bring this nightmare to an end – a swift victory by the Allies, the assassination of Hitler, some sort of stunning revolution. Certainly there were always rumors in the air. But we no longer relied on hearsay. This caution was my father's legacy to us, a warning that put us on alert, and would eventually save our lives.

Our apartment complex had three doors in the front and one in the rear. We began bribing Frau Hesse, the superintendent, to leave the rear door unlocked. Frau Hesse had once called us the nicest tenants in the entire complex. For fourteen years she had known us, from the time we moved into the building, and never did a holiday go by without some special gift or generous tip from my parents. It was customary in Berlin for doors to be locked every night promptly at eight; all tenants had keys to the front entryways, but very few had them to the rear doors. She said she would provide us with a key to this door, which would give us a safe exit if a Gestapo vehicle and driver were waiting for us out front. But things kept coming up and, despite our repeated requests, she could never seem to get hold of an extra key. In the meantime, she assured us that she was always at home, and if the door was locked, she would immediately unlock it for us.

We each packed a small bag with the barest necessities and hid them in Mama's bedroom closet. We decided to remain in the relative safety of our own home as long as possible, and if they came for one or both of us, we would make a run for it together. And together we mapped out an elaborate strategy, poring over the details many times.

We looked up a onetime acquaintance of father's, a black marketeer who was known to have access to forged German documents. From him, with the little money we had left, we bought Aryan papers for both of us. I got an identity card from the Technische Hochschule of the University of Berlin, Germany's best engineering school, which indicated that I had a temporary exemption from the draft. For Mother, there was the prestigious bronze *Deutsches Mutter Verdienst Kreuz*, the German Mother Cross, which was awarded to mothers who had produced three to five children for the Aryan nation. The Mother Cross endowed its owner with great respect; my mother, of course, having fulfilled the child bearing requirements, could have had one on her own merits except that she and her children were German, but not Aryan. Into our packed bags they went, the identity papers of the young student, Gerhard Peters, and his mother, Frau Ida Peters, holder of the Deutsches Mutterkreuz.

Chapter 4

Silent Night, Holy Night

December 24, 1942, Christmas eve, was a silent night on the streets of Berlin. But on this night God was there, and, with his blessing – a miracle, really – it would be a night of salvation.

Looking out from the balcony, I saw little traffic on our usually bustling thoroughfare. From other apartments there drifted the aroma of holiday cooking, the ripple of family laughter and togetherness, the swell of Christmas music. These were not my rituals, yet on this particular night I found them somehow comforting, those familiar sounds and smells of so many Christmases past, for I yearned for a time, even a moment, in which peace and beauty reigned.

My mother had just cleared the dinner dishes, and now she sat at the dining room table, writing in her leather-bound diary with a fountain pen. I loved to watch her during such quiet moments. She had the most extraordinarily intelligent, expressive dark eyes, eyes that seemed to contain the wisdom of the ages and that evoked confidence and trust in anyone who looked into them. Even with her husband dead, two of her children somewhere half a world away, and now cut off from everyone, she seemed ready for anything.

The shrill ring of the doorbell rent the evening quiet, as it had so many times before at Greifswalder Strasse, number 43. When I swung open the door, I saw Behrend and his Gestapo chaperon fix their solemn gazes on me. I knew I had just heard our front doorbell for the last time. There was nobody left but Mother and me.

As usual, Behrend was accompanied by a Gestapo man we had never seen before. He was a much older fellow than his predecessors, probably in his sixties, a replacement for the younger Nazis who, I fervently hoped, were freezing their asses off somewhere with the SS heroes outside of Stalingrad. On this occasion, Behrend tried to look particularly dejected, his voice oozing with compassion: "Young man, today I have the unpleasant duty to pick up your dear, good mother and bring her to the assembly depot," he stammered apologetically. "She is slated for deportation to a safe haven from all these bombings. Naturally, as you must be aware, because of her outstanding service to the Jewish community, she will command preferential treatment from the authorities."

I didn't see why the little bastard bothered with his lengthy explanation; I certainly didn't ask him for it. Pretending to go along with his palaver, I responded in a quiet, resigned tone. "I understand, Herr Behrend. But, sir, as you know, Mother limps a bit, so we'll need a little time. She will have to get washed, and I must help her into her special corset, and pack her things."

"That's all right, young fellow," Behrend said solicitously. The Gestapo man glowered and began to mumble that he wanted to get home – after all, it was Christmas. But Behrend waved his hand. "It won't be long. These people will be very cooperative."

"Thank you, sir," I replied. "Now how about a hot cup of Ersatz Kaffee, and a piece of Mother's plumcake?"

Not waiting for an answer, I steered them both into a now vacant sitting room at the front of the apartment.

My mother had been following our exchange from the other end of the apartment, and had already gathered up our things. Although she did walk with a pronounced limp – as a child she had been hit by a horse-drawn trolley – she moved with the speed of a much younger woman.

After supplying our messengers of doom with their refreshments, I rejoined Mother in her bedroom in the rear of the apartment. She opened the window and leaned out. "Frau Hesse, Frau Hesse, hallo!" she hissed loudly in the direction of the superintendent's apartment, her voice echoing through the courtyard. The superintendent's lights were on, so we knew she was at home. We quietly embraced. We had already discussed our next contact point – the apartment of Hans Loewenstein, a distant cousin, who lived a thirty-minute walk across town. Small leather suitcase in hand, Mother slipped out of the apartment's rear door.

I returned to Behrend and friend in the front room. "My mother will be ready in just a few minutes," I said politely. "Can I get you anything else? Oh, and here is today's *Abendblatt.*" I tossed the newspaper in their direction.

"Maybe you have some more coffee for me?" said the old Nazi.

"And I'll take another piece of that cake," mumbled Behrend, slouched in Papa's old armchair as though it were his home.

"It will take just a moment to reheat the coffee," I nodded, backing out of the room and making sure to close the door behind me. This was not unusual, since the room-by-room heating system of the day required that doors be kept shut.

I brought them refills. Now it was my turn. I paced the back bedroom for almost ten minutes, giving Mother an ample head start. And then I began my act. I tiptoed to the front of the apartment, and called loudly: "Mother, the gentlemen are waiting!"

Then, dashing silently through two foyers and two rooms, I returned to the back of the apartment and answered myself in a high, ladylike voice: "Yes, darling, I will be ready very soon, I've just come out of the shower." Again I crept to the front of the apartment, and called: "OK, I'll come and help you close your bag."

I crouched in front of the door of the sitting room and peeked through the keyhole. Behrend sat slack jawed, still drinking the bad coffee. The old Nazi had his face buried in the newspaper. I inserted the key and turned it silently, locking them both inside. I grabbed my knapsack, my money, and my papers from the bed where Mother had left them. I saw my home, my haven, my parents' home, and all that was ever dear to me for the last time. I closed the back door silently behind me. Lothar Orbach – all that I was, all that I knew – stepped into the night, into the unknown.

Then, sprinting down the darkened stairwell, I was overcome with the giddy feeling that we had outwitted Hitler's henchmen. But my elation was short-lived. When I entered the courtyard, I found my mother standing in the middle of the little garden, clutching her bag and weeping.

"Our great friend, the super, did not open the door for us, and she won't answer her bell," she sobbed. "I know she is in there, I saw her not even fifteen minutes ago, that horrible woman. How could I have trusted her? I should have reported her years ago when she was stealing flour from the Brother Groh's market!"

"Never mind that now, Mama," I said, trying to act calmer than I was. "There's no time for tears. Maybe we can find another key."

My mother regained her composure and grabbed my arm. "You're right, Lotharchen, let us make our way through the buildings. We have no other choice!"

We re-entered our building and rang the doorbell of the nearest ground floor apartment. The door was answered by a man who had known us since we had moved in, a grandfatherly type who used to slip me hard candy when I was a little boy playing in the courtyard. Mother opened her mouth to speak, but before she could say a word, he slammed the door in our faces and threw the bolt. The record player, barely audible when we first approached his door, suddenly blared Handel's "Messiah."

Floor to floor we rushed, pounding on doors and frantically ringing each doorbell; one after the other, all of our longtime neighbors turned their backs on us as brusquely as had the first one. These people had played bridge with my mother and father, they had stuffed themselves with my mother's pastries, they were the parents of my soccer friends. But that was in a different lifetime, before we had become Jews. Even those tenants who did not know us, knew when they saw us standing wild-eyed at their doorstep that we were undesirables of some sort, and that we were in trouble that they did not want to share. In the Nazi system, every individual was meticulously listed and categorized. Those who did not participate in party activities were foreigners, of whom there were no longer many left in Germany, or Jews.

Nobody dared to get involved. They all just stared at us through cracks in their doors, obviously annoyed that we had invaded the privacy and tranquillity of their Christmas Eve. At least they didn't try to hold us and deliver us to the hounds on our trail – that was something to be grateful for. It occurred to me that their savior was also a Jew, and that his parents had searched long and hard on this night for a refuge, a place for him to be born. But Berlin was not Bethlehem; here there were no mangers or wise men.

Then a great commotion broke out: the moment we feared had come. Finally wise to our scheme, Behrend and the Gestapo had forced their way out of the locked room and yelled frantically for reinforcements. "Everyone, everyone, be on the lookout for the escapees, the wretched Jews!" shouted the old Nazi, his voice echoing through the courtyard in the night air. "I demand they be returned to us immediately. Anyone who hides a Jew will be shot!"

The shouting escalated as we darted inside the last building. A manhunt was on for two enemies of the Third Reich, my mother and me, whose very existence imperiled the justice and welfare, the very foundation, of the exalted Thousand-Year Empire. It was so absurd it could have been a joke, but it wasn't funny. Like hunted animals we stood panting in the musty hallway of the third floor of the last building.

"Hallo!" croaked a small, thin voice that seemed to come from the heavens. Startled, we craned our necks to look up in the direction of the top floor and saw an old woman bent over the banister. A shock of silver hair framed her head like a halo, and even in the dim light, I saw on her face the most extraordinary expression: she was smiling, as though she had been waiting for us.

"Get up here, you two, make it fast!" she ordered as we climbed the final stairway and she ushered us into her one-bedroom apartment. "Else Mueller is here to help you, you are safe now. I'll show those pigs! They killed my poor Albert, they made him take his life! They told me if I spoke out they'd finish me off the same way!"

"Frau Mueller," said Mother in a hushed, urgent tone, "you must understand, you are our last hope. We are running from the Gestapo and we cannot go back down there."

"Of course, dear lady, I know everything. You needn't plead with me, it is my duty to help you. Jesus Christ has sent you to me on this Holy Eve." Mother began to cry, and Frau Mueller embraced her. "Don't worry, dear lady, I remember you very well. You have always been a good neighbor, with such a lovely family. Your boys were always so polite and helpful. Have no fear, my darling Albert in heaven is watching over us all."

Now her sad story came back to me. Her husband had been an official in Berlin's municipal government, in the tax department, and they had forced him, like all civil servants, to join the Nazi party. But Albert Mueller was a thinking man, a man with a conscience; he could not conform to their ideas and had committed suicide three or four years earlier.

The ruckus in the courtyard grew louder as more police and civilians joined the posse. Mother and I glanced at each other, and I could tell we were thinking the same thing: did this unassuming old woman, stooped over and barely bigger than a child, know what she could be in for? But we soon saw that she did. She hobbled to her bedroom and from the bureau drawer pulled out a swastika. She pinned it to her white apron where it stood out in sharp contrast. Perhaps this was the same emblem her Albert had been forced to wear. With one of her small, wrinkled hands she yanked up a corner of the Battenberg lace quilt that draped over her double bed, and with the other, she beckoned us.

"Both of you, quick, under the bed," she whispered. "Be still until I come to get you. Do not move a muscle or make a sound until I come for you, no matter what! Hurry now, I am going to open the front door so they won't suspect I'm hiding something in here."

As we scrambled under the bed, we could hear a mob downstairs, angry voices anticipating our capture. I could hear the voices vibrating with excitement; it could have been a foxhunt, with every good citizen eager to be in on the kill. We heard Frau Mueller fling open the door to her apartment and go into the stairwell. "Did you catch those damn Jews?" she shouted to the crowd that had gathered four flights below. I was amazed that such a big voice could come from such a small body. "They killed my poor husband, those damn Jews! They had the gall to ring my bell less than ten minutes ago. I should have stalled them!"

When the police finally came up to search her apartment, she repeated her story with great agitation. After one look at her official-looking swastika, they retreated with a respectful "Heil Hitler!" in her direction. They didn't even try to enter her apartment, though the door stood wide open the entire time.

Lying motionless under the bed, I could see the shiny black boots of our pursuers as they listened to Frau Mueller in the hallway. I was terrified, screaming inside, and yet it was all so unreal. We stayed under the bed for almost an hour. Frau Mueller's radio played "Silent Night" and "O Tannenbaum," and then one of Mother's favorites, "Es Geht Alles Vorueber." She squeezed my hand as we heard the refrain: *"Es geht alles vorueber, es geht alles vorbei, nach jedem Dezember kommt wieder ein Mai"* (Everything passes, everything ends, after December, comes once again May). I squeezed her hand back; yes, I swear, I told her silently, we will see another May.

Suddenly, church bells pealed throughout the city, heralding the holiday eve. At school I had loved to recite "Die Glocke" (The Bell), Schiller's epic poem that chronicled the life of man from birth to death. Now I began reciting it in my head. How poignantly Schiller had captured all those phases of life and all the upheaval between them – birth, youth, love, marriage, sickness, and finally death. But I just had started living and this could not be the end.

Out of the corner of my eye I could see two small feet in mustard-colored slippers approaching the bed. "Dears, all is quiet. They believe you escaped through one of the exits. You are safe," whispered Frau Mueller. "But let us speak very quietly, you know, for the walls have ears."

Mother and I crawled out from under the bed, our bodies stiff from the cramped position, the sheer terror and exhaustion. I blinked and looked around Frau Mueller's bedroom for the first time. In honor of the holiday, the room glowed with the flicker of candlelight, long white tapers in silver candlesticks, at least three on the bureau and two on each nightstand. On each stand was a handsomely framed photograph of her with her precious Albert. How young they looked, how carefree, how in love! There were no children, apparently; he was her whole world, and now her world was gone. No wonder she understood our plight so well.

First she embraced Mother and then turned to me. She held me in her arms and began crying. "Thank you, thank you," I murmured.

"Never mind, my son, I am happy to serve the Lord, to help you escape," she sobbed. "Yes, this is truly my holy eve, the first one I shall really celebrate since my Albert left me!" Suddenly she broke our embrace and her voice became steady and clear. "Listen here, my good neighbors, I don't know what the future holds, but you must survive this evil time. And we Germans also need to be saved from these thugs. We are all victims, but most do not know it yet. One day there will be a terrible awakening in this country, a day of reckoning will come."

She wiped the last of her tears and went into the kitchen to brew a pot of coffee, not Ersatz, but real coffee, which I hadn't tasted in a long time. She sliced me a thick hunk of holiday fruitcake. I ate it and wondered: What would tomorrow bring? I wasn't concerned with the entire future, just tomorrow.

Frau Mueller spoke as though she were reading my thoughts. "I'd like to have you stay here, but that would be very foolish," she said. "I suggest you get some sleep, and I'll wake you before daybreak. You can take Albert's key to the back exit. Just toss it away when you're out."

Just then we heard the faint, carnival-like music of an organ grinder who had been a fixture in our neighborhood for years. In honor of the holiday, he had come to the courtyard with his wizened little monkey, and was grinding out one Christmas carol after another, while shaking his collection can like a castanet. From Frau Mueller's bedroom window, I could see him swinging his flashlight in the darkness to find the paper-wrapped coins thrown to him. Usually, on such festive occasions, people were in a generous mood, but on this night, there was little response. The man and his monkey did not stay as long as usual and probably went in search of a happier building. Then, in the quiet, I kicked off my shoes and lay down on the bed beside my mother and plunged into a deep, dreamless sleep.

I was awakened by a gentle kiss on my forehead. "It's almost four o'clock, Lotharchen, you must get up. Your mother is already in the tub," said Frau Mueller softly. "After you have bathed, you will have something to eat and some real coffee."

I rubbed my eyes to look at this woman who stroked my hair and looked at me with such tenderness. Was she pretending that I was the son that she and Albert never had? A few hours earlier, she had been only a passing acquaintance, an old neighbor whose string bags of groceries I had carried up the stairs a few times. Now there was an eternal bond between us.

"God bless you," I said to her.

"And you, too, my dear," she replied.

Before we left, she made a satchel of food for us. And then she handed us the back-door key. "A good holiday to you, Frau Mueller," said Mother, embracing her one last time. "Now we can believe there are other good people out there, like you."

"I'm just being a Christian," she said quietly.

We crept down the four flights and entered the courtyard, so quiet after the previous night's tumultuous hunt for the two escapees. Then we made our way toward the back exit. With great care I turned the key, and the door to our freedom opened. The predawn air was so quiet and serene that I could hear the sound of my mother's breathing.

I saw her fumble inside her purse, and take something out of her wallet. Around her neck it went, the revered German Mother Cross. She put her arm around my shoulder, and, as always, I found peace in her warmth. Wordlessly she tugged at my sleeve and pointed toward the still-blackened sky. I looked up to see a million stars shining on us, Frau Ida Peters and her son Gerhard, on Christmas morn, the day of our rebirth.

But who was this Gerhard Peters? What lay ahead for him? I had no clue, and no time to ponder it. The dawn approached and it was time to move on, on into a new, uncharted life.

Chapter 5

A Very Busy Day

Mother and I had not merely undergone a name change. It was much more than that. We had to invent completely new attitudes, new postures, new family lore; we had to become masters of deception. The effect of every word, every gesture, had to be calculated, lest we give ourselves away. Our concepts of right and wrong were consigned to storage. In the back of my mind I knew something more: we might even have to kill to survive.

It had all seemed rather theoretical when we were planning our escape during our final months at Greifswalder Strasse. But suddenly it was all real. Suddenly we were walking through the streets of Berlin, homeless, just before dawn. And, in a perverse sense, as the Aryans Ida and Gerhard Peters, we were free for the first time from the prison that had been closing in on us for a long time. It was frightening, but it was also thrilling.

We were headed for the nearest public telephone, which was about a half mile away at the Arnswalder Platz, to alert my mother's cousin, Hans Loewenstein, that we were on our way as planned. On the way, I found myself saying good-bye to my neighborhood, to the part of town where the Orbach family had lived and were known by many. We passed my grammar school, the brick building where I had learned to read and write, the schoolyard where I had learned to throw a ball. I still prided myself on the many successful pranks I had played there – the time I put a huge beetle in Helmuth Hetmann's sandwich, the time I spiked our teacher's cushion with pins and needles. The teacher was furious, but none of my friends would tell on me. Those were good friends of mine.

Then we passed by my favorite bakery on the Pasteur-strasse, where every week I would treat myself to broken pastries at a discount, just five pfennig apiece, crumbled cakes that were still moist and fresh. Even as a small boy I always had a little pocket money, because I always found odd jobs, like collecting balls at the tennis club, or opening the doors of cars and taxis at the railroad station.

Right down the street had been Friedlaender's candy store, where ten pfennig would buy an assortment of broken chocolates, including the delectable chocolate covered orange peels and liqueur candies. On Kristall-nacht, after the good citizens had looted from Friedlaen-der's cracked display case, one boy in my class, Horst Meyer, bragged that he had stolen enough candy from the damn Jews to last him through the year.

I had spent hours in the playground at the Arnswal-der Platz; how forsaken it looked in the moonlight, without the children or the swooping Berliner *Spatzen*, the pigeons that never left the city, even in the dead of winter – cunning birds that always managed to find a warm berth. I watched them while I played in the sandbox, baking sand pies that we decorated with colored crayon shavings. "Cake to buy, don't pass it by!" we would shout. There we got our earliest lessons in business: haggling and bickering. "Ten rocks for the heart-shaped tart, five for the blue one, and if you throw in a couple of marbles, you can have them both!"

There were several ballfields near the playground, but the teenagers usually appropriated them, and between them and the *Pupe*, the groundskeeper, we younger ones were usually chased away. Walking or playing on the meticulously kept grass near the fields was strictly *Verboten!* The Pupe would shout at us, but we trampled on the grass just to irritate him. Once he chased Manfred into the street where he ran into a passing car and broke his leg.

I found a phone booth and called cousin Hans. He didn't sound too happy to be roused at five in the morning, but said that he would be waiting at his front door to unlock the entrance when we got there.

Ida and Gerhard Peters walked briskly. We stopped for a few moments in the Friedrichshain, one of Berlin's most beautiful parks, with its famous Fairy-Tale Fountain, which was even more picturesque in the breaking light of dawn. I had stood here so often as a little boy, hand in hand with Mama and Papa, looking at the sculpted figures of Snow White and the Seven Dwarfs, Cinderella, and the Frog Prince, standing tall with a big toad at his side. I used to sit astride this oversized frog, dreaming that I too might someday be a good-looking prince who could sweep a princess off her feet. And the plump Fairy Godmother with her magic wand: "Change me," I thought, "into an American, a Brit, anybody who is free. Or can you change them, my German brothers and sisters, into the old friends and neighbors they once were so that we can go home again?" Mother and I walked on in silence beneath the frozen treetops, both grappling with the unfathomable: this extraordinary city, serene, and a delight to the senses – how could the same people who had made it now want to purge it of some of its true children? Who could imagine Berlin without its Goethe, its Heine, its Einstein? I didn't want to think about Berlin without me.

By the time we arrived at the Landsberger Allee, the buses and trolleys had begun their morning rounds. I felt unsettled in the morning light, not sure I was ready for the dramatic transformation that had already begun. Cousin Hans, a stout fellow in his early thirties, looked a bit unkempt, but wide awake as he ushered us quietly into his apartment.

We knew that it would be unwise to spend more than a day with Hans, whose father had been picked up some months earlier, and who was in even more danger from spying neighbors than we had been in the Greifswalder Strasse. Standing over Hans's kitchen sink, Mother poured peroxide over my head to lighten my dark-brown hair and heavy eyebrows. She did not want to waste it on her own hair, which was even blacker than mine, because matron ladies did not stand out in crowds like young fellows out of uniform. I looked in the mirror and was startled to see Gerhard Peters.

The black marketeer, Herr Plaut, who had sold us our papers, had given us the name of a man in the Weissensee section who rented rooms for one hundred marks a week. Plaut said the man was an old bachelor, not in the least altruistic but very money hungry, who asked no questions, so many Jews were able to pass through there. Mother and I calculated that the few thousand marks in our possession would give us a roof over our heads for about six months. And once again, Mother repeated firmly: "Six months, and it will all be over. The Nazis will be finished!" I hoped she was right, because we couldn't hold out much longer.

At five o'clock that evening, we said good-bye to Hans, not knowing that we would never see him again: within weeks he, too, would be deported and exterminated. We decided to go out at rush hour, hoping to get lost in the crowds as we entered the Stadtbahn to Weis-sensee. The Weissensee railroad station, to our dismay, was only about three miles from our former address; a little too close for comfort, but we had no other choice. When we got on board the crowded train, a uniformed Hitler Youth leaped from his seat and clicked his heels. "Please, madam, take my seat!" he offered. Mother turned around to see who he was addressing; then she realized he was bowing to the "Mother Cross." It was truly worth the small fortune we had paid for it.

We arrived at the building on the Langhans Strasse, and walked up four flights to ring the doorbell of Herr Ulrich. A man answered the door but kept the chain fastened. I could see his eyes sizing us up through the crack in the door.

"What do you want, who are you?" he weaseled.

"Herr Plaut sent us," I answered. "He said that you have a room my mother and I could rent for a short time. We were bombed out in a big air raid in the Rhineland, we're just passing through Berlin."

"Well, get in here," he said gruffly, unfastening the chain. "I don't want to talk to anybody standing in the hall."

The first thing we noticed was the stench. Ulrich was a paunchy, bald-headed man in his fifties who looked and smelled as if he hadn't bathed in weeks. His plaid flannel shirt and baggy pants were covered with grime. The buttons of his fly were missing. When he talked he wheezed and coughed; he either had very bad asthma or emphysema.

"It's got only one bed, the room, and it goes for 125 marks a week," he said. "And you'll have to give me two weeks' rent in advance. The last son of a bitch ran out on me without paying."

I immediately gave him all he asked for, repulsed by the notion of haggling with him. Out of the corner of my eye, I saw my mother had covered her face with a handkerchief. We followed him up one more flight to a tiny room that was directly under the roof. The place was spartan, but, thankfully, it did not smell the way he did. Above the bed hung a large portrait of Adolf Hitler. I didn't give a damn; it was just what Ida and Gerhard Peters would want. We were exhausted, not from the short trip, but from stress, and went to sleep almost immediately.

We awoke early, as light streamed through the flimsy paper shades. Within minutes, we heard a loud pop, like a pistol, from the street below. I crawled over to the window on all fours, and moved the shade slightly to look outside. There outside our back window was the yard of a slaughterhouse. A small horse was sprawled out on the pavement, its last stop before a butcher shop. During our time at Ulrich's, I would watch many such executions.

There was no toilet in the room, but underneath the bed I found an old-fashioned chamber pot, which I handed first to Mother. I turned my back to give her some privacy, and, when she was finished she handed it back to me. I took the filled vessel over to the tiny washbasin, the only convenience in the room, and poured it down the drain.

From Ulrich's apartment came a blood-curdling yell. "Which idiot is pissing down the pipes, are you crazy?" he bellowed out of the window that was directly beneath our own. "My whole goddamn room is soaked and it stinks like hell!" Ulrich came storming upstairs, panting. He was still wearing the same flannel shirt and his fly was wide open.

"Only one night, and you're already causing me trouble!" he shouted. "That pipe needs to be fixed, and I'll be damned if I let the owner stick me for it!"

"But where are we supposed to go to the bathroom, sir?" I asked him, trying to sound polite.

"There's a toilet out in the hall, but I'm the only one who has the key. It's illegal for me to sublet to anyone, so I'll have to make sure the coast is clear before I let you in." So now we had to check in with him every time we needed to go the bathroom. We realized we would never last six months in this place. We had given Ulrich two week's rent. But where else could we go? We had learned one of the first lessons of the underground: never move on with just one address in your pocket, in case things don't work out there.

After nine nights and ten days in Weissensee, with constant air-raid sirens, about one hundred dead horses, and several dozen chamber pots, Mother awoke in the middle of the night, and bolted upright.

"I've got it! I've got it!" she exclaimed excitedly.

"What?" I mumbled.

"That woman's name!" she said. "It was Dudacy!"

"Of course, Anne and the Tante."

"Hedel!" said Mama triumphantly. "I'm going to call them!"

It struck me that both of us had completely blocked out the memory of Anne Dudacy. I realized that Mother must have known that the beautiful brunette was making a play for Papa. Under normal circumstances, we wouldn't have given her the time of day. Now, suddenly remembering her offer of help, we were ready to put our lives in her hands. Hardly able to sleep, we waited to call until early the next morning, hoping to catch them before they went to work.

As I dialed Anne Dudacy's number, my hands were shivering in the cold January morning. It rang several times before she picked it up.

"Frau Dudacy? Anne?" I stammered.

"Yes, yes, who is this calling at this hour?" The voice on the other end was terse and impatient. I was too excited to speak; there was too much at stake in this call. I handed the receiver to Mother.

"Frau Dudacy, this is Nelly Orbach, the former landlady of Herr Pieck, from the Greifswalder Strasse. ... Oh, good, you remember me ... how are you? ... No, we are not home anymore ... now it's just me and the boy ... my husband ... he's dead. You once invited me to come for a visit, isn't that right? I hope you understand me?"

For a few moments neither of us breathed. And then I watched a beautiful smile spread over my mother's face and, without being able to hear Anne Dudacy's side of the conversation, I knew what she was saying. Yes, yes, Mother nodded wordlessly. Anne suggested we come the following morning, giving her a little time to prepare a room for us, and to explain the situation to her son and daughter.

After she hung up, the two of us embraced in the phone booth in an explosion of relief. "God is great, Lotharchen," said my mother; "you must never lose faith in the Almighty!" By conventional standards she was not a very religious woman; she certainly was not schooled in the Jewish traditions. She seldom set foot inside a synagogue, and I doubted that she could read Hebrew. But Mother had a private God with whom she communicated in her own language. Each night before going to sleep she spoke to Him, praying for the safety of each of her children, invoking Heinz's name, then Manfred's, and lastly mine. When she said my name, I could hear the extra urgency in her voice. And, night after night, she closed her prayers with the same words: "Dear Lord, I thank You for all that You granted me today, all that You have granted me in the past, and all that You will grant me in the future."

Every night I waited to hear this prayer, feigning sleep to give her some sense of privacy as she whispered it. In the beginning I wondered what on earth she was giving thanks for. But, in time, the steadfastness of her faith became the source of my own perseverance. How could any deity refuse the prayers of such a devoted woman?

On our way back to Ulrich's, we stopped at a little bakery that served the wretched Ersatz Kaffee and day-old hard rolls, the only bread that could be bought without ration stamps. We sat for a while, dunking the rolls into the hot brew, and watched the Berliners hurrying to work, the soldiers heading toward the railroad station, arm in arm with girlfriends or wives. It appeared as though everyone had a place to go, a place in society, except the two of us. It didn't seem possible that there were no others like us left in Berlin. But where were they?

As we continued on, crossing the Antonplatz, I saw Herr Ulrich lumbering across the square in our direction. Gasping for breath as usual, he looked agitated as he approached us. "Look here, the Gestapo came to my apartment, to look around. Somehow they must know about you Jews," he wheezed. "They said they will come back tomorrow. You must find another place right away!" Ulrich began coughing and spitting blood on the ground. He took from his pocket a filthy handkerchief, and blew his nose; it was a disgusting sight.

"Look here, maybe the best thing for you is to go to one of those Jew camps, by your own free will. I heard when you volunteer they give you much better treatment. You get to eat and drink and you have a place to sleep; they have work for you, and they even pay you wages."

"Is that so?" Mother said icily.

Ulrich nodded. "Making the best of a bad situation, that's what they call it. And look, here's an idea. Leave your belongings with me, I'll hold onto them for you, and when the war is over you can pick them up! Won't be long now!"

I knew he was lying. The Gestapo never left and "came back tomorrow" when there was the slightest suspicion that a Jew was hiding; they stayed put until the Jew showed up. Either he had already ratted on us, or was about to. What we did not know was whether the Gestapo were there now waiting for us to return or whether this was a ruse by which Ulrich would relieve us of our belongings.

Then I saw he was wearing, under his overcoat, one of my three precious shirts, the blue cotton one that my father had given me on my eighteenth birthday, five days before he was shipped off to Sachsenhausen. The bastard must have gone through our things while we were gone!

Suddenly, it was clear. If the Gestapo were there, we would have no choice to turn ourselves in to a "Jew camp;" on the other hand, we would be able to take some of our things. Ulrich could get his hands on our things – and also avoid the risk of being found harboring Jews – only if he could fool us into fleeing. There was still a chance the Gestapo might be there, of course, but we would risk it. It was the first decision I had made on my mother's behalf.

Once he had our belongings, however, Ulrich might try for extra credit by turning us in. Our problem would be to escape Ulrich and his treachery and still keep our possessions, our only family remains. I knew I would say or do anything, absolutely anything, to get away from the slimy, and now dangerous, Ulrich. And I knew what I had to do. It would be my first act as an adult, an act I would never forget.

"Herr Ulrich, you have been a friend," I said smoothly, "and you have given us good advice. We will get ready to move on immediately, and thank you for allowing us to leave our belongings with you." My mother stared at me incredulously. I was adapting too well to this life of deceit.

We returned to the building together. No cars were about, no signs of Gestapo. We trudged up the four flights, Ulrich sounding as if he were about to pass out. I told him we would call him after we had finished washing up and taking inventory of our things. The minute we shut the door, my mother flew into a panic. "The Gestapo could be on its way this minute! And what has gotten into you, telling that cannibal that we will leave our things with him?"

Now it was my turn to calm my mother. "Mama, trust me. Everything will be all right. Let's get ready to go." We laid out our belongings on the room's only table, and I went out into the hall and called for Ulrich. While waiting for him, I gulped down the remains of an eight-ounce bottle of Immergut Milch – a milk substitute that required no refrigeration. I placed the empty glass container on the windowsill.

Ulrich's eyes lit up when he walked in and surveyed the pile of clothing. He probably planned to keep a set or two of my things for himself, and sell the rest along with Mother's. "Here are paper and pencil, sir," I said. "Why don't you sit here at the table and make a list of each item, while Mother hands it to me and I put it into the satchel? We will leave that with you, and take just the knapsack for the two of us."

"Very smart, my boy!" he said, trying to be ingratiating. "Travel light, that's my motto!" He sat down close to my mother, who struggled to maintain a smile.

"Two men's shirts, three undershirts, three boxer shorts," my mother called out stiffly. Ulrich obligingly wrote everything down. "Three pairs of men's socks. Two ladies' stockings. One knitted vest ..."

Ulrich wheezed and scribbled with intense concentration. I knew he was calculating feverishly, tallying up his take. When the list was nearly finished, I slowly backed away from the knapsack I was packing. Mother sensed immediately that something was up; by her look, I knew she was expecting something dramatic to happen, and that she was ready for it.

I took the empty milk bottle from the window sill and, turning suddenly, smashed it with all my strength over Ulrich's bald head. The glass exploded into a hundred flying pieces. Ulrich slumped over, his forehead on the table. His wheezing stopped. Blood began to ooze down both sides of his head and, as I watched from behind, trickled down behind his ears. He was motionless. The room was flooded with silence.

For a moment my mother and I stood there, unable to move or speak. Violence had become common in Germany, yes, but not violence by us. Mother looked horrified, first at Ulrich and then at me. Many years later I would remember this moment when Israel's Prime Minister Golda Meir told Egyptian President Nasser: "I can forgive you for killing my sons, but I can never forgive you for turning my sons into killers." I didn't know if I was a killer or not. And I would never know. But Ulrich remained silent and motionless, his blood now dripping from table to floor. We took our bags and fled.

Bolting down the stairwell, we could hear the noise of a marching band in the street. Just what we needed, another rousing demonstration of the Third Reich's majesty. A column of Bund Deutscher Maedel girls was marching by, dressed in their trim black skirts and white blouses with the little black scouting scarves. How pretty and healthy and clean they looked. A number of the girls appeared to be around my age, and for a moment I was worried that someone might know me. But nobody even glanced in our direction; they held their heads high, looking straight ahead, marching in perfect formation. They were singing an old German folksong, one of the same ones we had so often sung on the veranda of our apartment, and around the campfire during our summertime jaunts to the Mueggelsee:

"Out of the city's grayness we go,
rollicking through woods and fields
Who stays behind is a spoil-sport,
we're going off into the world!
Hei-lee, hei-lo, we're going,
going off into the world!"

After the line "going off into the world," *die Welt,* my brothers and I would always yell out the rhyming epithet *ohne Geld!* – "without money!" So did a lot of other German kids. These girls, however, were marching to a different drum, one beaten by an invisible but ever-present leader. They would not need "Geld." Almost involuntarily, I found myself singing along, my way, my vociferous "ohne Geld!" drowned out by their voices, lost among the trombones and the drums and the cymbals.

Yes, we certainly were "going off into the world," and "without money." The absurdity of it struck me. Not five minutes earlier I had committed a violent crime because I was a Jew trying to stay one step ahead of the Gestapo. And now I was singing along with a bunch of Nazi maidens, awash in nostalgia for my idyllic German boyhood. I felt ashamed. I felt angry. But I would not let them expropriate my memories. This was my song too.

A trio of girls holding a large swastika banner was passing right in front of us. And then, like all the other delighted onlookers who lined the street, we put down our bags and saluted it. Stretching out my right arm as high as it would go, I recited my trademark version: "The shit in Germany is piled *this high*!" How proud those three girls were to be the standard bearers. Their faces were flushed, their eyes burned brightly, their lips wet and parted. There was an erotic quality to it all.

We moved briskly down the street, trying to look purposeful, trying not to attract attention. The streets abounded with spies, mostly Germans trying to ingratiate themselves with the party higher-ups and, yes, even some Jews. It was best to trust no one. On the train I knew that we were both thinking about Ulrich. But to look back seemed pointless. What was done was done. It could only sap our strength and our resolve. So instead we talked about Anne Dudacy. "Maybe I was wrong about the Frau," said Mother haltingly. "Maybe I misjudged her."

"I'm sure you are right," I said, trying to convince myself as well.

"She was a smart woman. She predicted all of this. I remember her words, that the Jews in Germany were an endangered species. And she was good-looking, too."

"She was OK, nothing special." And then we grew quiet, holding onto the memory of my father, an honorable man, a wonderful man, who belonged to us alone.

After a few stops, we arrived at Frankfurter Allee. The Zorndorfer Strasse was a quiet street in a middle-class neighborhood in the eastern part of Berlin, not far from the station. A pretty blond girl opened the door of the apartment. She greeted us with delight, as though we were long-lost relatives.

"Oh, you must be Frau Nelly and Lothar! My mother and Tante Hedel have told me so much about you! Welcome, welcome!"

Her name was Sylvia and she was about seventeen. She looked like a younger, blonder version of Anne, but seemed a more easygoing sort, with a friendly manner and an open expression. She said that her mother had gone to the railroad station to pick up another one of her aunts who would be visiting from Koenigshuette, and assured us that our early arrival was no problem. "Please," she said, "think of this as your own home. Let me take you to your room."

She ushered us into a typical boy's bedroom, and then quickly ducked out to give us some privacy. The room must have belonged to her younger brother Andreas. A closet and several drawers had been emptied for us, and there were fresh linens on the two single beds. On the night stand were books by two of my favorite authors, Jack London and Tucholsky. Perhaps Anne had remembered that I liked to read.

As we unpacked, my mother had tears in her eyes, overwhelmed by this girl's hospitality, the warmth and cleanliness of the apartment, by the sudden, comforting normalcy of it all. There was a radio in our room, and for the first time in more than a week we listened to the news from the *Deutschlandsender*. As we knew from our top-floor room in Weissensee, there had been massive air strikes on Berlin, which the government tried to play down. They were finally admitting, however, that the courageous German Army of Stalingrad had been surrounded and destroyed by the Russians.

"Maybe it will all be over in a couple of weeks, by the time of my birthday," mused my mother. "Yes, that would be the best present I could get on the twenty-second of January!"

"Don't worry, Mama," I said, giving her a big hug. "It's going to be a great birthday."

"With God's help, yes, a great birthday," she said. But I could tell that she was not yet ready to believe that we were safe, that the worst might be over. And she was probably remembering other birthdays, on the veranda in the Greifswalder Strasse, being serenaded by her handsome husband and her three sons.

There was a knock on the door and in came Sylvia carrying a plate of cake and cookies and some fruit. "I baked something in honor of your coming. I hope it is edible," she said shyly. "I am just learning to bake in home economics class, and you are my first victims!"

"Oh, you sweet girl," said Mother, "I don't know how we can ever thank you."

Sylvia waved her hand; the Dudacys were a family of intense political convictions and, according to their ideology, harboring us was the right thing, the necessary thing, to do.

"No talk of thanks, what's ours is yours," said Sylvia. "The only thing my mother asks is, under no circumstances should you answer the telephone or open the door to anyone."

Sylvia kissed Mother on the cheek, and came over to me to shake my hand, her eyes unselfconsciously meeting mine. My first impulse was to look away, for it had been a long time since I had had the nerve to talk with an Aryan girl.

"Maybe you can bake a cake for my mother's birthday, it's coming soon," I blurted out, as awkwardly as a small boy.

"Why of course! Congratulations, Frau Nelly!" she replied enthusiastically. And then she left us to ourselves.

I filled up the bathtub and lay there for a long time. What a dream, a warm bath, a full washing. It was the kind of thing I had once taken for granted. Using a cake of soap with the gardenia scent I had smelled faintly on Sylvia, I tried to wash away the past weeks – the toppled horses, the smell of Ulrich, his gasping breath, his blood.

And then I started to think about my fetching new housemate. It was startling how my hormones ruled my thoughts; one minute I was anguishing about life-threatening dangers, criminal acts, and the next minute, I fantasized about Sylvia's creamy skin and wavy golden hair, about holding her in my arms. I was officially Aryan for the time being, so the race-mixing laws were suspended as long as my identity held. And if her own political beliefs were anything like those of her parents, "free love" would be taken for granted. But it would be insane to get involved with the Dudacy's daughter; there was too much to lose if things went wrong. I knew I had to find something to do with all the free time that lay ahead, so that I would have something to occupy my thoughts besides sex.

Mother spent the rest of the afternoon in the kitchen, preparing a dinner of potato soup with lamb shanks and turnips. This was the way she would make herself feel useful in the new household, for she was by nature uncomfortable taking from others. It was nearly dinnertime when a key turned in the door, and two women entered carrying large suitcases. The taller, fairer one nodded at me in a cordial manner, looking me up and down as though I were a great curiosity. The petite brunette I recognized as Anne Dudacy.

"Well! You're here already. I didn't expect you until tomorrow!" she said briskly. "Did my daughter get everything ready for you? I would have stayed home had I known!"

Anne spoke in a torrent of words. Her tone was very blunt, and she held nothing back. Some people were put off by her manner, but I would soon learn that there was no better friend than she.

"I hope it hasn't inconvenienced you too much that we came early," I said. "We had to leave our other place in rather a hurry – there was a problem. And I didn't want Mother to sleep in the streets tonight."

"No, no, Lothar, I'm only surprised to see you. This is my sister Hella – I have told her all about you. She will be with us for at least a week – she'll stay in my room."

"It is nice to meet you, Lothar," said Hella.

"You, too," I said, "but my name is now Gerhard, Gerhard Peters, and my mother is now called Ida."

"We'll get used to it if you will," laughed Anne. "So, Gerhard, come and help me with these heavy bags."

My mother came out of the kitchen, and Anne held out her arms to her. They embraced without words. I suspect they really were not sure what to say to each other.

"Well, it smells great," Anne finally said. "I seem to remember that you were a good cook. I'm hopeless in the kitchen myself, right, Hella?"

"Thank you, dear," said my mother, her voice choked with tears. And I knew that she was thanking Anne for much more than a compliment.

Just before we all sat down to dinner, Mother asked me to ask Anne for some matches, as we had left ours at Ulrich's. It was Friday evening, and while she still had a small supply of candles in her satchel, she liked to light them in honor of the Sabbath. It was one of the few rituals of Jewish family life in the Greifswalder Strasse that we had been able to retain, and it meant a great deal to us. Anne gave me a book of matches and a disapproving look. It was soon apparent that religion was not one of her favorite subjects.

"Gerhard, one thing you had better know about me: I don't believe in any of this hocus-pocus. I mean, you folks are supposed to be 'the chosen people.' Look what your God is doing to you. If He is really so powerful and just, He should not stand idly by and let all this happen to you. You give me Marx anytime – at least I can work with my hands and I don't have to wait for miracles. As Marx said, religion is the opiate of the masses."

I didn't answer Anne. I didn't want to antagonize her during our first night under her roof. And, also, I didn't know what to say to her, under the circumstances. I only knew that I felt differently, that my mother's nightly prayer soothed my soul and gave me hope, and that was enough truth for me. I remembered what my father used to say: never discuss religion, politics, or the raising of children with your friends. After all, this woman was a saint for taking us into her home, whether she believed in religion or not. So I said nothing.

Mother, always intensely attuned to her environment and to the wishes of those around her, took the solitary candle into our bedroom and shut the door behind us. She covered her hair with a shawl, waved her hands in a circular motion over the Sabbath light, and quietly uttered the traditional blessing. Finally, holding her face in her hands, she murmured the names of her children, one after another. A feeling of great peace flooded the candlelit room. We had made it through another week, a terrible week, to another Sabbath.

Now that Mother would no longer be alone in my absence, I decided I would take advantage of the darkness and go for a walk after dinner. I told everyone I would be back in a couple of hours. My mother knew I was desperate to get out and let me leave without reproach.

Heading down the Grosse Frankfurter Strasse toward the center of the city, I felt as free as a bird. It was an exceptionally clear night, cold, but not bitter. The streets were filled with people, and none of them knew me. Mostly there were women, often with children in tow; the absence of men was obvious and, among the very few that I saw, I realized that nearly all of them wore a uniform of one kind or another. This thought made me step briskly, for I had to show that I was busy like everyone else, that I had someplace important to go.

On the Koppenstrasse, about fifteen minutes away from the Dudacys', I saw a small sign in front of a narrow, rundown building, that said "Billiard Saal." I had never played billiards, but I loved Ping-Pong; we had played constantly on the makeshift table in our apartment. It was a good deal smaller than regulation size, but we made do. I had become quite proficient and rarely lost to my brothers or our friends.

I wrestled with my impulse to go inside. Maybe the place was a trap for idle fellows like me, with the Gestapo lying in wait. Maybe they were scouring the city for Ulrich's assailant. I stood outside, weighing the pros and cons, and youth won out. I had to see it once, just once, and before I knew it I was climbing the rickety wooden staircase. Even before I walked in, I could hear the clacking of the billiard balls, and the swift claps of the Ping-Pong paddles. To me there was great excitement in these sounds.

I had never been to such a place in my life. The smell of tobacco filled the air, and a jukebox played loudly. The whole place was shrouded in darkness, with only the individual tables illuminated by hanging lamps. At first I felt that all eyes were on me, as if all play had stopped because of me, but my imagination was playing tricks. The man sitting at the cashier's desk gave me a nod, and a few others looked up briefly before returning to their games.

I walked carefully around the billiard tables to the Ping-Pong room. There were six matches going. I moved carefully around the tables so as not to disturb the players. I wondered if I could hold my own with any of these players on the full-sized tables. I wanted to try, but I hesitated over starting a conversation with anybody.

Suddenly I felt a hand on my shoulder. My body stiffened and I swung around, ready to defend myself against any attacker.

"Hey, Lothar! What's with you, my friend?" In the dim light, I could barely see who was addressing me, but there was no threat in his voice. "It's me, Tad, from the factory!"

I was shaking as I tried to regain my composure. I realized that if I wanted to set foot outside the Dudacys', I had better toughen up, or I would have a nervous breakdown.

"Tad, you surprised me! It's great to see you!"

"Where've you been? I haven't seen you in ages!"

"Well, I had to quit the factory. My father died, and my mother got sick, family problems, you know."

"Yeah, I quit, too. Listen, follow me while I just finish this game in the billiard room, and then we'll talk, OK?"

I had never played caramboulage, the original billiard game. It is an extremely precise art in which one must touch the cushions and both red balls with the white cue ball. Tad appeared to be a real expert. He made several shots with his cue vertically in the air and hit the cue ball from the top, making it loop around two other balls, touching them one after the other.

On the table next to Tad's, a tall, dark-haired man played against a paunchy little one. Taunting each other's billiard prowess, they spoke German with what sounded like French accents. Since the fall of France there must have been a million or more French workers in Germany, which was to my advantage; the influx of all these non-Aryans made us less conspicuous. And yet something about these two men puzzled me: if they spoke German with such a heavy accent, why didn't they speak in French? The French were so proud of their culture and language.

Meanwhile, Tad had wrapped up his game with a series of fifty-two consecutive points, a feat I thought impressive until one day I watched him score 150 points in a row. His opponent, an older fellow, handed him some folded bills. "Next time give me a better handicap, boy!" he grumbled. "Twenty-five to 150 is not enough. I want at least an even chance to win."

"Anything you say, my friend," said Tad easily. "Next time."

Tad began setting up the table for a game. He handed me a cue stick, and as he stood close to me he bent his head and began to whisper. "Lothar, how the hell are you still walking around free in this city? It's supposed to be Judenrein."

"Tad, I don't think this is the time or place to go into it ..."

"Well, I'll let you in on something I've told no one else around here," he said tersely. "I didn't just leave the munitions factory, I ran away from induction into the army, so now I'm considered a deserter, a criminal just like you."

I was stunned, and flattered that he had chosen to confide in me. "And your mother? Are you still living with her?"

"She went back to Poland. And now I'm a *Taucher*, a diver."

"What does that mean, a diver?"

"I've gone underground," he said, and then he laughed. "There are a lot of us, we're like the goddamn rats in the city sewers!"

"I don't understand," I said. "How do you live?"

"I take home more money from this place than I did from the factory, and I make my own hours! I'm living with this woman, a beauty-salon owner whose husband was killed in the war, and she takes very good care of me."

"So you've finally found the right one," I said, remembering Tad's reputation as a lady's man.

"Well, she's the right one for now," he replied. "Be serious, Lothar, this isn't the time for romance – I'm glad to have a roof over my head. My girlfriend knows nothing about who I really am."

"But aren't you afraid to hang around a public place like this?" I asked him, but I was really asking for myself. "Couldn't there be military patrols where so many men congregate?"

"This place here is as safe as any other. In fact, it's safer. Johann, the owner, is a very sharp guy. He knows that many of the fellows who have the time to play here, day in, day out, are not too kosher, but he needs our business. It's in his best interest to be on the lookout for any potential problems."

He paused for a second and looked at me intently. He grinned and tousled my shock of peroxided hair.

"Hey, Blondie, you look great, just like me! So tell me, what have you been up to?"

I didn't know where to begin. It all seemed surreal, unbelievable – our Christmas eve escape, the dump in Weissensee, Ulrich, Sylvia …

"Tad, I'm still too nervous. I don't feel comfortable here."

"Relax. Johann warns us when anybody suspicious heads up the stairs, just the way he did when you entered. He has a mirror downstairs that he watches through a little side window. He's a Commie from way back, and he hates the Nazis as much as you and I do."

Tad motioned surreptitiously across the room. "You see that striped wallpaper? It covers a false door. Guys are constantly disappearing into that hidden room for all kinds of reasons. After Johann gives the all-clear signal, they come back out. The MPs drop in every few weeks, but in the three months I've been coming here, they have never caught a single person."

"Unbelievable," I muttered.

"Those guys at the next table, with the crazy accents? Believe me, they can't speak a damn word of French. They are Tauchers, Jews just like you. They bought French working papers, that's all. The tall one, Philippe, you see the bulge in his back pocket? That's a revolver, and you can bet he never goes anywhere without it."

So I was right about the phony Frenchmen. "He carries a gun? What if they catch him?"

"If they catch him they'll kill him or send him to a camp. At least his chances of survival are better with the gun," said Tad bitterly. "I'm buying one in the black market myself this week, and the first guy that tries to take me – bang-bang!"

A man tapped Tad on the shoulder. "Look here, are you guys playing or not?" he barked. "My friend and I are waiting for a table."

"I really should be going now," I said to Tad.

Tad walked me to the entryway. There I saw Johann behind his desk, looking me up and down.

"So where are you headed, boy?" Tad prodded. "What's the big secret? I've told you everything about me!"

"I'm not trying to be secretive, Tad, I trust you," I said to him. "OK, look. My mother and I escaped from the Gestapo, we've been on the run for nearly a month. Just today I think I killed our former landlord, and as of this afternoon we're being hidden by this Communist family — actually, a really good-looking bunch of women."

Tad gave me a huge grin. "Lotharchen, you have had a very busy day!"

"And my name isn't Lothar anymore. My papers say Gerhard Peters, and I'm a student in the Technische Hochschule," I told him wearily. "Really, I have to go. My mother worries about me every minute I'm out of her sight."

"Oh, bullshit! The night is still young! I'll talk to my girlfriend. She has lots of friends who are dying to hook up with a young guy like you. I'll set you up in a great situation. It will be safer for your mother and the Communist ladies if you're living elsewhere."

Tad was right about that. It had already occurred to me that the presence of a young man with no uniform in the Dudacy household was bound to draw more attention than yet another middle-aged woman. Not to mention the high cost of feeding one.

"I don't know, Tad," I said, slightly embarrassed. "To be honest, I'm still a virgin." And then I realized I had always expected my first time to be with somebody I loved.

"You're joking! Well, we'll fix that, too. Lothar – I mean, Gerhard – this city is full of lonely, really lonely women, with no one to look after them."

"But to use them like that ..."

"Who is using who? You have something they want, and they have something you want. Look, with Stalingrad gone, the Allies will soon land and this fucking war will be history, and if my luck holds out, I will be off to

America. But in the meantime, Taddeus the deserter is fighting this war in his own way. I eat well, I sleep with a nice woman, and I hustle pool for money. It won't win me a place in heaven, but it could be worse, right?"

It could be a lot worse. I did not know much about the kind of place in which my father had died, places like Sachsenhausen, Auschwitz, Treblinka, and I did not really appreciate the meaning of the word "ghetto," but I knew these places were like a black hole from which no one emerged alive. That was a lot worse.

Tad told me to come back the next day, Saturday, his biggest money day. He boasted that he won ninety percent of his matches, even when he gave his opponents big handicaps, and that the other ten percent he lost just so the suckers would keep playing against him. He said that he would teach me how to play, that the two of us would make a good team.

Walking back to the Zorndorfer Strasse, I felt something I hadn't felt in a long time: I felt alive. Reconnecting with Tad, a friend close to my own age, suddenly gave everything a new form and shape. He had already scoped out all the dangers and seemed to have everything all figured out. The billiard hall seemed like a good place to pass the time, and time was my enemy. I was going crazy with nothing to occupy my mind.

I had often wondered, during these last several weeks, if we were the last Jews left in Berlin. Now I knew where the rest of them were – like rats, crawling underground. Tauchers, Tad had called them. I supposed I was now a Taucher, too.

When I got back to the Dudacys' apartment, it was clear that my mother was very agitated. Sylvia sat next to her on the sofa, holding her hand, and she, too, glowered at me disapprovingly. I apologized and told them I had met a friend in the billiard hall, but I didn't go into any more detail. They had all been waiting for me before having coffee. Sylvia sat down next to me, which pleased me to no end. Despite her annoyance over my absence, she smiled at me with genuine delight. And then she passed me a plate of her crumbly cookies, and that rarity of rarities: a steaming cup of real coffee.

I raised my cup to Anne Dudacy. "I wish to thank you for everything, for all the kindness you have shown my mother and me today," I said solemnly. "I hope to reciprocate in good times, and may they come very soon." To myself I added "with God's help," but I didn't think that Anne would appreciate it.

"Prosit, to Gerhard!" said Anne, with a slightly sarcastic tone, but tears in her eyes. "If you want to be around to see the good times, young man, you had better watch your step in this city. It's like a minefield, full of spies and other dangers."

"That's right, Gerhard!" said Sylvia. "You must be more careful, think of your poor mother!"

Mother sighed and shook her head. "Ladies, I know my son is trying the gods, but he is a young man and he needs to live, to be with people his own age."

There was a pause in the conversation and suddenly Sylvia, with the radiance of inspiration, asked: "Do you play chess, Gerhard?"

"Oh, yes, he's quite good," Mother answered before I could disclaim any skill at the game. "He used to play a lot at the Jewish Children's Club on the Wehlauer Strasse."

In truth, I wasn't a very good player at all, but I knew what Mother and Sylvia were up to, and I wasn't about to protest. The thought of sitting across a chessboard from Sylvia for hours on end was very appealing.

"That's great," said Sylvia. "Why don't we play a little, if you're not too tired."

"Sure," I said. Tired? I was exhausted, but I was thrilled just to be near this girl. And, yes, I really wanted her to like me.

After we cleared the table, Sylvia set up the chessboard. She had put a pink angora sweater on over her plain house dress, and with her golden hair and bright blue eyes, she looked to me under the light of the chandelier like a spray of spring flowers, all pinks and yellows and blues. She took a white pawn in one closed fist and a black in the other, and then tossed them back and forth. "Which one, Gerhard, left or right?"

I took her right hand, and held it for a few seconds. "You get white, you get the first draw," she announced. Within moments, my ineptitude became obvious. "Gerhard you're making a bad move, your queen is in danger," she warned. "Change your move or I'll take her."

But I didn't care. My mind was off on other things. What was the loss of a queen with everything else that was happening in our world? Within the last few hours, our lives had ranged from darkness, degradation, and despair to safety and the warmth of human friendship. I was still decompressing.

"I'm really not very good at this," I admitted.

"I don't care," she sighed. "All the other boys are off fighting this, this despicable war. Some of them have even been killed already. I'm just glad for the company."

"What about your brother?"

"Oh, he's hardly ever home nowadays. And besides, he's totally immature – all he thinks about are sports and cars. I can't talk to him about, you know – life."

Did that mean that she felt she could talk to me? I hoped so.

After a few more minutes, both of us could hardly keep our eyes open. She asked if I would go to the movies with her the next day, Saturday, assuring me that she would pay. I hated to turn her down, but said I had agreed to meet Tad at the billiard hall to discuss some important business.

"Important business?" she said petulantly. "You would rather hang around some sleazy poolroom than go to the movies with me?"

"No, that isn't it, really," I said. "Tad is a very smart fellow, he knows his way around. There is a lot I need to learn from him if I am going to get through this."

"Well, just be careful, then," she said sleepily. And with that, she lightly kissed my cheek, and went off to bed.

That night I was vaguely aware that the air-raid sirens were wailing. Every building had an air-raid warden whose job it was to knock on every apartment door and order the residents down into their assigned shelters at night. For some reason, that night no one gave the order. So all of us stayed in our beds, and slept like the dead through the entire night and the all-clear alarm.

Tad was right. It had been a very busy day.

Chapter 6

Learning the Angles

When I arrived at the billiard hall the next afternoon, Tad was playing against two men who were tallying their combined scores against his. About a dozen bettors and onlookers stood around the table, watching the action intently and rooting for Tad.

In the Ping-Pong room, a young man sat on one of the tables holding two rackets and a ball. When he saw me, he whistled in my direction and waved his hand.

"You, over there!" he said. "My partner's late. Want a quick game? The table's paid for."

"It's been a while since I played," I said, "but sure, why not?" I had never played on a full sized table, but I beat him easily. He introduced himself as Heinz, and asked me if I were new in town. I gave him what would become my standard story: Gerhard Peters, recent arrival in Berlin after the family home in the Rhineland was bombed, transfer student at the Technische Hochschule.

"Well, Gerhard, you're good!" he said. "How about throwing me a ten-point handicap and we'll play for a couple of marks?"

So we did, and again I won. By the time Heinz's partner arrived, I had won two more games. Six marks wasn't much, but they were my first earnings since leaving the factory, and it was certainly a much more enjoyable way to make a living.

Tad had wandered in and, with obvious enjoyment, watched the final minutes of play. "Good game, my friend!" Tad said, shaking my hand. "But now come with me into the billiard room, where real men play for real money."

"I don't know how, Tad."

"That's no problem, Lo … uh, Gerhard. With me for a teacher, you'll be an expert in no time." I thanked him, and saw a big grin on his face. "That's not all you'll be thanking me for," he said slyly. "Ever been on a blind date?"

"Tonight?" I said nervously. "With who? Does it have to be tonight?" I had planned to leave the poolroom early. Sylvia had looked so sulky that morning, I told her I would go with her to a late movie after all.

"Don't be a fool," said Tad firmly. "She's very pretty and very nice, a friend of Ilse's. She and Ilse have planned a special dinner for this evening. She's dying to meet you."

"You do work fast," I muttered, wondering how I would tell Sylvia.

"Learn from me, kid," he laughed. "In this city, you're quick or you're dead. Things are changing by the minute, and every minute could be your last."

He said her name was Trudy and that she was about thirty. She worked as a hairdresser in Ilse's beauty salon. Her husband, a career army officer stationed in Poland, had been gone for more than a year and a half, and was open about the fact that he had other women. Tad said that she was very lonely, and that her husband tried to compensate for his neglect by sending her large packages of canned goods and other rations. She had more food than she knew what to do with.

"Go on, call your little friend and tell her you're spending the night at my place," said Tad. "Johann will let you use his telephone if I ask him. I tip him after every game I win." My brain was racing to absorb all that I was hearing from Tad. There was an angle to everything. Tip the billiard-hall owner so that you won't have to go out into the street when you need to make a call. Hook up with a lonely woman who has a pantry filled with food and no one to share it. A few things I had already figured out on my own: for example, never, ever write anything down. I had already memorized the Dudacys' phone number. If I were ever caught, nothing in my pockets would lead the Gestapo to them, or to Mother.

Tad introduced me to Johann, a grizzled older man who, with his Meerschaum pipe, knickers, and plaid shirt looked like something out of Brecht's *Three-Penny Opera.* Tad must have been a good tipper, because Johann slapped me on the back and croaked, "Any friend of Taddie's is a friend of mine! Go right ahead, kid, use my phone, just don't call England or America, y'hear?" And then he laughed and coughed right in our faces, giving Tad and me a whiff of stale tobacco.

Sylvia answered the telephone. I told her Tad was going to introduce me to an important fellow that evening, and that I couldn't go with her to the movies. I felt awful, but I just couldn't tell her the truth. "I hope you're not too mad at me," I said, consumed with guilt.

"If it is important for you, Gerhard, I mustn't hold you back," she said evenly. "What shall I tell your mother? Will you be coming home, or are you staying overnight?" She was such a smart girl; did she know there was more to my story than I had let on?

"I'll probably stay with Tad. He has an extra room and a bed for me to sleep in. Tell Mother not to worry, I'll call again tomorrow at about noon. And, Sylvia ..."

"Yes, Gerhard?" She never got mixed up and called me Lothar. She had never known the boy I used to be.

"Thanks, Sylvia. Thanks for being such a good friend."

"Good luck, Gerhard," she said softly.

Tad and I spent the next several hours in the billiard room. He pressed the chalk into my hand and taught me how to prepare my cue stick. He demonstrated how to hit two balls with the white cue ball, and touch the cushion at the same time. The rules of caramboulage and the score keeping sounded complicated, but Tad assured me I would get the hang of it.

"Gerhard, the main thing you've got to remember is, always play it nice and slow, and figure out the shot before you execute it," he said. "It takes only one point to win or lose the game, and that means winning or losing money." I was learning from a master. In the coming days, Tad would spend hours critiquing my shots and teaching me strategy. As he predicted, within a week I would become good enough to beat many of the guys who wandered into the billiard hall for a few beers and a few games.

But on that first afternoon it was difficult for me to concentrate, because my mind was on things to come. After a few hours of play, when Tad winked at me and said it was time to leave, my knees began knocking.

The two of us walked for about ten minutes, past the Frankfurter Strasse, in the same direction as the Dudacys', to Tad and Ilse's apartment on the Proskauer Strasse. When no one answered the doorbell, Tad used his key. It was obvious that a great deal of care had been taken to make the apartment especially nice for company. In the air was the strong odor of a pine-scented cleaner. Even the doorknobs gleamed. The place was charmingly decorated, all in ornate French provincial, with accent colors of garnet and silver gray. Ilse had created a very inviting home.

Tad said he was going to the bathroom to freshen up. He looked pretty fresh to me. Even in these times, when people wandered around looking ragged in torn and faded clothing, Tad managed to look neat and even elegant. Clothes hung perfectly on his well-sculpted physique. He did not look like a bum on the run, and I resolved that I wouldn't either.

Alone in Ilse's living room, I sank onto her comfortable couch. My thoughts turned back to her friend Trudy. What would she be like; would she like me? My anxiety, and exhaustion from the strenuous afternoon at the billiard hall, must have done me in; within moments, I had fallen fast asleep.

I slept for almost an hour. I was finally awakened by the sound of girlish laughter. When I opened my eyes, two very attractive women were smiling down at me. They seemed to be wearing a great deal of makeup, expertly applied. There was a strong scent of perfume, and a secondary smell that I remembered from when Papa and I used to pick up Mama from the beauty salon: the pungent odor of the permanent-wave solution.

"Come on, Gerhard!" said Tad. "We let you sleep, but now dinner's ready and we're starving!"

"Oh, I'm sorry!" I stammered as I rose to my feet. "Never mind, let me welcome you," said the blonder of the two women. "I am Ilse Hartwig, and this is my friend, Trudy Lipkow." We all shook hands. I was so nervous I could hardly meet Trudy's eyes. But her smile told me that she was friendly and easygoing. She had thick, lustrous golden brown hair, and an arresting figure. Ilse was also well built and impeccably groomed. She hung all over Tad like a lovesick poodle.

When the two women went into the kitchen to bring the food to the table, Tad cornered me and whispered, "What did I tell you?"

"Very nice," I said nervously, "very nice."

"Her no-good husband hasn't been home, even on a weekend pass, for at least six months!" said Tad with a leer. "You're in, my boy, you're in!"

"Stop it!" I hissed. "I don't even know her, I don't know what to do."

"With an older woman? Relax, kid, she'll do everything."

I checked myself in a mirror in Ilse's dining room. My hair was now quite blond, although it seemed to me that it had begun to thin slightly from all the harsh chemicals. I looked like a real Aryan. Well, almost. Aryans weren't circumcised. That was another thing I had to worry about.

Ilse put on some music, "Baccarole" from *Tales of Hoffman,* and lit the candles on the dining room table. Sitting down next to Trudy, I realized that her perfume was 4711, the same one that my mother used when she and father went to the Kulturbund, the Jewish theater. My mother used cosmetics only on special occasions, like her rare evenings out with my father, and all those wonderful parties. I tried to suppress the memories that washed over me. I still felt hurt by the disintegration of my world, but I had to rise to the occasion; I was about to dine with three mature dinner companions who were looking forward to a lighthearted evening.

In the center of the table was a large platter filled with steaming corned beef, sauerkraut, and potatoes. On the buffet server behind Ilse was a plate of pastries garnished with fruit. "This looks wonderful," I said. "Where on earth did you get all this meat?"

"It's from a can, but we fixed it up," said Ilse slyly. "And for that we give thanks to the German Army and its able Quartermaster Alfred Lipkow, who sends his Trudy lots of cans, but little else."

"Ilse, please!" said Trudy, and there was genuine embarrassment in her voice. She was blushing. "The gooseberry tarts I baked myself, upstairs in my apartment," she said to me, changing the subject.

Now, that was great news. Tad had neglected to mention that Trudy lived in the same building. If I did end up at her place later, I would not have to take any risks by venturing out into the streets.

"Taddie, darling, would you pour your friend some wine?" said Ilse, handing him a freshly uncorked bottle. "Gerhard, it's Ruedesheimer, genuine Rhine wine, awfully hard to come by."

The only wine I had ever had was homemade raisin wine at my parents' Passover Seder. But as the meal progressed, it became apparent that I held my alcohol quite well. The girls became very giggly, and Trudy began leaning against me. The flesh of her arm against mine was soft and warm. Tad would wink at me periodically across the table. I could see that he was massaging Ilse's leg.

After dinner, we moved into the living room, and toasted each other with shot glasses of Aquavit. Ilse put a stack of new records on the machine, and we sang along to one of the popular songs of the day, "Kauf dir Einen bunten Luftballon" (Buy Yourself a Colorful Balloon). The next record, "Die kleine Stadt will schlafen gehen" (The Little Town Wants to Go to Sleep), drew applause from Trudy; it was one of her favorites.

"Well, not only 'the little town' wants to go to sleep," announced Ilse, with an exaggerated yawn. "I'm exhausted. Let's leave the dishes for the morning, and say goodnight."

"Great idea, Ilse," said Tad, wrapping his arm around her waist. And without another word, they left the room, leaving Trudy and me on the couch by ourselves.

It was all so sudden. I didn't know what to say or what to do. My face was hot from the wine, and once again I found myself on the brink of the unknown. But Trudy was very cool. She rose to her feet and said: "Never mind what Ilse said, I'll clean up the kitchen. I'll be through in a few minutes, and then we can go to my place. All right?"

"All right," I answered.

While Trudy washed the dishes, I tried to busy myself with a crossword puzzle in one of Ilse's magazines, but I couldn't concentrate. I could hear Trudy humming softly, the song about the little town that wanted to go to sleep. It was very soothing, and for those few minutes, I reveled in the pleasures of a normal life – a full stomach, pleasant home, the sound of a pretty girl's voice. Maybe one day I would have a normal life again, go to college, maybe.

"Ready, Gerhard? Goodness, it's after midnight." Trudy walked over to the couch and tousled my hair. From the way she treated me, it was clear that Tad, the rat, must have told her I was a virgin. Trudy told me not to bother taking my coat upstairs: we were coming back to Ilse's for brunch the next day – smoked trout and potato salad, already prepared.

Trudy's apartment was as neat and clean as Ilse's, but not quite as elegantly decorated. The furniture was mostly Danish modern style, and clashed with a heavy Bleichroeder buffet, like the one we had in the Greifswalder Strasse. She put a blue crystal decanter and two fancy goblets on the coffee table. "Have some cherry liqueur, from Holland, Gerhardchen," she said, filling the glasses.

"Let's say 'prosit,' to our good health." We touched our glasses and sipped. She said she wanted to take a quick shower, and that I could take one when she was through. "I'll put on some nice classical records, Vivaldi, Mozart," she said. "They are very calming for the nerves, don't you think?"

"Oh, yes," I said. Were my nerves that obvious?

She brought me a man's housecoat – her husband's, I was sure. While she was gone, I slipped into it, leaving my boxer shorts on. I didn't know what I would do if she uncovered my secret below the belt. Perhaps I could convince her that I had needed an emergency operation because of an infection. It had happened to one of my old schoolmates, Kurt Luedtke. He had to be circumcised at the age of thirteen, and missed four weeks of school. He couldn't ride his bicycle for a month after that. But I would cross that bridge when, and if, I came to it. Just then Trudy came out in a pale blue, two-piece silk pajama set, faintly transparent. Between the woman, the wine, and the music, I felt like the king of France.

"Your turn to wash up," she said, her demure tone at odds with the sexiness of her attire. "I will be waiting on the couch for you when you are through." And she was.

Trudy showered me with compliments and kisses and caresses, and led me to the bedroom that had, mercifully, been darkened. She was very much in command of the situation. I was awed by the touch and scent of her body, her skin, her hair, her lips. I was grateful for her tenderness, and enthralled by her hungry attention. I'm sure it was the best the first time could be for a young man. For this one amazing night, I did not think of death, of war, or of danger. I did not think about yesterday or tomorrow. In Trudy's arms, I was a young man like any other, and I became totally lost in the moment.

The need to connect, to love and be loved, to taste whatever of life I could, was stronger than fear and despair. With my people starving and dying like flies, was it selfish for me to want only to live and to love? Perhaps, but I didn't see it that way. If my eventual fate were the same as theirs – and by the odds, it would be – there would be time enough to cry then, when hope and life were ebbing away.

The next morning, before we joined Tad and Ilse for brunch, I excused myself and went out into the street to call my mother from a public telephone. I had decided it would be best for her safety that I never call her from anyone's home. She was relieved to hear my voice and I assured her that I would be back later that day. At Ilse's table, I ate as though I hadn't eaten in days. Tad and Ilse watched with amusement. Trudy, sitting very close, looked for any excuse to touch me, dabbing a bit of mayonnaise from my cheek, and brushing the bread crumbs off my lap.

Reality intruded from the radio, which blared forth the usual rousing marches and patriotic folk songs, punctuated by frequent news reports. About every fifteen minutes, they would rebroadcast Hitler's latest fantasy, that the loss of Stalingrad was the alarm that had awakened the great German nation, that had rekindled the determination of every German man, woman, and child to stand behind their beloved Fuehrer. That would be followed by a speech by Goebbels, about the glorious Fatherland's endless victories. But, between the lines in the *Abendblatt,* one could detect a weakening of the great German war machine, especially in Russia. The Red Army had broken through Germany's iron ring around Leningrad. In the Ukraine and the Caucasus, many of the so-called "bread-basket cities" were retaken by the Soviets. The tide was turning in Africa, too, where the mighty Rommel was being rolled back. Yes, the end was nearing, but would it come soon enough to do us any good?

We did not talk about the war. If Ilse and Trudy already knew more about Tad and me than we had volunteered, they did not say. The war news was clearly upsetting to Trudy with her faithless husband. I knew nothing about Ilse's past, but it was obvious that she was deeply in love with Tad. Neither of them would jeopardize our arrangement.

The girls began to clear the table, leaving me alone with Tad, who was still in his robe. "Well, kid, you look happy," he said, smiling.

"I can't believe this is happening," I said. "I feel I'm dreaming."

"She's nice?"

"Very nice, very, very nice!"

"Has she asked you to stay?" he whispered quickly, as the two women came back to the dining room.

"Didn't talk about it yet." Trudy had put on new lipstick, and just looking at her made my heart beat faster. But I had promised my mother. "I hate to leave, but I have to go home now," I said, with real regret.

Trudy's face fell. "At least walk me back to my place."

We said good-bye to Tad and Ilse, and in the stairwell she said in a sorrowful voice, "I would walk home with you and meet your mother, but it isn't a good idea for me to be seen in public with another man. I hope you don't mind if we have to stay behind closed doors." Mind? I could live out the entire war locked up with Trudy.

"I don't judge you, Trudy," I said to her as we entered her apartment.

"Good, because you cannot imagine what it is like," she said, holding back tears. "Alfred was a bastard long before the war. He treats me like garbage, shows me no affection or respect, and leaves pictures of his little girl-friends lying around."

"I can't believe anyone would do that to you," I said sincerely.

"That's because you are an honorable person, Gerhard. And I'm still young, and with this shitty war, I deserve a little happiness in this life, a little tenderness, don't I?" She began to cover me with passionate kisses. It was time to go, but not quite yet.

When we were finished, I said, "You know, I'm on semester break for the next week or so. Maybe I could spend a couple of nights next time."

"Oh, Gerhard, that would be fantastic! I didn't dare ask you, because of your mother," said Trudy. "You can stay as long as you like – in fact, you can move in. I hate living here alone, especially when the sirens go off, I'm frightened."

"But what about your husband, doesn't he get some kind of furlough from time to time?"

"Oh, he does," she said angrily, "and then he stays with his girlfriend in Poland. I don't care anymore."

I told Trudy my mother was very understanding, and that I would be back later in the day with a few of my things. Just before I left, she pressed a set of house keys into my hand. She said that as a precaution I must never answer the phone or the door, and that she would go down to the shelter alone during air raids, lest the neighbors talk. Perfect. Those were just the precautions that could save a Jewish boy's life.

When I got back to the Dudacys', only my mother was home. She hugged me as though I had been gone for years. I wondered if she could tell there was something different about me. I didn't keep her guessing; without being explicit, I told her about my night with

Trudy, and that I planned to move into her apartment for the time being.

"Are you sure, Lotharchen? Is this the best way?" I knew my mother would always think of me as her baby, and now I was all she had left in the world.

"Mama, it's safer this way. If I were followed, I would lead them here. And you should see how much food this girl has. Maybe I can bring some."

"Lotharchen, they are such wonderful people, they treat me like family. Last night, when you didn't come, Sylvia took me to the movies in your place." Sylvia. I hoped that she would understand, too. "Lotharchen, will you at least try to call me every day?"

"Yes, Mama, you know I will."

"And you'll visit?"

"As often as I can."

"And you won't take chances?"

"Of course not." I hoped that would be true, but I wasn't going to tell her I planned to spend my days with Tad in the billiard hall.

I gathered a few clothes, a toothbrush, and a razor. I wanted to be out of there before any of the Dudacys returned. My mother would explain my departure much more gracefully than I could.

* * * * * * *

I settled into a life with Trudy, and, while it lasted, it was a very good life indeed. So this is what it must feel like to be married, to live with a woman, the way grown men do, I would think to myself. I did not dwell on it, but I knew this might well be my only experience.

I savored the serene rhythms of our domesticity. We spent a great deal of time quietly reading together,

entwined on the couch. Trudy had inherited a trunk full
of old books, some of them quite valuable, from her late
father. Among them were several books by Jewish
authors that had been banned, though I don't think
Trudy was aware of it. Our candlelight dinners were
delightful, and our lovemaking ... I know that Trudy saw
my body uncovered at least once – early one morning
as the dawn light streamed into the bedroom, but if she
noticed anything Jewish about me, she never said anything about it.

Trudy told me she was from Stettin, next to my own
village in Pomerania. She never asked me any questions
about my own life, and she was extremely protective of
me, making sure no one ever got near me – the mailman,
the meter reader, the air-raid warden. I was her treasure,
sheltered from the outside world. She would not let me
answer the door, even when she was expecting Ilse or Tad.
She made no new acquaintances, male or female, while I
was with her. She did not ask me what I did during the
day while she was at the beauty salon, and I never
confided in her. When a large carton of government-issue
food arrived the first of the month, she unpacked it
silently, and insisted I take some cans to my mother, and
to be sure to say it was a gift from her.

Trudy's birthday was March sixth, the same day as
my father's. She was thirty-one, twelve years older than I.
The four of us celebrated at Ilse's with wine and cake and
all the trimmings. Her husband didn't send her anything,
not even a card. Now that I was beginning to win money
at billiards, I bought her an imported silk scarf in a swirl
of rainbow colors, from Hertie's, a fancy department store
in the Alexanderplatz. It was rather extravagant, but I
wanted to get something special for her. She was always
giving me things, including clothing of her husband's that

she didn't think he would miss, and she would never accept my offers of food or money for the household.

Besides, I loved having an excuse to go to the department stores, which, despite the war, still had luxury goods that few could afford. My parents and I had always made the rounds of Berlin's finest stores just before Christmastime. Several times I actually sat on Santa's lap, and he would ask me if I had been a good boy. He never asked me if I was Jewish.

I spent almost every day in the billiard hall, from about noon until six. Under Tad's tutelage, I became one of the better cushion billiards players in the place. Only once during a two-month period did the army police descend upon the billiard hall. Johann gave a hand signal, and those of us who had something to hide from the authorities fled into the secret room. After Johann gave us the all clear – a triple knock on the wall – we all piled out as though nothing had happened. The games began where they had left off, the cigarettes were re-lit, the jukebox continued to play. One thing was clear, however; contrary to Goebbels' triumphant declaration, Berlin was not "Judenrein." More than a few of us were still there, hanging on for dear life.

Tad introduced me to the two pseudo-Frenchmen, our fellow Tauchers Philippe and Jacques. What their real names were I still did not know. I did know that they worked as handymen, and lived as squatters in an abandoned shack in a suburban bungalow colony on the outskirts of Berlin. Tad told me that a black marketeer had sold them French working papers and pistols, and suggested we too buy guns for ourselves. Like every other boy, I had played cops and robbers and pretended to shoot people, but I had never held a real gun in my life.

Another regular at the billiard hall was a stout, courtly little fellow named Etienne, a real French laborer.

Etienne had spent a year in a German prisoner of war camp, and was now employed as a handyman. He was always selling something, mostly food stamps or ration cards. Etienne would frequently treat everyone to what he said were day-old pastries – real Berliner delicacies like Liebesknochen, Schnecken, and Schillerlocken – which often tasted a week old, with the whipped cream centers gone slightly rancid. Betting and taking bets was Etienne's chief source of income, and he always carried a large wad of bills. He was forever lending money, at fair rates of interest, and usually on collateral, for a ring or a watch. He was a decent man, after his own fashion, and I never saw him have an argument with anyone.

Although he had a wife and children in Paris, Etienne lived not far from the billiard hall on the Neue Weber Strasse with a German woman named Kitty, a madam whose apartment also served as a *Puff*, or brothel. Etienne was her boyfriend, not a pimp or a partner. He always spoke of Kitty in a respectful manner, and never tried to fix up any of the men from the billiard hall with her girls.

One of the oddest of Johann's patrons was "Opa"– Gramps–Simon, a grizzled old fellow of at least seventy-five who played neither billiards nor Ping-Pong. He made his living as a cardsharp, playing at marathon poker parties all over town. Tad, who had the dirt on everybody, said the old geezer was consistently a big winner everywhere he went. Opa wore thick horn-rimmed glasses and didn't say much, but he seemed to take a liking to me, and called me "Sonny." He said that if I were a "good boy," I could accompany him sometime to one of those back-room, all-night, invitation-only card games where he earned his bread. I was fascinated, and agreed, though I wasn't exactly sure what he meant by a "good boy."

At the billiard hall, too, I met up with an old school friend, now a Taucher, who wore the most imaginative disguise of all – an SS uniform with all the trimmings. I first spotted him standing in the front entrance, wearing the dreaded black uniform, and nearly had a heart attack, only to discover that it was Horst Atlass, a darkly handsome Jewish boy a few years younger than I. Horst had always been a reckless sort. He had stolen the uniform, and a gun that went with it. He only occasionally spent time in the billiard hall, and what he did with the rest of his days, I preferred not to know.

The billiard hall became my world. I hated to miss a day. I would manage to lose myself completely in the games, in the daily routines of the place, and in the personalities of the men who drifted in and out of its rickety doors. Some of those men might hold the key to my survival; others might be dangerous.

In the evenings, Tad and I would often ride the subway together back to Ilse and Trudy. Sometimes we would take a stroll first, window shopping on the Kurfuerstendamm, the Ku-Damm, Berlin's most famous shopping street, its "Fifth Avenue." Aboard the trains, we behaved as though we were deep in an important conversation, and avoided eye contact with anyone, from the stern-faced policemen to the flirtatious females. At home, there was dinner on the table, the soothing strains of classical music, and a warm embrace from Trudy. And every day, I would call my mother.

So the days went. Were they normal? Not by the standards our family had once expected, but they were better than what might have been normal under the circumstances we were in. In fact, there was no "normal" anymore, and to me, those days were good. Neither my Mother nor I was starving or in any imminent danger. I was thankful for every minute I could breathe the free air. I would have been so proud to wear the mantle of my country, as my father had, and all those generations before him. Instead, stripped of my credentials, a German youth coming of age in a world in chaos, I found myself adrift, with little to believe in. I believed in the God of my mother's fervent nightly prayer, yes, but I could have used some sign of His presence, some sense that those prayers had actually been received. The decadence and deceit that surrounded me, that had begun to swallow me, were the antithesis of the holy Torah. I had broken almost every one of the Ten Commandments, and was bound to break them many more times before all this was finished; it was impossible to picture the day that my life could resume the course my parents and I had assumed it would take – the *derech ha'yashar*, the straight path, the path of righteousness.

The only commandment I continued to uphold was to honor my father and mother. This injunction I clung to, and the solace it gave me supported me when all else seemed to fail. I called my mother every day, and visited her faithfully each week. Of course, I also wanted to see Sylvia, who hugged and kissed me whenever I appeared at the door. This girl still made my heart do flip-flops, for, despite my life with Trudy, I was still in many ways a shy teenager. It was as though the boy who visited the Dudacys and the man who spent the nights at Trudy's were two different people. I was becoming adept at living a multiple life with multiple identities.

During one of my visits, my mother begged me to spend the night. She felt cheated that our time together was always so brief. When I agreed, Sylvia asked if we could finally have our long-awaited movie date. In her usual understanding fashion, my mother urged us to go.

She said that it was enough for her to know that I would be coming back to sleep under the same roof with her that night.

It was a rainy, windswept evening, but any evening without the wail of the air-raid siren was a beautiful one. Sylvia and I went to see *Krach um Jolanthe*, an absurd little movie about a pig on a farm, and we laughed. We held hands in the theater, and also while walking home. By the time we arrived, wet and shivering, Mother had already gone to bed. Sylvia brewed some tea, and we stayed up talking for hours. Her mother, she said, would be out until late that night at a secret meeting. In fact, Anne was seldom at home. She remained an active organizer for the Communist party, and was always passionately involved in one sort of clandestine political action or another. Sylvia also suspected her of being "passionately involved" with a young man from the party. Sylvia's own attitudes were a good deal more conventional than her mother's, but she did not judge her mother's behavior. She was still an attractive woman in her forties, and her husband had been away for a long time.

Sylvia said she was amazed at how different I looked from the day I had first arrived at her door. My hair was now completely blond, and I had trimmed my heavy eyebrows considerably. The substantial meals at Trudy's and the beers in the billiard hall had added some bulk to my lanky frame. She told me I looked wonderful, and I returned the compliment.

"Surely you have boyfriends," I said. "At work they must fawn all over you."

Sylvia sighed. "Oh, Gerhard, you know better! At work, there are mostly women. The boss is close to seventy and married. This stupid war has taken all the boys, good and bad. No, I can't imagine where my true love is, Gerhard." Hanging in the air for both of us was the unspoken question: "My true love, could it be you?" There was so much genuine feeling between us, but so much that stood in the way: the war, our religions, the delicate circumstances of my mother's stay in her home – a situation I dared not jeopardize. We played chess for a while, and this time I beat her twice.

Suddenly I remembered that I had not let Trudy know I would be spending the night with my mother. I called her on the phone, and I heard the relief in her voice when I told her where I was.

"Very well, but I will miss having you next to me, Gerhardchen," she said, her voice already sounding sleepy. "Say hello to your mother from me."

"I will, Trudy."

"Until tomorrow, then."

"Until tomorrow."

She was a sweet and understanding person, and I cared deeply for her, but Tad had hammered it into me how foolish it would be to allow myself to fall in love. And it was a good thing he had, because that was the last time I would ever hear Trudy Lipkow's voice.

By the time we got up the next morning, Sylvia and Anne had already gone to work. Mother made me some scrambled eggs out of powder I had brought from Trudy's army supply. After a leisurely breakfast, I kissed her good-bye and headed for the billiard hall. That day, I was on a hot streak, winning every game I played. Exhilarated and with about eighty marks in my pocket, I took to the streets with Tad at our usual dinnertime departure hour. Tad had had a good day, too. We agreed that we should use some of our winnings to buy gifts for the girls, for the coming weekend was Easter.

But just before we turned the corner onto Proskauer Strasse, we saw Ilse running toward us, her eyes wild with terror. She was dragging my satchel, bulging and heavy; she was sobbing, and completely out of breath. The three of us ducked into the nearest apartment building.

"It's over!" she cried. "It is all over!"

"Ilse, what happened?" I begged her. "Where did you get my bag? Is Trudy all right?"

"You can't come back, not ever!" she gasped. "Trudy's husband arrived from Poland today! He has new orders, he will be stationed in Straussberg, and can commute from home."

She looked at Tad, her eyes filled with love and anguish, and it was clear that without being told, she had known the truth about him all along. Ilse, unlike Trudy, was a single woman and it was nobody's business if she had a lover staying in her apartment. But this lover had a secret, and could not risk exposure to the eyes of the army officer who was moving back in upstairs. There was no way Tad could go back there either.

"I love you so much, Taddie," she wept. "What will happen to you?"

"Don't worry about me, I'll be fine," he said in an even tone. "You're a good woman, Ilse. Now just take care of yourself, you hear?"

Once again I was amazed by Tad's cool demeanor under pressure. I was so shocked by this sudden turn of events that I felt as though my legs would buckle under me, and I could hardly speak. I was lucky, damn lucky, that Trudy's husband hadn't walked in on me wearing his clothes – or in bed with his wife.

"Gerhard, Trudy brought your bag down to my apartment. She sends you her love, but asks that you do not try to contact her, not under any circumstances."

I nodded. "Give her my love, too, and my thanks, for everything," I said hoarsely. For everything. The first and only taste of adulthood I had known, maybe the only one I would ever know.

Ilse told Tad that she would hold onto his things in her apartment for a little longer, and call him when she was sure that Trudy's husband would be gone for the day. Maybe, just maybe, they could have a few more moments together.

I walked away to give them a chance to say good-bye. They clung to each other, kissing and whispering. I was fortunate not to have to go through such a parting with Trudy. This sudden ending of our life together was probably the best way it could have happened.

We walked out of the building, and watched Ilse head back home. Her shoulders were slumped, and her thin legs wobbled. She turned around to give us a dejected wave, and with all the makeup smeared or washed away by her tears, she looked haggard and old. She and Trudy were good women. They were looking for love, but they had also given it, generously and purely. They were our kind of Germans.

Night was falling. I didn't dare go back to the Dudacys' for the second night in a row, especially with another young man in hiding. It was just too dangerous. We turned around and went back where we had come from. I gave Johann my satchel to hold under his desk. "How long will you need to leave it here, dear boy?" asked Johann pleasantly. He had become my bosom friend, too, since I had begun earning enough money to tip him.

"I don't know, Johann," I said miserably. "I really don't know."

"Trouble with the girls, eh?" he said. "Ach, don't worry, young fellows like you. Plenty of fish in the sea, especially nowadays."

Tad and I picked up our pool cues. Wordlessly, we subdued our passions with the game. For the first time ever, I beat him. That told me, despite his cavalier attitude, how much he had really cared about Ilse. For me it meant no more hearty meals, no more safe haven, no more candle-lit nights with Trudy. But I still had my mother and Sylvia's affection, while Tad had nothing.

I had not spent any evenings in the billiard hall, and had no idea how crowded it became after dark. Many of the patrons now appeared to be working men trying to get away from their wives. I recognized no one, until Etienne came sauntering in, carrying the usual cake box filled with rotting pastries. Even though we had gone without dinner, Tad and I declined. We had lost our appetites. We saw Johann whisper something to Etienne, and both men laughed. Etienne walked over to us with a twinkle in his eye. "L'amour, l'amour!" he sighed, slapping me on the back. "You two boys have some troubles, I hear."

"Yes, we have troubles," I said miserably.

"I have some nice perfumes, I'll sell cheap, they'll love it! You'll kiss and make up, voila!"

"Not a chance, my friend. We've been kicked out for good."

"So where do you sleep tonight?"

I looked questioningly at Tad, because my instincts told me I should not reveal how unsettled our circumstances really were. Basically, we were out on the street again.

"Well, do you have a place to sleep tonight?" Etienne repeated.

"Sure," lied Tad, "but it's so damn far away ..."

Etienne nodded sympathetically. "And naturally, you're tired, you're all done in, after your ordeal today. Why don't you come with me, back to Kitty's?"

"You're kind, Etienne," I said, "but we couldn't impose on you like that."

"Sure, Etienne, we'd love to!" Tad broke in, throwing me a withering glance. "Just for one night, at the most two."

"It's no imposition at all, and you can call it home as long as you like," said Etienne easily. "There are always empty mattresses on the floor, plenty of them."

Of course. I had forgotten. Kitty's place, my new home, was a whorehouse.

Chapter 7

Houseguests

"Mon Dieu, what miserable faces on you two young-sters!" said Etienne with a hearty laugh. "You must have been spoiled rotten by those German ladies of yours!"

Tad and I sat glumly across from him at a table in the Glocke, a restaurant a few doors down from the billiard hall, trying to eat before heading over to Kitty's. The bill of fare was *Stammgericht*, modest fare that could be had without ration cards. Many people with big appetites and limited ration cards came to rely on those extra portions. Stammgericht was typically potato soup, or vegetables cooked in lard. Sometimes, if you were lucky, there were mussels or some other delicacy in a well-seasoned sauce.

But it was a far cry from the fare at Trudy's table, or at Ilse's. Besides, eating in restaurants could be hazardous; people sometimes ended up with full stomachs and hand-cuffs on their wrists. Military police regularly patrolled the city's restaurants, especially during peak hours, and Stam-mgericht, for us illegals without food stamps, was com-monly referred to as "The Last Supper."

The uniformed police were not the only danger. Spies and turncoats also laid in wait in the more crowded food establishments. Every Taucher soon learned the names of Stella Goldschlag and Rolf Isaacsohn, the glamorous Jewish couple who were notorious informants for the Nazis. The beautiful, blond Stella, especially, had a talent for ensnaring lonely young men, gaining their confidences, and then leading the Nazis to the hiding places of a whole network of their families and friends. The only way to avoid being hooked by Stella and her ilk was to keep moving – never to eat in one restaurant too often, or to sleep in one place too long.

Kitty's four-story apartment building on the Neue Weber Strasse was, predictably, on the shabby side. Judging from the bustling lobby, Kitty's was not the only brothel in the place. Moments after Tad and I entered with Etienne, a pretty girl approached us and offered her services for only five marks.

Kitty was a short, round woman in her thirties with dyed platinum hair and heavy blue eye shadow. Etienne explained our predicament, and she immediately welcomed us. When I got a closer look at Kitty, I saw there were deep worry lines in her brow, but in her face there was also a great deal of strength and compassion. The apartment was dingy and without frills; the neighborhood did not warrant an opulent bordello. Etienne showed us to a tiny room with one small window, bare of furnishings except for two rattan chairs, and two mattresses on the floor. I assumed they used this space for overflow customers on particularly busy nights.

"Hey, does this mean we'll have to take care of the really hard-up customers if no girls are available?" Tad laughed. Etienne started to guffaw along with him, but stopped when he noticed the stricken look on my face. I had never been inside a place like this before in my life. I knew that my mother would be most upset about my latest change of address, but there was a certain irony to it: my esteemed government was trying to exterminate me; the policemen, who I had been taught since childhood would protect me, were now stalking me; the churches and social services organizations, supposedly a nation's angels of compassion, were silent; so if a madam was willing to risk her life by hiding me in her brothel, I was not about to complain on moral grounds.

Etienne unfolded a bridge table and two additional chairs. He covered the table with a red-and-white checked tablecloth. Sure enough, he couldn't wait to get a card game going. "I got this tablecloth when I worked as a waiter in an Italian restaurant in Switzerland," he declared. "Just look at the international ambiance we have here this evening: un homme de Paris, a Polish deserter, and a Jew from Berlin!"

Etienne was sharp. I had never told him anything about me. He gave us a key for the bathroom out in the hall, which he claimed was never used by the girls or their customers, since there were bathrooms adjoining each bedroom. Despite Etienne's assurances that we were safe, I was unnerved by the continuous parade of men, many in uniform, past my door. I could only hope they were too preoccupied to take any note of us. Kitty's girls were constantly passing through as well. All of them were very young, and some were quite pretty. They always knocked before entering, handed some bills to Kitty, and left quietly. I would soon discover that the girls who worked for Kitty loved her and trusted her completely. She explained that nearly all of them had been abused or abandoned by their families, by the men in their lives, or by brutal pimps. She gave them a fair cut, and shielded them from violent or otherwise dangerous situations. Kitty spent much of her day seated next to the telephone, with a bulging appointment book on her lap. She would give the callers her prices, the names of girls, the times available, and the room numbers. Everything else went on discreetly behind closed doors, and I never heard or saw much of anything.

Later that night, I slipped out to call my mother. She was, of course, aghast at my new situation. As a law-abiding woman, though liberal in many ways, she set high standards for herself and for me. She had yet to come to grips with the fact that she and I, in this new order of things, were shady underworld figures. Maybe in the old days we could have felt some sense of moral superiority or higher social standing, but those days were gone. We were all in the gutter together.

For the next couple of weeks, Tad and I stayed at Kitty's. She was generous to a fault, and insisted on sharing her food with us as well. Once, when I beat her at cards, she became insulted when I hesitated to take the few marks she had bet. She said that we could be with any of her girls, too, for free. But neither of us felt right about it; we were, after all, housemates. During the day I would go to the billiard hall, where I was now known as the high-school truant who was hard to beat. And at night I would lie on the lumpy straw mattress, Tad snoring beside me, and think about Trudy whenever I wasn't slapping off bedbugs.

Our evenings at Kitty's were quite sociable, and there was always someone to chat with, or something to do. We played Dame or Muehle, popular German board games of the day, and, from time to time, Etienne would enlist Tad and me to sort food stamps, and food and clothing ration cards. I didn't know where he got them, or how he went about selling them; I did know they were very valuable, and it was a money-making enterprise.

One night, Tad walked in with Leo Eckert. Eckert was something of a legend in the underground, a father figure to the underprivileged and to people on the run. He was the man who had sold false French papers and weapons to the Tauchers Philippe and Jacques. Etienne asked Kitty to clear out a private room for us. It was interesting to see how completely he dominated this strong woman, and how she seemed to love it. She immediately acceded to his every wish.

Eckert was an older man with wild gray hair who resembled Ben-Gurion, or maybe Trotsky. He looked as if he had a bit of the Bolshevik in him. He opened his briefcase, and carefully laid two small revolvers on top of a table. I could read the name on the smaller one, "Walther." The larger one had no inscription. Eckert got right down to business.

"The Walther will cost you 625 marks, which in-cludes twenty-four rounds, and the Italian one you can have for 350, including ammunition," he said. "And don't think I am making any money on you guys. I just want to see to it that everyone of us is armed and ready when the shit hits the fan, and I think it's going to be soon."

Tad and I looked at the guns while Eckert continued to offer opinions about the political situation. "My fellow Germans, my compatriot morons, are too scared and too stupid for a revolution," he complained. "Ja, through the grapevine they say the Allies are planning an invasion somewhere in Italy this summer. It's about time that goddamn Mr. Roosevelt got over here. It can't be too soon for us."

Tad reached for the sleeker, more expensive model, the Walther, and caressed it. "Look here, Leo, I like this one, but my girlfriend has my money stash, and I have to wait until she gives me the signal to come and pick it up."

"Don't worry about it, take the gun, I trust you," Eckert replied. "These guns aren't a luxury for you guys, they're a necessity." Eckert turned to me and pointed to the remaining gun. He gave me a paternal nod. "Don't be afraid of it, my boy. It's your friend, maybe your best friend. Take it."

"Sure, I'll take this one," I told Eckert, and handed him several weeks worth of my billiard winnings. Now my life was in my own hands. I would make my own law, and answer to no one. I confessed to Eckert that I had no idea how to load or shoot my new acquisition, and he assured me he would show me everything I needed to know. After he loaded the gun and gave me the necessary instructions, cautioning me always to leave the safety on, I slipped it inside my pocket. Leo was right: a new sense of security, of being in control, had replaced the feeling of helplessness that I had become accustomed to. I was now armed and dangerous.

In the warm spring days that followed, with our new guns buried in our back pockets, Tad and I became outright cocky when we strolled around Berlin. Had my mother known of the chances we took, hanging around outdoor cafés and flirting with the waitresses, she would have been horrified. One afternoon, after leaving Kitty's place, we were surprised to see the streets filled with crowds of people in holiday dress, and Hitler Youths in their parade uniforms. Loudspeakers blared speeches and marching songs, and most of the shops were closed. Easter Sunday had already passed, so we couldn't imagine what the fuss was all about. When we reached the Grosse Frankfurter Strasse, we finally remembered.

An enormous banner stretched from one side of the street to the other, proclaiming in big black letters, *Wir gratulieren unserem Fuehrer zum Geburtstag!* April 20, 1943 – it was Hitler's birthday, now the grandest of all German holidays. It appeared that Tad and I were in the thick of it, crashing his party. We decided to forgo the poolroom

and take advantage of all the commotion to remain out-
doors, bathed in the sunshine of a gorgeous day. So many
swastikas fluttered over the streets and plazas that people
didn't even bother to give the traditional salute. Over the
loudspeaker came the booming voice of Goebbels, singing the Fuehrer's praises.

We looked silently at these smiling citizens, returning
their friendly nods as we sauntered by them. The Germans today were one big, happy family. Husbands in full
Nazi regalia strutted alongside beaming wives. Little boys
in sailor suits walked hand in hand with girls wearing
garlands in their hair. And here were Tad the deserter and
Lothar the Jew, in the midst of all this picturesque folly.
"Happy birthday, Adolf, you son of a bitch," Tad hissed,
"and may this one be your last!"

The circle surrounding the Alexanderplatz was closed
to all traffic because of the festivities. Tad and I spotted an
empty table at the popular Berolina Haus Café and sat
down. The place was so busy that it was fifteen minutes
before the waitress approached us, and fifteen more before
she brought my dish of ice cream and Tad's iced coffee.
Normally that kind of delay would have made us edgy, but
today the German folk so obviously relished this celebration that they were looking for no unnecessary distur-
bances. The usual Gestapo patrols were conspicuously
absent.

Staring at us quite blatantly as they stood waiting for
a table were two girls, one very blond with braids, and the
other brunette, wearing identical sky-blue dirndl dresses.
They had the classic, healthy, Aryan look about them, but
they were definitely not pretty. With their plump figures,
they were the prototypes of future Teutonic mothers.

"Ladies, won't you share our table?" Tad called out.
Delighted expressions spread across their faces as they

trotted over to join us. Like the gentlemen we were, Tad and I rose, pulling out the two empty chairs for our new friends.

"Thanks, this is great, we've been waiting such a long time, and it seems no one is leaving!" the brunette gushed. "We heard that this place has the best iced coffee in Berlin."

"I can vouch for that, girls!" Tad said, flashing one of his winning smiles. "This table is meant for four, and we would love to share it with such lovely ladies." The blond giggled and fluttered her eyelashes, but did not say a word. Clearly the brunette was the leader of the two. "My name is Ursula," she said, "and this is my sister Johanna, but everybody calls her Hansi."

"I am Tad, and this is my cousin Gerhard. I hear by your accent that you are not from Berlin."

"Well, actually, we are from a small village in East Prussia, outside of Koenigsberg, but now we live here, that is, in Dahlem Dorf. Do you know it?"

"Of course," I broke in, turning my attention to the quieter sister, who looked at me with the eyes and intelligence of a cow. "That is the most elegant suburb of Berlin. You girls must be millionaires to live there."

"Not really," Hansi answered shyly. "Our father is the assistant to the governor of our province, and he was transferred here. I think our villa once belonged to a Jewish professor or scientist, who knows, and after the government booted him out, they moved us in."

"Well, that is exciting!" I blustered, feeling my face grow red. "You must be very proud of your father, a real VIP in the party."

Ursula nodded vigorously. "And you? You look like two real *Berliner Jungen*, so friendly and helpful! No uniforms for you?"

"Uniforms? Today is a holiday from uniforms, from work, from school, from everything!" hooted Tad. "I go to medical school in Berlin, and my cousin here is a student at the Technische Hochschule, so we're both on spring break. And all we're thinking about," he continued with a leer, "is enjoying this gorgeous day with two enchanting sisters, and having a damn good time!"

The girls bought every word of it and slurped on their *Schlag*-covered ice coffees, demolished big servings of pie, and then ordered second helpings of everything. The sisters said their parents were spending the evening at a bash for Hitler's birthday at the Adlon Hotel, and that afterwards a chauffeur was whisking them directly to a high level Nazi conference in East Prussia. They would be away for at least ten days. Ursula and Hansi said that they had told their parents they couldn't come along because of their jobs at a nearby kindergarten, jobs obtained through one of the Nazi party's women's organizations in which they were active. But the truth was, these two peasant girls only wanted to be on the loose in the big city, out from under the eyes of their parents.

"Who wants to go to the movies?" Tad asked. "At the Muenz Strasse they're showing an old Pat and Patachon."

I loved the Swedish comedy team. "OK by me. How about it, Ursula?" I didn't bother asking Hansi, because I knew she would go along with whatever her sister wanted. Ursula did not hesitate for a moment. "All right, what's to stop us?" she said gaily, rummaging through her handbag. "But you boys are students and we are both working, so I insist we pay for ourselves."

That was a relief. I had already been worrying about how we would pay for their extra desserts. Berolina Haus Café wasn't cheap, and after our defense expenditures a few days earlier, we had barely enough money for our own bill.

The movie theater was filled with schoolchildren on holiday who roared at every caper and pratfall of Pat and Patachon. The sisters sat next to each other, with me on one end next to Hansi, and Tad next to Ursula. Out of the corner of my eye I could see that Ursula was already snuggling with Tad; Hansi would occasionally give me a moony-eyed glance.

Dusk had fallen when we got outside, and the streets were still crowded with families who had spent the day at the parade. Long lines of people waited patiently at all the bus and trolley stops; you could tell by their genial expressions that everyone had had a wonderful day. I noticed that Ursula and Tad were holding hands. Then he turned to me and said nonchalantly: "Hey, Gerhard, do you have to go home tonight? Ursula has invited us to Dahlem Dorf. I don't have to be home, but if you can't come with us, I won't go either."

I was dumbfounded. Tad was a smooth operator, but she seemed to have made this ridiculously easy for him. Heaven knows what they were up to while they were in the movie theater. Ursula looked at me with pleading eyes. "I don't know, I'll have to check with my mother," I mumbled, my brain racing, trying to anticipate all the lies we would have to invent if we were to spend any amount of time with these girls. "If I don't do some studying during this school break, I could flunk out and get drafted. Don't get me wrong – I'd like nothing better than to fight for my country, but Russia is a little too cold for my taste."

The previously reticent Hansi tugged at my sleeve. "Gerhard, you must come! We gave the maid the week off, and our parents took the chauffeur! And the Jew left thousands of books in his dusty old library, surely you'll find something for your studies. Please, Gerhard, I don't want to be a third wheel with them." She was breaking my heart. Hansi yanked my arms with unexpected strength and pressed me against her chest. The girl was built like a wrestler. She had gesticulated with such force that one of her glossy braids came undone. I thought of the food that had padded her, the clean and comfortable bed she slept in peacefully each night, the library filled with untouched books. It was a far cry from Stammgericht and the threadbare mattress that Tad and I shared on Kitty's cold, hard floor, with mice and bedbugs crawling over us.

From a telephone booth in the Alexanderplatz Station I called my mother. I hadn't spoken to her in nearly a week, and was lucky to get through because the lines had been cut by recent air raids. I could hear the relief in her voice. She said things were fine; as I knew she would, she had become a surrogate mother to everyone in the household. I told her I would be out of the city overnight, and not to worry. "How can I not worry, Lotharchen?" she said, her voice trembling. "You are my whole reason for living, and if you keep taking such risks ..." I promised her I would be careful. When I got off the phone, Tad had one girl on each arm.

"So what's the story, Mr. Peters, are we going to Dahlem Dorf?" he asked, smirking. "Or maybe your Mommy wouldn't give her little boy permission?"

"Cut it out, Tad, you know I am going, I just had to tell my mother not to expect me. But I will have to do some studying."

Hansi's milky blue eyes twinkled and she grabbed me once again. "Oh, goody, goody for me, goody, goody for you," she squealed in English, singing the current hit tune from America. Ursula began singing along with her sister, and the two girls reeled giddily around us as we headed toward the Stadtbahn, destination Dahlem Dorf.

The train was so crowded that we were strap-hangers most of the way, pressed tightly against each other. As we got farther from the city's center, we were all able to sit down. Several older people seemed to enjoy watching us as we jostled each other and laughed. As we got to our stop, they nodded and smiled at us approvingly.

In the pitch darkness of the wartime blackout, I could see little of the beautiful tree-lined neighborhood of Dahlem Dorf. Several minutes after leaving the train, the girls led us down a private road with no street sign, and then down a narrow path. Ursula opened a squeaking wooden garden gate, and we walked another two hundred feet through a portico overhung with evergreen vines. Just up ahead, past the gardens fragrant with mint, we could dimly see the contours of an enormous villa.

"Hansi, I need some light to find my keys," said Ursula. "Feel for the switch on the wall behind the holderbush."

The faint light illuminated only the entryway, leaving most of the place still cloaked in darkness. After Ursula unlocked the door, Hansi pushed me into the house first, and then she and Tad and Ursula followed. "This is it," said Ursula.

Tad and I stopped dead in our tracks. The circular foyer was inlaid with a magnificent black and white checkerboard marble floor, surrounded by silver-gray marble walls that led up to a dramatic cathedral ceiling. The ceiling was painted with an elaborate mural, reminiscent of Michelangelo's Sistine Chapel, an image I had seen in library books. The figures reached for each other with outstretched arms around the sphere of a sky-lit tower. The builder of this house had not only great wealth, but also a great sense of beauty.

The girls led us up the grand, carpeted staircase to a guest room, and Ursula switched on a Tiffany lamp on the nightstand. In the room were two heavy brass beds with goose-down covers and an ornate French provincial chest of drawers. The adjoining bathroom had fixtures that seemed to be pure gold.

Ursula scurried away for a few moments and returned with her arms loaded with underwear, socks, and two heavy velour robes. She put new toothbrushes and razors on the vanity in the bathroom.

"Father's things should fit both of you, and there will be plenty of time to launder them before he and Mother return," she said coyly. "Hansi and I are off to freshen up before dinner. We'll see you in about an hour, yes?"

"Yes, yes, lovely ladies, thank you!" Tad said heartily, turning to me with an enormous grin even before shutting the door behind them.

"Shit, I've never seen anything like this place!" he hissed. "I hope the poor bastard they stole it from will make it through this wretched war and reclaim his property."

"Yes, and I hope that we make it through tonight," I said nervously. "At least without the girls discovering our weapons, or any other interesting details."

"Just keep the lights low, my boy," Tad laughed. "Luckily, your Hansi doesn't seem to know one end from the other."

Searching the room, we discovered that one of the bureau drawers had a lock, so we put our guns and papers inside and hid the key high inside the closet. Tad said that I could have the first shower while he stretched out a bit on the bed. As I stood in the fancy stall, I felt numb and altogether lost. I wondered what Trudy was doing, if she and her husband had picked up their miserable life together where it had left off. Sometimes, when I thought about her, I could feel her thinking about me too. "What the hell are you doing here?" I suddenly found myself saying aloud. "Who are you? Do you even know any more?"

"No, I don't know," I answered aloud in a lifeless tone. "I don't know, I don't understand this whole sick world." But I could not afford to dwell on the past, on the way life might have been; it brought me down and dulled my instincts. I forced myself to be in the present. How old was Hansi, the Viking maiden? Was she a virgin, and what were her plans for the night? Whatever was to happen, one thing was certain: at least tonight I would not sleep on the floor with the vermin. I dried myself, shaved, brushed my teeth, and sprayed myself generously with a Nazi's cologne.

While Tad got himself ready, I drifted off for a few minutes under the goose-down covers. Then the two of us put on the Nazi's robes over our undershirts and boxer shorts. Mine was burgundy, Tad's a golden brown, each embroidered with a fancy gold coat of arms.

"Very elegant, just like Goering, Nazi pig number one," Tad declared as we looked at ourselves in the mirror. In stocking feet, the two Tauchers descended the staircase, like an emperor and his minister.

We followed the sound of classical music thundering from the radio, and found our way into a spacious parlor. Several groupings of brocaded couches and chairs in rich tones of maroon and blue were artfully arranged around the room. Tad and I sank down into an overstuffed sofa. A large Rococo buffet was crammed with crystal and silver. Three of the walls were hung with massive oil paintings of battle scenes, while an onyx fireplace graced the fourth.

With a burst of cloying perfume, Ursula bounded in gaily. She wore a red and white polka-dotted housecoat that buttoned down the front, and looked ridiculous in this opulent setting. Next Hansi came in carrying a large tray of frankfurters, pastries, and wine. She, too, had changed into a plain blue housecoat with a little half-apron, and looked like the wife of a peasant farmer, or even a maid.

"Look at these big, fat 'specials' prepared by the butcher back home on our farm!" said Ursula enthusiastically. "Our Hansi is a wonderful cook. You'll love her potato salad. She puts in apples, onions and pickles, which makes it tart and sweet at the same time." Hansi blushed and busied herself with pouring the wine into four cut-crystal goblets.

"Prosit, Gerhard," she said shyly, raising her glass. "It's a Mosel, do you like it?" I sipped the wine and nodded my approval. The girls beamed at me and began wolfing down the hot dogs. Tad and I ate with more dignity. After several hot dogs, Hansi licked her fingers and switched off the radio. Then she wheeled in a record player, one of the latest models, which could take a stack of up to ten 78s that automatically played one after another. They had a collection of the latest titles, American imports like "Broadway Melody," "A-Tisket, A-Tasket," and "There's a Skeleton in the Cupboard," by my favorite, Count Basie. "Where did you get all these great records?" Tad asked. "They are hard to find nowadays."

"The Jew left them," said Ursula. "He had tons of records, especially classical, but we don't go for that highbrow stuff."

"Yes, tons of records, the best records!" Hansi broke in. "'Alexander's Ragtime Band,' 'Hold That Tiger,' 'In the Mood'... do you know them?"

"Of course we know them, Schatzi!" I held up my glass and shouted. "A 'Prosit' to the Jewish professor, who was so gracious to leave us his records and this beautiful house! Without this inheritance, we, the invincible German youth of today, would not be able to dance the night away! So thanks to you, the Jew! Bottoms up, friends and countrymen!"

Tad and the girls roared and guzzled their drinks. I started to feel giddy and strange, not yet from the wine but from the absurdity of the situation. Prancing around the room, I began to sing at the top of my lungs, over the sound of the record player: "*Trink', trink' Bruederlein trink, lass' doch die Sorgen zu Haus.*"

It was a raucous beer-drinking song, the German equivalent of "Forget Your Troubles, C'mon Get Happy." Ursula leapt to her feet and pulled Tad up with her, whirling him around. I grabbed Hansi by the midriff and spun her several times around the room, her blond braids flying. Suddenly she turned pale and staggered away from me, throwing herself back onto the sofa. "You are too fast for me, Gerhard, I had a glass of wine and one of those big frankfurters!" she gasped. "Ursula, please, switch the record ... let's start with something slower, like 'Let Me Call You Sweetheart,' or the one with all the English waltzes."

One of those big frankfurters? She had had at least three. Ursula stopped kissing Tad long enough to dab at Hansi's forehead with a damp napkin, and to change the music. Soon my bloated date rose to her feet and began to dance with me in a slow, romantic fashion. Her braids kept tickling my nostrils and I sneezed.

"Gesundheit!" Tad shouted, the girls joining him in peals of laughter. For the next few hours, we ate and drank and listened to the Big Bands, dancing and singing just like our American counterparts across the sea. But I kept thinking that these two good-natured sisters, were they to discover our true identities, could, and probably would, send us to our deaths.

It was after midnight by the time Ursula and Tad drifted upstairs, and Hansi began to yawn and snuggle close to me on the couch. "I'm tired, Gerhard, all that wine," she said thickly. "Please help me up the steps." Arm in arm, we staggered up the long staircase. With laughter coming from the bedroom Hansi shared with her sister, we continued down the hall to the room that had been assigned to Tad and me. I excused myself to use the bathroom. When I returned, Hansi was sitting in one of the ornate chairs and staring at me balefully as I slid into bed. "I don't know what to do, Gerhard, I am so frightened!" she whimpered. "I never did anything like this before, I hardly know you! All the girls say 'Oh, it's wartime, forget the old rules, Hansi!' But I don't know. Maybe if I just lie next to you, would that be all right?"

"Sure, sure," I nodded, just wanting her to be quiet. Hansi's girlfriends were right about one thing, though. In this new Germany of ours, the old rules were all relics of a dimly remembered past. If Hansi had never dreamed that someday she'd be in this situation, well, neither had I.

"Oh, Gerhard, you're so understanding, so special," she murmured, snuggling up next to me. Within moments, I fell asleep.

It must have been nearly dawn when I woke abruptly with Hansi kissing me, her hair cascading over my face and chest. Still half asleep, I gasped for breath and pushed her away.

"You don't care about me, Gerhard!" she sobbed. "Nobody ever loves me, everybody loves Ursula. Oh, I am so ashamed, I want to disappear, I want to die!" I felt badly for the girl and kissed her gently, but that seemed to make her cry even more. "If you want, I'll stop," I said.

"No, Gerhard, no, please don't stop," Hansi blubbered, her nose leaking, her chest heaving. But I did stop, and went back to sleep.

Late the next morning I awoke to cloudy and rain-swept skies, a day in stark contrast to the one before. Hansi walked in carrying a tray of ham and eggs, rolls, and coffee, and put it down on the night table. Her hair was tightly braided again, and she wore another homely housecoat.

As we ate, she told me that she and Ursula had already called in sick to their jobs at the kindergarten. Ursula had asked that she and Tad not be disturbed. With the weather so dismal, they planned to spend the whole day in bed. "I hope you are not mad at me for last night, Gerhard," she said timidly. "I suppose I am not too good at this sort of thing."

"You must be a virgin," I said.

"Well, yes," she replied haltingly, "and no." Sniffling once again, Hansi launched into a complicated story about being raped by a married cousin in East Prussia. I could not follow all of its twists and turns, and some of it seemed too fantastic to be true. But after a while, she loosened her hair again and climbed back into bed. This time, I did not stop.

The dark, chilly day passed like a languid dream, punctuated by food and sex. It was evening by the time we left the room and went downstairs. Ursula and Tad never came out at all.

"Tomorrow my sister and I will have to go to work, but we are so hoping you boys will stay," said Hansi as she washed the dishes and I dried. "I know it's a lot to ask, but will you stay, Gerhard, dear?"

"I don't know, Hansi, Mother will kill me if I don't start catching up with my studies," I said.

"Never mind, wait until you see the Jew's library!" she insisted. "While we are gone, you can have the run of the house!" Hansi grabbed my hand in a proprietary manner and led me down the corridor. She motioned ahead to a pair of elaborately carved pocket doors. "To tell you the truth, I don't even know what he's got in there. We're not big readers in our family," she said. "Why don't you get started while I tidy up the kitchen and make us dinner? I promise not to disturb you." Hansi was pulling out all the stops. She was desperate for me to stay.

It was a struggle to pry open the library doors. Clearly, this room had been abandoned for some time. Cobwebs and thick layers of dust had settled over the cherry wood paneling and the glass-encased bookcases that extended from floor to ceiling on all four walls. Each wall had a brass rail to which a ladder was affixed, and a book stand that attached to the sides of the ladder. My eyes roamed the shelves, which were crammed with heavy leather volumes whose titles I could not see in the dim light. I was once an avid student, a lover of German literature and poetry. That was before Hitler decreed I could no longer go to school. I was not always a hustler of no fixed address; I was a scholar who belonged in a room like this.

The professor must have been an attorney or a politician, for one full wall of the library had nothing but heavy, leather-bound books of law and legal history. Another wall was filled with the literature I had devoured as a schoolboy only a few years before. The complete works of Schiller, Goethe, and Heine; Tucholsky, Schopenhauer, Deeping; Chronin, Werfel, Zweig, Zola, and Kafka. There was a German translation of Margaret Mitchell's *Gone With the*

Wind, and several volumes of the Zionist ideologies of Herzl and Jabotinski. The Nazis had long ago banned many of these works, and burned them in public bonfires.

Climbing up several rungs of the ladder to examine the top shelves, I saw that many of the titles were embossed in Hebrew. Rows and rows of Jewish books, destined for the flames but somehow never confiscated, the Siddur, the Tenach, Tehillim, the Talmud. I suddenly remembered a line from the poem "Jehuda Halevy," by Heinrich Heine: "How barren, how lonely and forgotten is the Wailing Wall," he had written, "without its Jewish people praying there." My fingers caressed the holy books, leaving streaks in the dust. I did not know much Hebrew; the ancient religious tomes had held little appeal for a thoroughly modern German boy who had popular literature to read, soccer games to play, and movies to attend. And yet as I stood on that ladder, I felt a need to connect with God, and with my people, from whom, until this moment, I had felt very far removed. Leafing through the prayer book I managed to find the 23rd Psalm, and read it in a halting whisper: "The Lord is my Shepherd, I shall not want; He leadeth me to green pastures …"

Faith, compassion, truth – all I had lost – it was all here. What nobility, what courage, what wisdom my faith had brought to mankind! Was that what had threatened the Nazis, was that why they wanted us out of the way?

A section in the back of the prayer book listed the dates of all the major Jewish holidays, past and future, from the year 1925 until 1975. Fifty years, a mere blink of an eye in history, but, to me, an eternity. I would be just past my fiftieth birthday in 1975, not yet an old man. Damn it, I wanted to become that man, balding, gray haired, pot-bellied, perhaps, and maybe the father of a family. But how could I get there from here?

I looked up 1943, and saw that it was around the time of Passover. Passover, the one holiday of the year that my none-too-traditional family observed to the hilt. My father made a great show of conducting the Seder, dressed in his ceremonial *kittel* – the white robe that was to have been his burial shroud, rather than the striped urn filled with his ashes from Sachsenhausen. I knew all the melodies of the Hagaddah, knew by heart its tale of the deliverance of the Jews from bondage in Egypt. Passover, a fragrant holiday table, laden with my mother's delicacies.

When I spied an oversized, illuminated Haggadah and took it carefully off the shelf, I began to feel I was no longer so alone, no longer fearful and adrift. I began to turn its pages, and remembered how my father had lifted his cup of wine and sung the "V'Hee Sheh'amda." Never before had its words held such meaning for me as I recited them out loud, boldly and with fervor, in the twilight in Dahlem Dorf: "And God's promise has been the support of our ancestors and ourselves, for in every generation some have arisen to annihilate us, but the Most Holy, blessed be He, always delivered us from their hands." And I heard the same voice, the same fervor, with which I would have recited "Kaempfe, Blute!"

Suddenly, I began to cry, my tears flowing freely, and, in embracing the book, I embraced my father, my family, our past, our faith. For the first time, I understood our need to pray, to find solace and comfort in talking to God as hope and strength begin to wane. "*Dayenu!*" I whispered hoarsely in the language of the Haggadah. "Enough, already! Please, God, save me, save us all!"

I would return to the library again and again to gain solace from the holy books, for Tad and I ended up staying in Dahlem Dorf for nearly ten days.

Ursula and Hansi left for work early the next morning, telling us not to answer the doorbell or the telephone. After a huge breakfast, Tad and I explored the house from top to bottom. We found aged cognac, fresh fruit, and real coffee. We found the religious ceremonial objects that had been left behind by the professor and his family, gleaming Sabbath candlesticks and silver goblets for the sacramental wine. We went down into the basement that had been transformed into an air-raid bunker with toilet, bath, and sleeping capacity for six. Stacked inside its storage room were several hundred cans, including meat, vegetables, fish, fruit, and even caviar. The dire shortages of food that plagued the general population certainly did not apply to the Nazi elite.

Each day, while the girls were gone, Tad and I ate as much as we could, trying to build ourselves up for the days ahead when food would be scarce. We immersed ourselves in the forbidden books, snooped in the forbidden drawers and engaged in forbidden discourse. And at night, when they returned eagerly to the roost, we transformed ourselves into the most charming, solicitous Aryan house guests two Nazi princesses could want. As the days and nights continued, the girls became more possessive. Ursula began to plan for the day we would return to meet their parents. She said more than once that their father was very influential, and that his connections could greatly enhance our careers. Although Hansi still had little to say, she had overcome her shyness, and followed me around like a puppy. I told her I could not make any romantic plans for the future until after I graduated and became established in my career as an engineer.

Not a word we ever said to them was the truth, and they suspected nothing. Only one night was there a close call. Ursula found a loose bullet from Tad's gun on the bedroom floor and became very inquisitive over how he would have such a thing in his possession. In his usual offhand way, he said it was a souvenir from his brother, who was serving in Russia with the Wehrmacht. Then he gave her one of his high-voltage smiles, and she melted contentedly into his arms.

On Saturday, the day before their parents were due back, Ursula and Hansi left for the morning with a lengthy shopping list for a farewell dinner. Hansi had given me a radiant smile when I patted her behind as she rose from our bed that morning, unaware that she would never see me again.

As soon as they left the house, Tad and I sprang into action. We found two medium-sized suitcases in one of the closets, and began to fill them with as much as we could carry. In went enough food to keep a couple of Tauchers alive for weeks: two pounds of coffee and one of butter, two bottles of Hennessy cognac and one of curacao; from the bunker, a dozen large cans of meat, and many more of sardines and fruit. For my mother, I took the Sabbath candlesticks and two brand new housecoats from Hansi's closet with the tags still on them. The father's clothing had fit us both so well that we took almost everything he had left behind while he was at his conference. There was even an armband worn only by air raid wardens that would come in handy. The gold earrings, opal ring, and eighteen carat gold watch from Ursula's bureau drawer would have suited Sylvia nicely, but they would be more useful to us if sold on the black market. Etienne would see to it that we got a good price for them. I packed about a dozen books, including the Haggadah and the Hebrew prayer books. I had learned something in Dahlem Dorf – that the God of Israel was with me, even there. These holy books would provide the strength and the inner peace I would need in the dark and dangerous days ahead.

I had never stolen anything before in my life. I felt guilty as I filled those suitcases, yes, but I felt this house and its contents were more rightfully my inheritance than that of its current inhabitants. The Jewish professor and his family had been deported as my father had been and had probably met the same fate. Wouldn't he have been pleased that I was a guest in his home, treasuring his books, and taking back his candlesticks to observe the Sabbath? I hoped so.

We took our guns from the locked drawer in the bedroom, put on our coats, took the luggage and left the Jewish home, the Nazi palace. "A good Sabbath, Hansi; *Shabbat Shalom*, Ursula!" I thought, as we went out the door. "You won't run out of food, there's still plenty of clothing, and you'll never miss the books, but maybe you'll miss us!"

We boarded the Stadtbahn back to Berlin, and sat in the baggage compartment surrounded mostly by women with babies in carriages. Soldiers also entered the car, dragging their duffel bags, but their attention was diverted by the noisy children. Tad and I agreed that it would be unwise to bring all this loot to Kitty's. As much as I knew Mama disapproved of me bringing anyone to the Dudacys' apartment, there was no other choice. We huffed and puffed our way from the Frankfurter Allee station to the Dudacys' apartment. Anne opened the door with a long, searching look at Tad.

"Frau Ida, your Gerhard is here," she said dryly, "with a friend."

Mother rushed to the door. I could see the panic in her eyes. "It's OK," I told her. "It's Tad, you remember, I told you about him."

"Did anyone see you? The neighbors, it's Saturday, they're all home."

"Ida, you worry too much!" said Anne Dudacy, grinning at Tad. "So tell me, are you also one of those 'chosen people'? You don't look like one."

"You're quite right, I'm not a Jew," Tad replied. "Let's just say I'm a Polish-born deserter who missed the last boat to New York."

"Well, then, you will surely stay for dinner. I happen to have made some Polish soup, *gzcur*, with sourdough, garlic, and onions."

Sylvia came walking into the living room, wearing a coy smile. She made a beeline in my direction, and gave me a big hug. Out of the corner of my eye, I could see Tad eyeing her cascade of golden hair and her trim figure. But on his face was an expression I had never seen before. Tad was jealous, not because I had gotten a hug from a pretty teenager, but because he was all alone. Nobody cared if he lived or died. And I had the support of these three wonderful women – one of them, my mother. Even when days, or weeks, went by when I did not see them, they sustained me.

The three of them looked on in disbelief as Tad and I dumped the contents of our suitcases onto the dining room table. Anne was delighted with the coffee, the butter, and the pile of cans, and her lips trembled when Tad slowly fastened the gold watch around her wrist. Mama cried when I handed her the candlesticks. She was crying because they were beautiful and symbolized her way of life that seemed to have been eradicated; also, of course, because she knew I had stolen them.

We used the candlesticks to light the dining room that evening. For some reason, it felt like a celebration. Here we were, in Berlin, capital of the Third Reich, center of the Nazi Empire, the mouth of the volcano, the eye of the storm. My government had pledged to destroy me and my religion and my culture, but here I sat with my mother and our friends, Jews, gentiles, Communists, together at one table, singing Jewish songs and Polish songs, songs of revolution and dissent. For a moment my thoughts turned to Hansi and Ursula, whose dinner hour tonight might be a bit glum as they sat alone in their stolen villa with more food than two people could possibly eat. Well, our table was not empty, either. And, thank God, neither were our lives.

Chapter 8

Stacking the Deck with Opa

Tad and I were now back to cold reality – the filthy straw mattresses on the floor of Kitty's cathouse. Two new tenants had set up camp in Kitty's spare room during our frolic in Dahlem Dorf – Philippe and Jacques, the phony Frenchmen from the billiard hall. Once again Etienne had collected a couple of lost sheep, offering them shelter after a fire from some incendiary bombs destroyed their wooden shack on the outskirts of town. Never too ebullient to begin with, Philippe and Jacques were downcast. All their money and belongings had been lost in the blaze, and they were hungry. We realized our spate of luck was over and we were only a few steps behind them.

"You guys ever thought of breaking into a grocery store, like Reichelt's, or Gebrueder Groh?" Philippe asked. "We could grab the ration stamps, and whatever we don't use for our own food we could sell in the poolroom, like Etienne does."

"Robbery, huh? You're talking dangerous business here," Tad said after a moment's reflection. "Anyone who gets caught stealing, especially during the blackout, usually gets shot on the spot."

"I agree with Tad," I said. "There must be a better way."

"It is obvious that you two Romeos are not as hungry as we are," Jacques said dryly. "On the days I get to eat, it is that lousy Stammgericht, and I am so goddamn nervous about the Nazi patrols that I can hardly swallow. I may not look that bad, but I'm in pain. I think I need a doctor."

"He's right. We've got to do something," said Philippe in a desperate tone. Philippe worried me. He appeared to be a very troubled man who would try to solve all his problems in one swoop. "Tomorrow, we'll break in somewhere. The next day might be too late. Didn't you read in the *Voelkischer Beobachter* that just yesterday they arrested about thirty commies? I hope Leo Eckert wasn't one of them, because I need more ammunition. All my bullets went up in the fire." The man was out of control.

"Look, Philippe, if we act rashly, we will get caught, and that will be the end of it," I said to him, speaking in a slow and deliberate fashion. "Let's get some sleep, and then we'll talk about a robbery, all right?"

"Sleep if you can," groused Philippe. "I'm too hungry."

The next morning, we had a pretty good breakfast, courtesy of Anne Dudacy. We shared the sandwiches she had packed for us with Philippe and Jacques. Then Etienne brought us some hot chicory with Immergut milk substitute. Every time I saw an Immergut bottle I would see the broken head of Ulrich in Weissensee.

It had been a while since Tad and I had been to the billiard hall. Philippe and Jacques warned us that the MPs had stepped up their patrols, and that they had been forced to duck into the secret room several times during our ten-day absence. And sure enough, that morning, just as we got to the door, we saw two uniformed officers leaving the place, heading in the opposite direction.

"Tad, Gerhard, welcome back! Where the hell have you been?" Johann greeted us like long-lost sons. Perhaps he had missed our tips. "Back with your girls?" he asked, pumping our hands.

"Different girls," said Tad, smiling broadly. Johann shook his head. "Lucky bastards," he said, and he was right.

The tables were already bustling with the usual cast of shady characters. This morning, even Opa Simon was there, this time with his younger brother Arthur, a man of about sixty-five. Wearing his usual inscrutable smile, Opa sat serenely behind his thick glasses and watched a pocket billiards game between Arthur and a regular named Martin, a volatile ex-convict whom I had been warned to steer clear of. Martin's sullen face was contorted with anger. Clearly he did not expect that the newcomer Arthur, who was at least twenty years older, would be such a good player. One rack of balls after another, Martin was trounced by the stooped retiree, and a great deal of money was changing hands, most of it ending up with Opa.

After Martin had lost more than a hundred marks, he had enough sense to stop. But he thrust his cue menacingly in Opa's direction. "I'll get you, you old bastard, for matching me up with this brother of yours!" he shouted. "You knew I didn't have a chance! Come hell or high water, I'll win back every pfennig from you, or else!"

Martin left the billiard hall in a huff. He had spent more than ten years in prison, something to do with an armed robbery in Pankow which was why he was never drafted into the army. His tone frightened me, but Opa did not seem in the least distressed. The old man just sat there, beaming and counting his money. He looked up, and our eyes locked.

"Ach, you have returned, young master Gerhard!" he said. "I was hoping to see you again."

"You were?" Why, I wondered.

"You need a little extra pocket money, you are a student, is that not right?"

"Right."

"Well, how would you like to play in a card game tomorrow night? My brother Arthur has other obligations, and I need a partner."

"OK," I shrugged. "But I can't afford to lose much. I must take care of my mother."

Opa's face broke into a huge grin, showing a mouthful of dentures on the top, and a few brown and twisted teeth remaining on the bottom. "Lose? Are you kidding? No one ever loses, playing Opa's way. Tonight you will come to my house for your first lesson. You can even sleep over, I have a couch."

"I don't know," I said.

"I used to be an army cook, during World War I. I can still make a good pork and beans." Opa leaned his face close to mine and said to me in a low voice, "You do eat pork, don't you, Gerhard? Is it OK for you, pork?"

That old bastard. "Of course, I eat everything. I'm a growing boy, can't you tell?"

"Very good. Eight o'clock, then. And come alone."

"What about my friend Tad? He's a quick study, too."

"No," he said tersely. "I train one partner at a time. Gets too complicated otherwise." And with that, Opa put his arm through his brother's, and the two of them shuffled out into the street. When I told Tad that Opa had invited me to spend the night at his house, he warned me to be careful, but he didn't tell me not to go. Everything we did carried risks; if you were paralyzed by them, you might as well turn yourself in to the Gestapo.

Opa lived on the Lange Strasse, not far from the billiard hall where we both now spent most of our days. That night, he ushered me into his tiny apartment, clearly delighted that I had accepted his invitation to join him for dinner, but obviously there was more to it than that. The crooked old cardsharp had something in store for me, and tonight, he promised, I would find out what it was.

Opa's apartment was littered with magazines and newspapers piled in every corner and, although I had never seen him smoke, a collection of dirty ashtrays gave the cluttered rooms the musty odor of tobacco. The floors were sticky with grime, and the tattered carpet in the living room showed more floor than rug. Opa noticed my distasteful expression as I glanced around the dingy apartment, and steered me to the dining room table. "Just in time for supper, my young man, I hope you brought a good appetite!" he said in a jocular tone. "Notwithstanding my deficiencies as a housekeeper, you will see that I am an excellent chef, and I have made an extra portion for you, because young people are always hungry."

He had tried to make the table look presentable. It was set with a moth-eaten tablecloth, two large china plates with faded blue-and-gold borders, some tarnished, unmatched silverware, and carefully folded toilet-paper napkins. Using the severed sleeves of an old jacket as pot holders, Opa carried a steaming, black iron pot to the table. In the absence of a serving spoon, he tilted the pot gingerly and managed to pour a heaping portion of fragrant pork and beans onto my plate without spilling a morsel. I hesitated a moment before digging in. The smell was delicious but unfamiliar because pork, of course, had been taboo in my family. Also, Opa's apartment testified that hygiene was not his strong suit, and I could not afford to get sick.

Opa poured a smaller pile onto his own plate, and slid into a chair next to mine. He scooped up a large spoonful and gummed it noisily. I noticed he wasn't wearing his uppers, so each mouthful took a great deal of chewing before he finally gulped it down. "Eat and be merry, Gerhard, you will love it!" he sputtered between swallows. "You'll never want to leave here after you get a taste of Opa's dinners!"

When I finally got the nerve to take a bite, I was surprised at how good it was. I had a second helping, and for dessert, some homemade applesauce and a slice of marble cake. Opa watched approvingly as I ate. With his beady little eyes behind thick glasses and his pointed woolen cap, he reminded me of one of the Seven Dwarfs.

"I like you, Gerhard," said Opa abruptly. He sat back in his chair and folded his arms, his eyes never leaving my face. "Well, more accurately, I need somebody like you, somebody who has to make a living, honest or not, and who isn't afraid to take a few risks. And you are not afraid, or are you, Gerhard? No, I don't think so. Otherwise you wouldn't be sitting in this dump, now, would you, consorting with an old criminal?"

I was suddenly wary. Just how much did this guy know about me? In the billiard hall, I was the cocky high-school kid who liked playing hooky and earning a little extra pocket money at the gaming tables. But maybe Opa's experienced eyes had seen me differently, perhaps he could see that I, like the other Tauchers, was playing for the highest possible stakes, for my own life.

"No, Opa, I am not afraid," I said, pushing away my plate and turning toward him. "What do you have in mind?"

The old man nodded. "Good, we get right to the point. I am seventy-six years old. I have made my living playing cards since before you were born, my boy, long before these Nazi assholes came to power. I have traveled the length and breadth of this city, everybody knows Opa. Yes,

I'm an old dog, too old to learn new tricks. I need a partner. My brother – you met Arthur – is moving to Schoeneberg. He has made enough money to buy a house for his family. You will soon see, you can't miss playing Opa's way, you will make out very well. I have made many connections over the years, I have many friends. Most of them are retired, and they can afford to lose a few marks."

"So listen closely. Here are a few tricks of the trade, from that senile fool Opa. First of all, I bring my own cards to these games, that's the key. And second, I am not at all as nearsighted as my eyeglasses would have you believe. These lenses are just for show." He thrust his glasses at me so I could examine them. "A friend made them up for me when he worked in the Zeiss factory, you've heard of them, the company that makes the camera lenses. You see? Heavy loupes, enlargement instruments, like the jewelers use. And, boy, if you ever squeal on me, I am as good as dead. Now I am in your hands forever. You are my accomplice, my partner, my new brother. You see now how much trust I have put in you?"

The hairs at the back of my neck began to bristle. What the hell did he want from me? I sat at the edge of my seat. "Come on, Opa, what's the deal here?" I said, trying to seem calm. "Lay it all out on the table for me."

"Calm yourself, young man, patience is the mother of success," he replied evenly. "In this business, you must control your emotions at all times. Help me clear the table, and I then I will reveal the tools of my trade. You shall have all your answers in due time."

I carried the dirty dishes into the kitchen, dumping them into a slimy sink that swarmed with cockroaches. Opa carefully wiped the tablecloth. He took a large key ring out of his pocket, and unlocked the bottom door of an old armoire in the corner by the window. As the door of the armoire swung open, I could see at least fifty decks of cards, neatly stacked in five piles of about ten each. These were all new decks with the cellophane covers still intact. Playing cards were expensive and had become increasingly difficult to get. He must have had a good source in the black market.

Opa took two decks from a pile, and then opened a different drawer from which he took a razor blade and several long, sharp, hat pins. He then returned to the table and spread everything out in front of him. "Now then, Gerhard, we begin. Sit across from me, watch carefully, and don't ask any questions. When I am finished we will discuss everything. First tell me, do you know how to play poker, Skat, or Meine Tante, Deine Tante, or will I have to teach you from scratch?"

"We played those games at home almost every evening, my parents, my brothers and me," I answered. "I was always pretty lucky." The tableau flitted through my mind like the last vestiges of a dream: Papa's deep belly laugh as he showed us his hand, my brothers' good-natured horseplay at the table, Mama's eyes sparkling when she looked at all of us. I didn't feel so lucky anymore.

"With Opa you don't depend on luck alone," he smirked. "We make the cards work for us! It takes some very careful preparation but, after that, good fortune will surely smile upon you and me." Opa painstakingly slit the plastic covers of both packs with the razor blade, preserving the seal on each package. Then he slowly pulled out each of the two decks and pushed them toward me. "These two decks are completely new, am I right?" he declared. "Inspect them very closely – thirty-two cards and two jokers in each deck, starting from the seven and going up to the ace. All in good order, right?"

I scrutinized all sixty-four cards piece by piece, with a great deal of care. Opa watched me silently. We must have sat this way, without conversation, for a good five minutes. Finally I said: "That's right, sir, there is nothing wrong with these cards. I checked each one, as you saw, slowly, front and back. I am convinced these are new cards."

"Aha. Now, kid, take Opa's magic spectacles with the five-power loupes, the ones I wear only for the games. Now tell me what you see." I placed his glasses on the bridge of my nose and held up a couple of the cards. I gasped. Now, under the extreme magnification, small scratches were clearly visible in varying configurations at the top and bottom of each card.

"This is unbelievable!" I gasped. "You can't even feel it with your fingertips! How the hell did you do this?"

"Here's the secret," he said dryly. "You see this design, the row of little octagons that borders the back of each card? Well, those little octagons tell you what the card is."

"You've lost me," I said.

"Look, it's easy. When one of my little scratches appears inside the first octagon, for example, that means the card is a seven. When it's in the eighth octagon, it's an ace, and so forth. Get it?"

"But when we play, I won't be wearing those thick glasses," I pointed out, "everyone knows I don't wear eyeglasses, so how will I see the markings?"

Opa took a deep breath. "Look, you don't have to see the markings, because you're the player. At my advanced age, I am retired from playing, they just let me hang around the games, for old time's sake. Everyone knows that poor Opa is practically blind, ha-ha! No, it is I who will look at the backs of the cards of your opponents, and then signal you when to bet and when not to, either with my pinkie, or my hand on the cheek, or, if I sit next to you, sometimes with my foot, or some other such sign. We will make up different clues before each and every game, as we go along, so as not to create any suspicion. Before betting or doubling, always pay attention to me, just play very slowly and deliberately. Sometimes I might make a mistake. Just don't get nervous, ask for a drink, or get into a bit of conversation if I'm not ready with a signal."

"My God," I muttered, shaking my head. "My father should see me now."

"Gerhard, spare me the righteous shit," Opa retorted sharply. His gnomelike face suddenly turned twisted and ugly. "Now let's lay our cards, the real cards, on the table. One hand washes the other, am I not correct, young Master Peters, the new boy on the block, the spoiled student from the Technische Hochschule, who has the money to play from his rich Nazi parents? Let the others buy your line of crap! Opa sees all, remember? Opa and his magic spectacles! To me you look like a boy on the run, perhaps a Jew-boy on the run?"

I was flabbergasted, but managed to retain my composure. The arrogant bastard was blackmailing me to be his accomplice. By telling me he knew what I had to hide, he was assured that I would be a reliable partner in his crooked scheme, and that I would never betray him. But I was also relieved to have it out in the open; the uneasiness I had felt earlier when I was only suspicious that he suspected was now gone. Now, the anxiety of uncertainty had been replaced by the weight of a new bondage.

Opa reached into his pocket and pulled out a lapel pin bearing the Nazi swastika. "By the way," he added, "sometimes I'll wear this bonbon, depending on which crowd we are playing with. I wear it in the subway and on all public transportation, to assure myself of a seat, and when you travel with me it will give you some protection, too."

"Well, sir, I have no choice but to accept your offer, for more reasons than one," I said slowly. "I am badly in need of money, and you have made certain assertions about me that I am unable to disprove. But just remember that I am not scared of anybody, dear Opa." With that, I lifted my jacket, and caressed the pistol that bulged out of my rear pocket. Maybe I was at the old man's mercy, but I had to let him know that I was not totally helpless.

"Oh, put that thing away, I knew I could count on you, my boy!" Grinning fiendishly, Opa grabbed my hand and pumped it heartily. "And I know you will be Professor Opa's quick and clever student. So let us now begin to practice the art of cards. Our first lesson will be to create signals for tomorrow's game."

"Tomorrow? Already?"

"You told me you were a quick study! What's the matter, are you getting cold feet?"

"No," I said. "I just didn't think ..."

"It's not your job to think, Master Peters. You let Opa do all the thinking." Opa spread the cards out on the table and began speaking, but my thoughts were elsewhere. Only a few years earlier, I had dreamed of attending a university, of becoming a philosopher, or a poet, or a builder of bridges. I had dreamed of becoming – something. Suddenly I felt a wave of grief. Inside, I heard my voice promise, "I swear, when this is all over, if I live to see the day, I will never cheat or steal or lie again!"

"Peters, wake up! Are you listening?" barked the old man.

"Go ahead, Opa," I answered grimly. "I'm all yours."

"Excellent," he said. "Now remember, don't get nervous if I am not ready with a signal." Slowly and methodically, he showed me detailed signals for the next day's game. His index finger on his nose meant "double," index finger and thumb held together meant "get off," and so forth. It was two in the morning by the time he was through drilling me, and I was exhausted. I could not imagine where the old man got the stamina.

Before stretching out on the tattered velvet couch, I pulled it carefully away from the wall. Several telltale splotches on the wallpaper behind the couch indicated that the vicious bedbugs I had learned to avoid at Kitty's were living and breeding there. Thankfully, they gave me a one-night reprieve. I awoke the next day to sunshine streaming through the thin window shades, and to the aroma of fried eggs, onions and potatoes. Opa hobbled out of the kitchen wearing a filthy undershirt, with a spatula in his hand. "Greetings, Gerhard, it's almost noon," he said in a jocular tone. "I let you get your beauty sleep, before your big debut this evening."

I couldn't believe it. The apartment had been as quiet as a tomb all morning. I realized that if I could overlook the cockroaches and the filth, Opa's place had the potential to be an excellent refuge, much safer and more secluded than Kitty's. Clearly no one cared if the old coot lived or died. No one looked in on him, and he was beholden to no one. If we were traveling together to and from the late night card games, would he not need me to escort him home? I resolved that if Opa asked me to move in with him, I would try to overcome my revulsion and say yes.

Opa said he was out of real coffee, but he had brewed me a cup of the bitter chicory. Over brunch, we listened to the radio; the newscaster denounced the British for parading before cameras the thousands of German soldiers they had taken prisoner, and there was more of Goebbels' insufferable ranting, as he boasted of the great and still-unbroken strength of the Wehrmacht. Watching

Opa as he sat across from me noisily chewing his food, it occurred to me that he might be another closeted Jew, or half-Jew, especially with the given name of "Jacob Simon." But like the master card player he was, he betrayed none of his emotions as he listened to the radio blare. Opa's true identity would always remain a mystery.

The card game that night was to be held in Charlottenburg, a suburb in the western part of Berlin. On the train, Opa wore a blind man's armband, an insignia of three yellow dots on a black background, and brandished a cane. He pinned on his swastika, and held me to his side like a seeing-eye dog. A group of solicitous Hitler Jugend fawned over us, clicking their heels respectfully and offering us more space than we could use. It never failed to amaze me that these young Nazis could have such excellent manners, and yet be imbued with such a murderous brutality.

On the train, Opa quizzed me on the signals. Despite his advanced years, he had a mind like a steel trap. When he saw the sweat on my forehead, he patted my hand and told me not to worry. He promised that I would do fine, that I was already much better at this than his brother had been at the beginning.

Our host was a widower by the name of Wilhelm, a retired postal clerk who seemed to be an old friend of Opa's. Wilhelm had equipped each of the three rooms in his apartment with a round table that seated eight, so that three games could go on concurrently. He escorted Opa and me to a table in the living room, and introduced us to the other six players who were already waiting eagerly at the table, all of them men in their sixties or seventies. Wilhelm asked before the games began that people refrain from political discussions, as he wanted no arguments in his home. Then he retired to one of the other rooms to join a game there. I suspected he knew that the other players at our table were doomed to lose their shirts.

Each player had a porcelain saucer filled with coins, with a thick pile of ten, twenty, and one hundred mark bills stacked underneath. Opa sat directly across from me. He fumbled in his pocket and pulled out two decks of cards, so expertly re-wrapped that no one would imagine they had been tampered with.

"Wilhelm asked me to bring some new cards, he was all out," rasped the old man. "Now don't you fellows play too rough with them, they cost a lot and Wilhelm wants to use them again."

"You're not playing?" one of our tablemates inquired politely.

Opa pointed to his thick lenses and shook his head. "Wish I could, but I have to be content with accompanying my nephew here. No, these old eyes are practically useless, just like the thing in my pants."

Everyone laughed, and the banker, Heinrich, broke the seal and began shuffling the first deck. We played with two different decks, one blue and one red; while one was being dealt, the other was shuffled, so as not to lose any time between hands.

"Gentlemen, high deals, the play is as usual. Let me explain it to the new kid here," Heinrich declared, and turned to me. "Gerhard, we're playing five-card stud only, dealer sits out, six play. Ace is high. One mark to ante, a pair or more showing, two marks; limited to five raises." He was staring at me, and I was nervous.

Opa had given me three hundred marks to put under my plate, to show that I had plenty of money to enter the game. My first hand was lousy and I bailed out fast. On the next hand, I got a nine down, and my second card was another nine. I could not raise without a pair showing. The third card was a queen, and the fourth a ten. Another man showed two jacks and doubled. I stayed in. My last down card was a third nine. All the while, Opa was reading my opponents' cards and my own from the scratches on the back. Emil, the player next to me doubled. I watched Opa casually pass his index finger along his nose, never changing his genial expression. I redoubled to sixteen marks. Emil paid the raise and the other four guys dropped out. There were more than seventy marks in the pot. Emil's two pairs lost to my three nines.

With each hand, I became more confident. Opa was a master. All I had to do was glance at him out of the corner of my eye, and remember the prearranged signals. I only played when I had at least a pair; I raised only when I knew I'd win, but sometimes Opa's signals made me lose. This was good, of course, because it eliminated any suspicions. On my first day as a professional cardsharp, I left the game with over a thousand marks in my pocket. At Opa's apartment I gave him back the three hundred marks he had advanced me, and we split the rest.

"Listen, give me another fifty for Wilhelm, and I'll throw in fifty," said Opa. "I promised him a cut for the house."

"So he's in on it, too?"

"Of course he's in on it. He keeps the games going, always adding in some different guys, cronies of his from the Catholic church, or from the Red Cross. He does a lot of volunteer work, you know."

Opa took great pleasure in caressing the bills and laying them out in neat piles.

"See, isn't this better than that crappy old pool hall? Much safer too," Opa chortled. "What a profitable day this twenty-second of May has been, very profitable indeed!"

"Are you kidding? Today, the twenty-second of May? Shit!"

I had forgotten my own birthday. I was nineteen years old. Before, when a Berliner had such a birthday, there were parties and dancing, a memorable night on the town with family and friends. There I sat in a pigsty with a certifiable old lunatic, counting money we had stolen from a group of pensioners. This was manhood?

"Congratulations, dear Gerhard!" said Opa after I told him. "In honor of this special day, I am going to brew us a nice pot of real coffee!"

"Real coffee? This morning you said you were all out of coffee."

He gave me one of his sardonic smiles, and said, "Your Opa is always full of surprises, isn't he?" Indeed he was.

I would live with Opa, on and off, for the next six months. The old man was genuinely grateful not to be alone, and over time, I believe he developed a sincere affection for me, but there was no way he could be trusted. More than once I left his apartment in the morning with less money in my wallet than it had held the night before.

Neither of us, however, would ever forget the time I had a little surprise for him. It happened a couple of months later, just after I helped my mother move temporarily out of Anne's apartment in anticipation of a visit from a nephew who had become a Nazi. I managed to find her a place to stay through the kindly meatlady, Frau Schreiner. The cramped refuge was Frau Schreiner's little-used business office. She assured us that she was the only one who had the key; she occasionally sent some of her employees there to pick up or deliver papers, but promised not to do so while Mother was there. The problem was, the office had a sink, but no toilet. There was a bathroom on another floor, but she didn't dare go wandering around the building, especially at odd hours.

Offensive as it was to her strong affinity for hygiene and propriety, she knew she could always urinate in the sink, but when it came to solid waste we had to be more ingenious. Once again, the crinkle-papered Nazi hate-sheet, the *Voelkischer Beobachter*, came to the rescue. I would buy it regularly to ensure my public standing as a propa-ganda-loving patriot, then leave it with my mother, who would use a few pages as toilet paper and then carefully wrap everything in the rest of the paper. I would drop in on her almost daily, carrying, as usual, my briefcase like a real student, and place the carefully wrapped package inside. Then I would dispose of it in a garbage can far away, so as not to alert the policemen or spies to the presence of a Taucher in the vicinity of Frau Schreiner's office.

On one occasion, I forgot about the bundle in my briefcase, and brought it back with me to Opa's. In the middle of the night, I was jolted awake by Opa bellowing at the top of his lungs. "I don't believe this! You bastard, what are you, some kind of a pervert, bringing shit into my house?" he screamed. With one hand, he switched on a table lamp, and in its light I saw him standing over my open bag, holding high in the air his other hand, com-pletely slathered with shit. The old man let loose at me with a string of the foulest curses I had ever heard in my life. It was a glorious moment; it could not have gone better if I had planned it. One of our family's favorite sayings immediately came to mind: "*Wer Dreck anfaesst besudelt sich!*" – Who touches filth, becomes filth – as I would be admonished when I tried to hang around with neighborhood ruffians. In dear Opa's case, he was deep in it long before he opened my briefcase. But he never put his nose – or his hand – in my business again.

Chapter 9

Warmed by an Old Flame

Opa was right. I was much safer living with him than at Kitty's, and less likely to get arrested at one of his floating card games than at the billiard hall. The money was better, too; we played several nights each week, and often I won as much as thirteen hundred marks, before Opa's split.

But I was too young and too restless to spend all of my time in that bug-infested apartment, watching Opa meticulously doctor his endless stacks of playing cards. Despite the risks, I was still drawn to the billiard hall. Tad continued to preside over the tables, but he wasn't making much money now because he was known to be so good that few people were willing to play or bet against him even with a significant handicap. In fact, he told me that he was on the verge of succumbing to Philippe's ongoing harangues about planning a robbery, until he got an unexpected call from his old girlfriend Ilse. Both Ilse and Trudy felt it was safe for Tad to come back: Trudy's Nazi husband was still at home, but he detested Ilse and refused to set foot inside her apartment. So while Tad remained practically penniless, he informed me with a broad smile, he was no longer homeless, hungry, or horny.

Tad said that Trudy asked about me constantly, and even cried when she mentioned my name. She was desperately unhappy. At night, as I sprayed Opa's room with Flit, the foul-smelling insecticide, I thought longingly about the good life with Trudy. She was trapped with her contemptible husband, and I was trapped with Opa and the bedbugs. I was thoroughly jealous that Tad and Ilse were able to pick up where they had left off.

It was now June. In the late spring sunshine, Berlin was still a beautiful city, with the trees and flowers in full bloom. I was alone, walking to the pool hall feeling rather lonely and dejected, when I heard a voice behind me call a name that made me freeze in my tracks. It was my own.

"Lothar! Lothar Orbach!"

I had passed a new milestone in my life: the sound of my real name frightened me to death. No one had used it, except my mother, in many months. I reached around to my back pocket and put my hand on my pistol. Then I slowly turned around.

Standing behind me was a strikingly beautiful young woman with her thick blond hair worn in a *Dutt*, a braided bun that was a popular hairstyle with all the Nazi maidens. I was sure I had never seen her before in my life. But how did she know my name?

"I'm sorry, Miss, you have mistaken me for someone else. Good day," I said, trying to keep a steady voice. Then I turned around and started to walk on.

"Lothar, I've frightened you, I'm sorry!" the voice grew more urgent. "Don't you know me?"

My hand still on my pistol, I turned around again.

"As I said, Miss, I'm not ..."

Her voice went down to a furious whisper. "Erika, Erika Weissmann, don't you remember me?"

Of course I remembered Erika Weissmann. What young man can forget his first fierce crush? What young man can forget being stood up on a date by the haughtiest, most beautiful girl in the whole school? But Erika Weissmann was a classic Semitic beauty, with gleaming black hair and a figure that was already voluptuous in the seventh grade. This woman was model thin, almost gaunt, with eyebrows tweezed in a thin line, and hair the color of wheat.

I looked closer, into her eyes. "Oh, my God, Erika."

"Yes, it's me," she said dryly. "Still alive and kicking, but probably not much longer."

"Same here," I said. "Where are you living?"

"No place, as of yesterday. I was staying with a friend, a Polish foreign worker, and last night they arrested him. I spent the night behind some bushes in a school playground. Isn't that something?" It was something. Erika, the first child of a wealthy family, had a reputation for being rather spoiled, but I had found it part of her charm. I could not imagine her living on the streets.

"What about your parents?" I asked her.

"They were picked up in January, from the factory," she said. "I never saw or heard of them again. I've been a Taucher ever since." Her face was devoid of any expression. Her voice seemed disconnected from her body, like a zombie. It was as though she had strangled all of her emotions in order to survive. This is how I would be, I thought suddenly, if I didn't have my mother.

"What are you still doing here?" she asked me. "I heard your brothers made it to America. I thought you and your parents had affidavits, too."

I was about to tell her the convoluted story of my life, when an uneasy thought ran through my head: she could now be a Gestapo informer. Anybody could be one.

Erika instantly caught my hesitation. "That's right, Lothar, either one of us could be a spy. So we have to make a decision here, about whether or not we are going to trust each other. I don't think you are a spy, because in school, even though you were a bit on the wild side, you always had strong convictions. I could be a spy, but I'm not. We have enough enemies without turning on each other. I detest turncoats like my former schoolmate Stella. Have you heard about her? I don't know how they live with themselves!" By now every Taucher knew the name of Stella Goldschlag, the blond Jewish seductress who ensured her own safety by turning in her old friends.

Erika had failed me once. She had promised to meet me at a movie theater for a date and never showed up. The next time I saw her at school, she ignored me completely. Her girlfriends giggled when they looked at me. I was heartsick about it for weeks. But that seemed so long ago, so absurd in light of our current situation. I decided to believe her.

"Let's get moving," I said to her. "We've been standing in one place too long, and the street is crawling with MPs." She hooked her arm through mine, and we began walking. How this would have thrilled me a few short years earlier. I stole a look at her profile. In some ways, she was more beautiful now, but I felt only confusion.

"I need a place, Lothar," she said. "Please help me."

"Why can't you go back to the Pole's apartment? The coast is surely clear by now." She shook her head. "The neighbors, I am sure they told the authorities that Woitek was harboring somebody. It's because of me they arrested him."

I couldn't bring her to Opa's. I wouldn't bring a dog there. And I didn't dare endanger my mother by bringing her to the Dudacys'. There was only one other choice.

"I'll meet you back here in half an hour," I told her. "I have to talk to somebody."

Her face searched mine. I could see the fear in it. "Can I trust you, Lothar?" she said.

I smiled. "Who stood up who last time?"

She grimaced. "Oh, my God! I'd forgotten about that!"

"I never did," I said honestly.

"I'm sorry," she said, her contrition convincing.

"A half hour, then. And be careful around here, it's a red-light district."

Erika looked exasperated. "At this rate, that might be my next move."

Indeed, it was to Kitty's house, about two blocks away on the Neue Weber Strasse, that I was headed, but I couldn't bring Erika there without Kitty's approval. Kitty, seated as usual next to her ringing telephone, greeted me with hugs and kisses, and a loud "Hello, stranger!" She said that Etienne was in France for a week, visiting his family. Within seconds she was cheerfully offering me a cold drink, a pastry, even a girl, in case I had changed my mind. When I told Kitty what I really wanted, she did not hesitate.

"A place for your old girlfriend, of course! How nice that you are together again, finding true love in these times!" I tried to explain that Erika was never really my girlfriend, but Kitty was hearing none of it. She had gotten a romantic notion into her head, and was delighted that her humble abode, and it was humble, would be the site of our reunion.

"Philippe and Jacques are still here, so she will have to share the room with them," said Kitty. Her face assumed a thoughtful expression. "I've never had a girl here before who didn't work. You tell your girlfriend she mustn't ever feel uncomfortable, no one will ever pressure her, although I would appreciate it if she didn't socialize with the other girls."

I kissed Kitty and thanked her. If ever there were a hooker with a heart of gold, it was Kitty. As I walked quickly back to Erika, I suddenly felt very masculine, very potent; I had rescued a maiden in distress. Kitty's romantic fantasy, I realized, was taking hold in my brain.

Erika was standing there, waiting for me. Her hands were clenched.

"OK," I said, "it's all arranged. For a few nights, anyway. It's not exactly fancy, but it's better than sleeping in the bushes." I heard a small cry escape Erika's lips, like the sound of a small animal, bleating. It was the sound of relief.

Kitty was waiting for us at the door even before we rang the bell. She probably had some kind of a mirror or intercom system rigged in the apartment that signaled every arrival. Kitty, who was barely five feet tall, looked up at Erika, and grabbed her hand. "Welcome, dear. Hmm ... don't let the clients see you, or they will be beating down your door!"

I had not told Erika where we were going. She looked confused, but only for a moment. She was a Taucher, like me, and caught on quickly. All that mattered to her was survival.

"Thank you very much, Fraeulein Kitty," she said. "I promise I won't cause you any trouble. I am not the world's best cook or housekeeper, but I will help you in any way I can."

Kitty beamed, and I knew that Erika had said exactly the right thing. Kitty and her girls earned the money to put food on the table, but everyone was too busy to prepare it. Kitty took Erika to her own bedroom, and flung open her closet and bureau drawers. She told Erika to take anything she needed, including underwear. She saw that Erika had come with nothing besides the clothes on her back. Kitty even offered Erika the use of her private bathroom, which none of the working girls were permitted to enter.

Sprawled out on the mattresses in Kitty's spare room, Erika and I talked for hours. We shared our memories, we looked back on who we had once been before we were forced to reinvent ourselves. We counted up who was alive and who was dead. At times Erika seemed like a complete stranger, her appearance was so different, and the coquettish manner she had affected in junior high was gone. There was no trace of the little Jewish girl I had once known. But I understood why she had changed; I too had changed a lot, maybe more than I had ever thought I could. I wondered what she saw when she looked at me.

She had noticed how I had reached for my back pocket when she surprised me in the street, and asked me if I carried a gun. "Yes," I told her. "I am not going out quietly. I plan to take some of Hitler's bastards along."

She nodded approvingly. "You're still the way you were in school. Remember when Herr Schwartzman beat you with a bamboo stick? You had a sweater stuffed inside your pants, and after he hit you over and over, you just turned around and asked him if he was finished. We all laughed, and Schwartzman went berserk!" The memory made both of us smile, but only briefly. That had been child's play; now there was no audience to cheer us on, no one to comfort us – or even notice – if we were caught.

I decided not to go back to Opa's that night. I thought Erika would feel more comfortable her first night at Kitty's if I were there too. When Philippe and Jacques came in from the billiard hall, I introduced them to her and made it clear that she was in the same boat as the rest of us – a diver but without a boat, so to speak. At first they seemed a little dubious about sharing the room with a woman, especially a head turner like Erika. But she made it clear that she wanted to be treated like one of the boys, and she didn't blink an eye when the three of us stripped down to the underwear we wore to bed.

Erika had borrowed a long nightgown from Kitty. She lay down on the mattress and faced the wall, and I slid in next to her. I didn't know what to think or what to expect, but the warm body wedged next to mine made it impossible to sleep. Then Philippe, as usual, began to snore – huge, rolling thunderclaps of snoring. The sounds that had driven me crazy other nights, tonight I found reassuring because now I could investigate the situation with Erika.

The situation was quickly clarified when she turned around to face me, and her mouth sought mine. When I put my arms around her, I found a small towel folded behind her back. She had come prepared. Our lips were locked together for what seemed like hours. We moved silently, barely breathing. This girl, who would not give me the time of day a few years ago, was giving herself to me completely now. Was it the war, loneliness, gratitude, fear? Did it matter? We were alive, my Taucher girlfriend and I, and they had not been able to keep this moment from us.

The next morning, I tiptoed out of the room without waking Erika or anyone else, and went straight to Opa's house. I knew he would be annoyed that I had not come home the night before, or even thought to call him. Opa sat at the kitchen table clad in his grimy undershirt and boxer shorts, and glowered at me. "You Schweinehund!" he bellowed. "Are you stupid, don't you realize we have a game tonight? We should have spent yesterday evening preparing! Where the hell were you?"

I didn't want to give Opa any more information than was necessary. "Relax, Opa, we have all afternoon to get ready. I promise I'll come back early from the billiard hall."

"You irresponsible asshole, you'll get caught there, you and your brainless bunch of friends." Opa knew we had plenty of time to prepare our signals for the next game. The truth was, he was lonely, and jealous of my other friends. But he probably did have protective feelings toward me and was genuinely concerned when I didn't come home. He knew I was bound to come back eventually, unless I was caught, because I had taken to leaving my winnings in a hollowed-out floorboard in his closet until I could get them home.

After a quick, icy bath in Opa's slimy tub, I left for the billiard hall. Tad was already there, playing against the thug, Martin. Martin was obsessed with beating Tad, but even with a seventy-five point handicap, he still couldn't win. With each point he fell behind, Martin exploded in obscenities. Tad did not flinch, just continued playing, point by point, until the match was finished. But Martin was dangerous, and I really didn't like being around him.

Philippe and Jacques rushed over to me the moment they came in. "That was some babe you brought over last night," said Philippe. "What's her story? Where did you meet her?"

Tad had just finished his match and was eager for all the gossip as usual. "What babe?"

"Ssshhh," I whispered. "She's one of us, I know her from school. She needs help."

"So is she your girlfriend?" Philippe asked.

"I don't know," I said. "I would like her to be."

"Someone else to worry about?" sighed Tad. "Another mouth to feed? How you love to complicate your life, Gerhard."

Philippe's anxious face began twitching and his huge Adam's apple bobbed. "Ja, we've all got problems! Look at Jacques, how skinny he is! Sometimes he can't walk. The guy needs a doctor! We need money!" He was right. Jacques was emaciated, and seldom spoke anymore.

"I know what you're getting at, that robbery business again," I said to Philippe. "Look, you come up with a good plan, and Tad and I will be the first to come on board."

"It might be sooner than you think," Tad said dryly. "Remember the guy who sold us the guns, Leo Eckert? He told me the Nazis arrested thirty known Communists last week, a whole red 'cell.' It's only a matter of time before they go after Johann, and that will be the end of this place."

"Leo? Is he still free?" Philippe asked anxiously. He was the only reliable source of guns and ammunition.

Tad nodded wearily. He seemed uncharacteristically pessimistic. Perhaps he was worn out after a morning with the abusive Martin. "Leo's OK, for now. But he can't go on forever. Neither can we," he added glumly, the first time I had heard him sound genuinely depressed. "They'll get us all if there isn't an invasion of Europe soon."

Philippe was delighted whenever anyone shared his gloomy outlook. "You better believe it! The worse the war goes, the more vicious these bastards get. What's with these people, are they hypnotized or something?" Jacques was nodding at his friend's every word. Then his face went white and he doubled over, clutching his stomach and moaning.

"Let's get out of here," Tad whispered. "I can't take another minute of this."

We decided to go for a stroll on the Ku-Damm, with its many diversions and large midday crowds to get lost in. From a phone booth, I called Erika at Kitty's and asked her to meet us outside. As we walked to meet her, I tried to cheer Tad up. I did not want him bringing down Erika's already shaky morale.

Luckily, the one thing that could lift his mood was the sight of a pretty girl. His face brightened as he watched Erika strut out of the front entrance of Kitty's building. Today she wore her platinum braids in another classic German style, one coiled tightly above each ear. Her mouth seemed to be locked in a straight line. Alone in the world, Erika had little to smile about.

Tad suggested we go to the Café Wien, a Ku-Damm watering hole, popular for its specialty, Schwarzwaelder Kirschtorte, an outrageously rich Black Forest cake spiked with cherry liqueur. He said his birthday was two days away. So Tad was a Gemini, too. I had never been much for astrology, but maybe that was why he and I had adapted so readily to our false identities. I also now understood why he was depressed. He was several years older than I, about to turn twenty-three. There was not much to celebrate, and he had no one to celebrate with.

"Not Café Wien," said Erika sharply, matching our long strides with her own.

"Why not?" I asked. "Their Kirschtorte was the best. I'm not sure they even serve it anymore, since the war. My mouth is watering just thinking about it."

"Don't be fools, over a piece of cake! *She* goes there!" Erika said flatly, glaring at both of us as though we should understand what she was talking about.

"Who?" I asked.

"You know, Stella. She and her boyfriend are regulars at Café Wien, it's one of their hangouts."

"What are you talking about?" asked Tad. "Who the hell is Stella?"

"A Taucher who doesn't know Stella Goldschlag, that's a first!" muttered Erika.

"You'd know her if you were Jewish, Tad," I broke in. "This girl is one of the biggest informers in Berlin. The Nazis have nabbed hundreds of Tauchers because of her."

"And how does she do this?" Tad asked.

Erika's face filled with disgust. She seemed almost obsessed with Stella. I think it was because Stella was probably one of the few girls that the beautiful and snobbish Erika Weissmann had once actually admired. "She's a devil who looks like an angel, that's how. She's blond, beautiful, like a movie star, and doesn't look at all Jewish; my best friend Ushi and I went to school with her, and the boys fell all over Stella. Well, today she passes herself off as a Taucher, like you and me, ingratiates herself with people, and once they get comfortable enough to tell her their secrets – like where they live and where their Jewish friends and relatives are – she and her lowlife boyfriend, Rolf Isaacsohn, hand them over to the Gestapo. Ushi was one of their victims!"

"Just like old Behrend, the bastard who tried to pick up my mother," I muttered. "They should all drop dead."

Tad shook his head. "How can this be?" he said. "How can Jews turn on each other at a time like this? Can't you trust your own people?"

"Don't be naive, friend," I retorted. "There's always a skunk in the best of families, even among us chosen folks."

"I pray that the whole lot of them will go straight to hell," said Erika bitterly.

"And I pray we don't meet them there," I said, only half joking. Unlike Stella, my friends and I protected each other fiercely, but in other areas of morality, sometimes our damnation seemed inevitable.

We boarded a subway at the Alexanderplatz, and got off at the Charlottenburg Station to bring us closer to the Ku-Damm without spending too much time walking the streets. As we passed the Joachimsthaler Strasse, I noticed a group of young men standing outside a public men's toilet.

"What's going on there?" I asked Tad.

"Now I'll call *you* naive," he replied. "They're all homosexuals, you know, arsch-fickers."

I tried not to stare, but couldn't help myself. Sex, in all its permutations, was of endless fascination to me. "Weren't they all supposed to be arrested?" I asked.

"Right," said Tad. "And Berlin is supposed to be free of you guys."

Erika wrinkled her nose in disgust. "I think it's sick."

"Unless they are caught in the act, there is no real way to ferret them out," said Tad. "But if they do get caught, the word is that they're sterilized or castrated, and then thrown into a concentration camp."

"So aren't they taking big chances," I asked, "loitering in broad daylight, with policemen all over the place?"

"Of course. But most of them are desperate for money, just like Kitty's girls, and they have found something to trade in. They hang around outside those toilets for survival, not for love. Well, maybe a little of both."

"What makes you such an expert on this subject?" said Erika. She acted as though she didn't like Tad at all. Or maybe her antagonism masked an attraction?

"Who said I was an expert?" he replied cagily. I looked at Tad. He was handsomer than any of the young men across the street, and, with his golden curls and delicate hands, I suspected he had had his share of propositions from men. Crazy Martin in the billiard hall often cursed him with the word "homo." It might have enraged some macho types, but not Tad. He was an egalitarian soul, resolutely blind to the differences between people, and he would not have been apologetic had that been his sexual preference.

It was such a glorious day that we decided to stop in at the Zoologische Garten, Berlin's immaculate and beautifully landscaped zoo. We looked like three young Germans on summer holiday, slurping on Langnese Ice and wandering among the mothers and children. Everyone was friendly, and we exchanged pleasantries about the weather and the monkeys, anything. A hyena screeched, a lion roared. Children of all ages skipped and twirled and chortled around us, their clothes pressed and their golden hair gleaming. They looked so happy and well-cared for.

But where, where were all the Jewish children, on this sundrenched day so perfect for an outing? The zoo suddenly became sinister. Tad and Erika and I looked at each other, and could read each other's thoughts: these animals, well fed in their clean cages, are better off than the Jews of Berlin, because the Nazis consider them higher forms of life than us. Wordlessly, we left the park. The chestnut trees were budding, and flower boxes outside the apartment windows were sprouting lilies, marigolds, pansies, peonies – but the beauty and normalcy that surrounded me felt like an affront. How could the flowers bloom when people were dying?

There was now no time to go on to the Ku-Damm. I needed to go back to Opa's and establish the signals for that night's scam. My first date with Erika after our passionate night together had been a big disappointment. From the moment she joined Tad and me, I sensed that she was keeping me at arm's length, just as she had years before. She had given me her body, but not what I wanted most of all – her heart.

Later that evening, in a sweltering apartment some-where east of the city, Opa and I had our best night ever. When we returned to the apartment I shoved a fat wad of bills under the rickety floorboard. The old man loved nothing more than money, and he was beside himself with glee.

It was Friday night. After Opa went to bed, I found a small candle and lit it. I encircled the flame with my hands, and said the Sabbath blessing the way my mother did. And then, in a voice barely above a whisper, I sang the Sabbath melodies that I remembered from my father, beginning with "L'Cha Dodi," the hymn that welcomes the Sabbath Queen. By now I was crying quietly. I knew I would never see my father again, but I wanted to sing his songs, in full voice and unafraid.

I did not visit Erika for several days after that, to give both of us a chance to sort out our feelings. When I finally got up the courage to visit her at Kitty's, I saw that she had kept her word; the apartment was immaculate, a far cry from the way it had been before. Two old end tables in the living room were now covered with crocheted cover-lets, and there were subtle changes in the arrangement of the furniture. Erika's taste was written all over it.

My heart pounded as she walked toward me. Her hair, for the first time since we were reunited, was long and loose and, with the cascade of waves framing her face, she looked more like the girl I had known in school. I was smitten by her, and longed to kiss her the way I had during our one incredible night together. But she greeted me with restraint. She gave me a warm smile and a quick hug. It was clear that she wanted me as her friend, but not as her boyfriend. I wondered if we would ever be together again.

"So how is everything?" I asked her, feeling some-what awkward.

"Lothar, I am so grateful to you. Kitty is a wonderful person. She even put up a small cot for me in her own room, so I don't have to stay with those two guys in the back bedroom."

"What about Etienne?"

"He's still in Paris. I promised I'd leave the room to give them some privacy when he comes back next week. Kitty says it doesn't take very long!"

I returned her mischievous smile. But my heart was heavy. If Erika was now in Kitty's room, it was even less likely that we would spend the night together. "I'm happy for you, Erika," I said. "The place looks great."

"Yes it does, doesn't it? I'm cleaning and cooking for the first time in my life. We always had a housekeeper at home. And you know what? I'm pretty good at it!"

"Yes, she is, Gerhardchen!" said Kitty as she entered the room, and Erika looked relieved. Another person's presence was bound to delay, if only for a short while, any intimate conversation between us. Kitty threw her arms around both of our shoulders, squeezed tightly, and sighed. "Both of you, such treasures! So gorgeous to-gether! One day, when all of this is over, I want to dance at your wedding. I have never been to a Jewish wedding! Gerhard, you must work hard and become very rich. I want this princess to marry a wealthy man. You'll have children, beautiful children."

Kitty had definitely read too many romance novels. "Erika is definitely a treasure," I said carefully, "but we can't think that far ahead. It is enough to get through today. Tomorrow will have to take care of itself – right, Erika?"

"Absolutely," she said firmly, fixing her eyes on me. "I never think about marriage, or children, never!" I returned Erika's pointed stare, and nodded my head. I knew she was right. As Tad had always cautioned me, we could not afford to complicate our lives by falling in love. But I wondered if she were being completely honest. If she really cared about me as I cared about her, would she be able to control her emotions this way? Maybe her heart was still so broken, after being orphaned, that she was not ready to open it up. Or maybe, as several of my friends in school had warned me, Erika was just spoiled and superficial. Whatever the reason, it still hurt. For the second time, my dreams had been dashed and my heart had been broken by Erika Weissman.

Kitty invited me to stay for dinner, a rabbit stew Erika had made. I had never eaten rabbit before, and was a little skittish about sinking my teeth into a fluffy white bunny like those in our backyard in Pomerania. But it turned out to be delicious. Several times during dinner, Kitty was interrupted by the demands of her work – the ringing phone, a girl who needed change for a large bill, a traffic jam of men in the hallway. I would never have expected the sheltered Erika Weissman to be so at home in a brothel, but now I saw that she was keenly intelligent and remarkably adaptable. Just like me.

Erika walked me to the door. In the hallway she melted into my arms and gave me the ardent kisses I yearned for. "I love you," I whispered into her hair, but she put her fingers to my lips.

"Shhh," she said. "You mustn't use that word. Not now."

"That night ..."

"It was beautiful."

"And will there ever be another like it?"

"I would like that," she said, her voice hesitating, "but only if we have an understanding. We are friends, comrades. Boyfriends and girlfriends moon over each other, they fight, they break up. We don't have the luxury of all that. We can't do that. We are bound together, we need each other to stay alive."

I nodded and turned away so that she would not see the tears in my eyes. Erika and I did spend more nights together, some of the most wonderful nights of my life. But I never said the word "love" to her again.

That night on my way back to Opa's I got caught in a sudden air raid. In my pocket I always carried the air-raid warden's armband I had stolen from Dahlem Dorf. I slipped it over my shirtsleeve and entered an apartment building on the Landsberger Allee. While the tenants made their way down to the shelter, I barked orders and sprinted up the stairs in the opposite direction.

After reaching the fourth floor I opened the door to the laundry-utility room, which in most Berlin buildings was directly under the roof. A woman saw me there and asked me where I was going. I told her to get down to the shelter immediately since I had smelled smoke and, as the air-raid warden, it was my duty to inspect further. I grabbed a pail of water and insisted she go immediately to the shelter.

I stepped out onto the black-tarred roof. It was a gentle summer night, balmy and moonlit, but searchlights slashed the serenity of the summer sky. The Royal Air Force flew overhead, bombs fell around me, the siren screamed its warning. I felt oddly calm. For some reason, I knew I would be safe, that the city would be reduced to rubble, but that I would live, maybe to tell the story as the last Jew in Berlin. That night I thought of myself as dancing on top of a volcano that was constantly erupting, always looking for the spots around the edges where I would not be engulfed in the flames.

Chapter 10

From Street to Sanctuary

By late summer 1943, life in Berlin had become conditioned by the constant pounding of Allied air raids. Each morning, people crowded anxiously in front of updated lists of the dead or missing. Sometimes I felt oddly triumphant when I contemplated the fact that neither my name nor my mother's could be found on any casualty list because we did not exist. Perhaps it was better that way.

Now, even basic services such as water and electricity, let alone telephones and transportation, were routinely disrupted, and repair crews worked round the clock to restore the city's ability to function. The Nazi propaganda machine raved on about the victory to come, but the message was received with growing disbelief, even contempt. Recognizing the danger of a surly city population, the regime made sure that basic food supplies – especially coffee, eggs, milk, meat – now extremely scarce in the countryside were still available in Berlin. Extra allotments of real coffee were offered after especially heavy air raids.

As the environment became increasingly difficult for the normal citizenry, it brought, ironically, certain benefits for us illegals. The perpetual blackouts that inconvenienced the average citizen provided us a protective cloak which enabled us to roam at night with greater freedom. Servicemen, no longer so proud of their service, were more likely now than before to wear civilian clothes when on leave or off duty so that we who had no uniforms became less conspicuous. And, while the average citizen would feel the shortages, we, who had long ago been forced to develop new and additional sources of life's necessities, were in some ways better prepared to cope than they.

* * * * * * *

I still spent most of my nights at Opa's, where my greatest expense was a weekly spray can of Flit to keep the bedbugs at bay. I knew I was lucky to have found such a safe place, but life with Opa was getting oppressive. As summer gave way to fall, the card games dwindled to only one every few weeks, yet Opa demanded my constant presence, cursing and screaming at me every time I left the apartment. His behavior became more irrational by the day. Sometimes I worried that he might follow me and make a scene in public; but Opa knew I would find a way to take him down with me if he turned me in. And the old guy wanted to live, though I couldn't imagine what he had to live for.

Being with Erika always lifted my spirits. She had become Kitty's personal assistant, helping her with her appointment book, and keeping the apartment in order. Occasionally we would spend the night together at Kitty's. I loved holding her in my arms, but I accepted her decision not to get serious with me. It seemed pointless to plan for the future, anyway.

Philippe had taken it upon himself to mastermind a serious robbery, as if a sack full of food stamps were the answer to all our problems. Sometimes he just sat around and played with his gun, aiming it randomly, like a child's toy. Jacques was a bag of bones. Erika said she thought he was servicing some of Kitty's clients out of sheer desperation. Desperation, squalor, duplicity – it had become a way of life, my way of life, and it seemed that decency, decent people, no longer existed. At least not in Nazi Germany.

And then I met Hans Scheidt.

He was one of the silver-haired gents who played cards from time to time at Wilhelm's apartment. He lived next door, in the same Sybelstrasse building. Hans seemed different from the other card players. The brown eyes behind his horn-rimmed glasses were intelligent and compassionate. He dressed neatly and carried himself with quiet dignity, never using profanity or even lower class Berliner slang like the rest of them. He was the exact opposite of Opa except that he, too, was very lonely. Hans had lost his wife in 1938 after a long bout with cancer. There were no children.

Hans told me he had worked as a schoolteacher for more than thirty years when he was abruptly demoted to custodian. Apparently the school authorities had decided that he was not qualified to educate the superior children of the Third Reich. Although he was over sixty and ready to receive his pension, they kept him on at the school because they needed help in all the trades. Hans stayed because he needed something to do with his time.

Hans seemed to take an instant liking to me, and I to him. He enjoyed hearing tales of my teachers and courses at the Technische Hochschule, all of which were, of course, complete fabrications. On several occasions, he urged me to come back to Sybelstrasse for a visit, after school. I decided to accept Hans's invitation, coming late enough in the afternoon so he would not suspect that I was not really attending classes. He was clearly delighted to see me, and brought out his best china to serve me real coffee and pastries, delicious cream puffs that he proudly announced he had bought at the Konditorei Kranzler, one of the best bakeries in Berlin.

Hans's apartment was sunny and clean. The flowered curtains on the kitchen window, though faded, bespoke a woman's touch. Hans sighed that his late wife, Emmi, had been such a talented Hausfrau that he never even peeled a potato until she fell ill. In the years since her death he had become a competent cook and housekeeper, but he yearned for companionship. He took me into the living room to show me a portrait of the two of them that hung on the wall above an upright piano.

"When the Lord does not bless you with children, and you are everything to each other, then it is very hard," he said, his voice catching. "She played so beautifully, Beethoven, and especially Liszt. I haven't got the heart to sell the piano. No one would buy it now anyway. People are no longer interested in the arts, all they want is food, cigarettes, and clothing. The intellect, the art of meaningful conversation, the riches of our German culture, it has all been lost."

Our conversation began very cautiously. We spoke in vague terms about how difficult it was to have any real life in today's Germany, verbally dancing around each other, trying to get a fix on each other's politics.

"Nowadays, many of the students at the school, they seem so, I don't know – bloodthirsty," Hans said tentatively, keeping his eyes on my expression. "I love the Fatherland, too, but my God! Human kindness, what has happened to human kindness?"

"Yes," I said emphatically, and saw his face flood with relief. "Many terrible things have happened in the name of this insane national socialism. Perhaps if we had opened our mouths when it still counted, things might have never gotten this bad."

"Ach, Gerhard, only one time did I open my mouth, and I have been paying for it ever since," he said quietly. "On Kristallnacht, it was just after Emmi died, they came to the school and beat up one of my colleagues, Grossman, a Jew, beat him to a bloody pulp right in front of his students. The other teachers and I, we just stood there like morons, we said nothing, we did nothing. Well, afterwards, I registered a complaint with the school administration. That's when they took away my job and made me a janitor. And believe me, I was lucky. If it had not been for my cousin Heinrich, who's a party member and interceded for me, I would have been arrested for sure."

"But why have we lost our humanity? Is it something about us Germans, something within us?" I asked him.

He shrugged his shoulders. "Who knows? Sometimes I think we have no foundation for inner peace. If you look at the Teutonic concept of gentleness, you see that Wotan and Donar think of it as weakness. So we worship strength, power, marching, and uniforms, and now it has become like a religion. Yet Goethe, Schiller, Heine, our poets, revealed man's deepest soul, and captured man's noblest visions. And many of them were Jews! As a Christian, I say, to turn our backs on them is to turn our backs on ourselves."

Then, after a pause, he continued, staring at the portrait of him and his wife. "No, we cannot tell. It seems we Germans have the worst and the best in us. We know that what we have today is not the Germany we loved yesterday, but we cannot know what tomorrow will bring." Then, looking me squarely in the eye, "It is too late for me, but you, Gerhard my boy, I hope you will live to see Germany restored. Yes, you must make it so."

Smiling, Hans put his arm around my shoulder in a fatherly way. "Gerhard, you are a breath of fresh air in a polluted world. A young man like you gives me hope for our country's future! It is a relief to speak frankly, to take off this mental straitjacket that we are forced to wear day in, day out. Yes, it is the silence, the silence that is choking me."

I had no answer. We sat and quietly sipped our coffee. Someday, perhaps, I could tell him that I was glad, in some crazy way, to be one of the victims; there were only two sides, and I could not be on the other. I sometimes even pitied them for having nothing to believe in. My own conscience was clear, in spite of all the lying and stealing, for I was keeping alive in my heart the memory of the Germany I remembered. But, for the moment, I had revealed all that I was ready to reveal to him.

The afternoon with my new friend passed quickly. He was so well educated that there seemed to be no subject he could not discuss with authority. Yet he was not at all dogmatic in his beliefs, and was a good listener. He must have been a wonderful teacher. Before I left, he handed me a small bag containing two leftover cream puffs. "One for you and one for the blind fellow, your uncle," he said. "I hope you will come back again soon, maybe even stay overnight. We can go to the National Gallery, if you like, or some other museum."

"That would be great," I said. "But of course I would bring my own food."

"Nonsense. I eat Stammgericht every afternoon in the school cafeteria, so my ration card is more than ample. And I have a spare bedroom. I am alone, as the saying goes, alone like a stone."

Alone like a stone. I took a long look around the gracious apartment, and at Hans's kind, open face. Charlottenburg was a bit out of the way, much farther from the center of Berlin than Opa's, farther, too, from my mother and the billiard hall. I wondered how Hans would feel about a house guest who stayed longer than one night, perhaps much longer. But I didn't think we knew each other well enough yet for me to broach the subject.

Riding the subway back to the center of Berlin, I found myself unable to stop fantasizing about what life might be like under Hans's roof. It was a matter of mental as well as physical hygiene. Being in the company of a decent human being like Hans Scheidt had put me back in touch with myself, with Lothar Orbach, the happy optimist who lived on, quietly and secretly, buried inside Gerhard Peters. It was a constant effort to keep Lothar's spirit soaring underground. But I clung to that spirit because, without it, who would I be?

I would be Gerhard Peters, of course. His skin had begun to fit me very well. Charming, manipulative, adaptable, an expert liar, a blithe con man, and an ever more promising thief. No family, no religion, no education, no known address. Bombs exploded around him, yet he remained always unscathed. The country was plunged into a dark, enveloping nightmare; but for him, it was one long, decadent party.

For example, there was Eva. Eva – I never learned her last name – was the proprietor of a busy, family-style restaurant on the Frankfurter Allee at the corner of Boxhagener Strasse. She was in her late thirties, with a rather pretty face, and shapely legs, but she must have weighed over three hundred pounds. She was so enormous that children sometimes peered inside the restaurant's bay window just to catch a glimpse of her. They pointed and laughed, and then ran away.

The first time I went into Eva's restaurant, I ordered the Stammgericht of the day, ate it quickly, and as usual got out of there as fast as I could. The fare was nothing special, some kind of bland stew, but I noticed she had waited on me personally and given me an unusually generous portion. With the card games drying up, I had little income. A filling meal, free of charge, was not something I took for granted.

The restaurant was closed on Sundays and Mondays. On Tuesdays, there was usually a big crowd to blend into, and the food was always fresh. After I had eaten there a few times, she began to serve me better dishes that normally were obtainable only with a ration card, like pork or goose. Even though this particular restaurant was a bit of a trip from Opa's apartment, it became worth going out of my way to eat there.

After I became a Tuesday night regular, she invited me to sit with her at her private table, in a darkened corner of the restaurant. She told me that her husband was a prisoner of war, that he had been captured in Tunis but was now being held in England. She didn't seem to be too upset about it; at least, she said, the war was over for him, in a way, and he would eventually be released rather than shot down somewhere. When he returned, he would rejoin her in running the restaurant, which was in a prime location and appeared to do a very good business.

In return I told her my usual yarn about being bombed out with my family and relocating in Berlin, that I was still a student and temporarily exempt from military service. This resume usually satisfied my fleeting acquaintances.

Eva would beam at me while I wolfed down her cooking, her puffy cheeks glowing like two pink balloons.

As big as she was, she moved with surprising speed, leaping to her feet to clear the table and bring me dessert. I could not help but stare up at her huge breasts when she stood over me, and then at her massive behind when she turned around to go back into the kitchen. With each step, her flesh shook like a mountain of Jell-o.

Interestingly, the few times I brought Tad in with me, Eva barely acknowledged us and served us only the basic Stammgericht. She had nicknames for everybody who walked into the restaurant, and referred to Tad sarcastically as "The Flying Dutchman." She made it very clear that she disliked him. I wasn't sure why; maybe his movie star looks made her uncomfortable. Me, she called "The Little Student."

One Tuesday evening, I came in at nearly nine o'clock, well past the dinner rush. The last patrons were about to pay for their meal. Eva's full cheeks were flushed and there were beads of perspiration on her forehead. Before I had a chance to sit down at a table, she grabbed me by the arm.

"Little Student, I have a surprise for you. I hope you are good and hungry," she whispered in my ear. "I am about to close. Tonight we will have a nice, quiet dinner in the back. You won't believe it, I just got in some fresh beef, much too good to serve in the restaurant, and I have fixed it up special, just for you and me!"

Without waiting for an answer, she steered me firmly into the kitchen. Two elderly women wearing hairnets stood at the sink, their forearms plunged into the sudsy water. The place was spotless, with gleaming pots and pans hanging from the ceiling. Alongside a large pickle barrel, a card table had been set up, covered with a lace tablecloth and two place settings.

"Dear ladies, don't worry about those last few dishes," Eva said to them. "You may go a few minutes early." She turned to me and winked. "They are so annoying," she hissed. "I have to tell them everything ten times before it gets done." The two kitchen workers were gone in a flash. Eva excused herself and disappeared into the bathroom, leaving me to inhale the aroma of the beef, slathered in onions, sizzling on the stove.

About ten minutes later she emerged, clad in a pink and white striped outfit that could only be described as a tent dress. The dress was quite short, showing off her legs, her best feature, and its plunging neckline revealed an enormous cleavage. With her pink lipstick carefully applied to match her outfit, and her beady, blue eyes set deep inside her fleshy face, Eva was, at first glance, grotesque. Yet the more I looked at her, the more I could see that this was a woman who was confident about herself and her body, no matter what others thought. After a while, in fact, I even began to find her appealing.

"What a day it's been, I'm hungry as a horse!" she chortled, her hands on her hips. "Now then, we begin with a nice hot bowl of lentil soup, and then go into the main course."

Eva and I each slurped down two bowls of soup. Then she uncorked a bottle of red wine that she declared was the finest one in her wine cellar. I wasn't much of a drinker, and the wine was too dry for my unsophisticated palate, but each time I took a few sips, she leaned over and refilled my glass without asking. Most of the bottle, however, she drained by herself.

We barely spoke a word as we cleaned our plates. Roast beef, potatoes in gravy, peas and carrots, topped off by apple fritters – it was the best dinner I had had since the beginning of the war.

There was barely enough room for our legs underneath the small folding table, and I could feel the heat of her fleshy thighs enveloping my knees. "The candles, oooh, I forgot the candles!" she exclaimed. She stood up quickly, and had to steady herself against my shoulder before staggering across the room. It took her several matches to light two large wax candles that she had propped up in aluminum foil on the counter. She switched off the overhead lamp in the kitchen.

"Do you like to dance, Little Student?" she murmured as she sank to her knees in front of me, her breasts spilling into my lap. "I am an excellent dancer."

"I'm sure you are, Eva," I said nervously. I sat frozen to the spot. So I was expected to sing for my supper after all. I needed food, and she needed a man. It was just that simple.

"How about opera, dear heart, do you like opera?" I nodded. "Good, then," she said thickly, "because I sing, too!" She rose to her feet and weaved into the bathroom. A few moments later, the door swung open. First, I heard her voice:

"Tra-la-la-la-la, To-re-ro-re-ro, Stolz in der Brust, Sieges bewusst; traaa-la-la-la-la …!" It was the aria from *Carmen*, sung in a strong and surprisingly sweet mezzo-soprano. And then out came Eva, completely naked, in all her astonishing glory, pirouetting around the darkened kitchen and waving an old woolen blanket in front of her like a matador.

"This is the dance, my little Don José, the dance of Carmen, just as she used to dance in Seville – or was it Madrid? – and painted by Rubens," she crooned, draping the blanket in front of her and curtsying. "What do you think?"

"Amazing," I said truthfully. This scene would be firmly etched in my mind for the rest of my life.

Eva folded the blanket and laid it on the floor in a corner of the kitchen. She spread herself across it and beckoned me to climb aboard. From the efficient way in which she approached this ritual, it was clear that I was not the first hungry customer to be rewarded with a candlelight dinner, music, and a heavy *digestive.*

Through much of the fall and winter of 1943, I remained a late-night patron of Eva's restaurant. Each time, I would be sent home with overflowing doggie bags of meats, casseroles, and other delicacies. I brought them to my mother and the Dudacys, or sometimes I shared them with my friends, but I never revealed how they were acquired. After a few months, I could no longer bring myself to continue our arrangement. I had no doubt that Eva would easily come across another young man whose stomach rumbled. I later learned that her husband wasn't a prisoner of war after all. He was an invalid, at home in their Berlin apartment in a wheelchair.

Now, all major German cities were being bombed constantly, by the Americans by day and the British by night. In Berlin, entire neighborhoods were burned to the ground. Some of these bloody infernos I saw with my own eyes, because I was more afraid of being captured by the Gestapo in a bomb shelter than I was of the falling bombs.

Nobody was more fatalistic at this point than Tad, whose reactions to situations always seemed to mirror my own, only he took everything a step further. He still lived with Ilse, but was feeling stifled by her devotion. He had begun spending time at a popular nightclub called the Vier Jahreszeiten, the Four Seasons. It was known as a hangout for soldiers on leave, and a pick-up place for underage girls. The place had had its liquor license revoked and then reinstated several times by the Sitten Polizei, as Berlin's Vice Squad was known. It seemed to me not the safest place to go, but Tad insisted it was as safe as any place else. He began working on me to go with him, tempting me with talk of pretty girls and great dance music.

"We'll find a table near the emergency exit," Tad insisted. "They have to keep it unlocked in case of fire or an air raid, and if something happens, we'll just make a run for it."

"And what if there's a Gestapo guy waiting at the exit?"

Tad smirked. "There's always your trusty gun, right?" Tad had had some marksmanship practice during his early teens in Poland. He knew I had never pulled the trigger of a real gun, and that the whole idea made me nervous.

"I don't know, Tad; if anything happened to me, my mother ..."

With unusual sharpness, he snapped at me. "Look, Gerhard, your mother has had her life, her marriage, her kids. What have you had? Nothing! This might be it for us, boy, this might be the only chance we get! If you want to spend the rest of your life like a cockroach in that old man's apartment, with your face buried in your books, that's your business. I'm not going to force you to do anything."

I didn't know if Tad was right or wrong, but I went back to Opa's and unearthed a clean sport shirt, a pair of knickerbockers, and a brown safari jacket. I had stolen them all from the Nazi's cedar closet in Dahlem Dorf, and had been saving them for a special occasion.

When I got to the crowded entrance of the Vier Jahreszeiten, Tad was already waiting. He looked me up and down, and gave me an approving smile. The doorway was mobbed with teenagers waving their identity cards. All the girls had to prove they were over eighteen, and the boys over twenty-one, unless they were in uniform.

My sophisticated outfit made me look much older than my age, and they did not even ask me for identification.

The place was dimly lit and filled with cigarette smoke. Waitresses hurried through the crowds carrying trays of drinks, nuts, and crackers. The band was playing a fox-trot, some German song I had never heard before, and you couldn't hear yourself think above the music, the shouting, and the laughter. I was relieved to see that quite a few other young men were in civilian clothes, more than the predictable number of plain clothes Gestapo agents. It was an easy place to get lost in.

A waitress ushered us to a large table with two empty seats. I noticed there was no emergency exit near us, but there was a sign with an arrow pointing to the restrooms.

With us at the table sat four girls and two soldiers. When there was a break between songs, we all introduced ourselves. Next to me was a girl named Charlotte, with her friend Marie on the other side of her. Both striking brunettes, the girls seemed to be extremely young, even though they were chain smoking and wearing heavy makeup. Tad asked the waitress for a Pilsner, and I ordered a Berliner Weisse mit'n Schuss – a sour beer with a dash of fruit juice. I asked the girls if we could buy them drinks, but they said they were sticking with sodas. I figured they were worried about getting drunk or sick.

When the band began to play "Tango Nocturno," I decided to ask Charlotte to dance. This was a song I had danced to many times, with busty little Inge Baruch at our apartment on Greifswalder Strasse.

Charlotte smelled of 4711 cologne and moved on the dance floor with a sensuousness and grace surprising in such a young girl. At first we danced with decorum, but in time we moved closer and even exchanged a few kisses.

When we came back to the table laughing and holding hands, Tad had moved over a few seats to sit next to Marie, and they were nuzzling each other. He looked up long enough to give me that grin I now knew so well.

"That's right, kiddies, have a good time!" he boomed, pulling me down next to him and patting my knee. "Life's so short, who knows where we'll be tomorrow?"

Several feet away, the two soldiers had become immersed in a deep political discussion with the two other girls at the table. As the night went on, Charlotte and Marie had one more drink each, and there was more dancing and kissing, groping and giggling. It was not hard to see which end of the table was having more fun.

The band started in on a *paso doble*, which was not my cup of tea, but Tad pulled Marie to her feet. As they whirled around the dance floor, Charlotte started to light another cigarette, but put it away when I told her I would rather be kissing her. After a few minutes of necking, Charlotte excused herself to go to the ladies' room. With Tad and Marie still on the dance floor, I turned my attention to the other foursome at the table. For the first time, I noticed that one of the soldiers, who looked about my age, had a cane hooked over the back of his chair. I tuned into his conversation and heard him talking about being wounded on the Russian front.

Suddenly there was a huge commotion. People were shouting and running in all directions. I had lost sight of Tad and Marie and couldn't make my way to the exit which, from the crush of bodies, appeared to be locked anyway. It was my worst fear realized, a police raid.

I slid off my seat, walked quickly in the direction of the arrow painted on the wall, and slipped into the first door I came to. Now I was in the ladies' room. Dozens of terrified teenaged girls cowered before me, clutching each other and weeping. Underneath the stalls, I could see lots of little feet crowded together. Charlotte's were surely among them. It took me a moment to realize that the girls were staring at me in terror; they thought I was an undercover vice cop.

"It's OK, it's OK!" I said in a loud whisper, but they continued to whimper and back away from me. Then I noticed a narrow door with a key sticking out of the lock. I lunged for the key, unlocked the door, and thrust myself inside. It was a tiny, dark closet, barely bigger than a locker, crammed with mops, brooms, and janitorial supplies. There was no way to lock it from the inside, so I grabbed the doorknob and pulled it toward me with both hands, holding on with all my strength.

For a few moments, things were relatively quiet. Then the girls began to shriek again and a gruff male voice yelled out from a few feet away: "That's it, girls, out with you! Let's see those ID cards! We're not leaving until the last stall is empty!"

I couldn't control my trembling inside the cramped space and prayed I wasn't making the door shake. A large spider was crawling over my knuckles, but I couldn't let go of the door to brush it away.

So this was how it would all end – in a janitor's closet in the ladies' room of a sleazy nightclub. All our planning, all our hopes for the future, dashed in an instant for the sake of a slow dance, a few kisses, a whiff of perfume. I was too scared to breathe; my stomach began to churn and I almost wet my pants.

Right outside the closet I could hear the girls pleading. "Oh please, sir! I will be eighteen in December, that's barely a month away," one of them sobbed. "My father will make it worth your while, you'll see, just let me go!" another whimpered.

Even with the spider crawling up my arm, I held the door so tightly that anyone who tried it from the outside would think it was locked. "Remember the Maccabees," I told myself. "Think of all the Jewish heroes!"

Then, finally, there was quiet. I waited a few minutes more and opened the door. The first thing I did was run to the toilet – I couldn't have waited a moment longer. I heard someone step inside the bathroom. She stood in front of the sink for a long time, humming to herself, probably fixing her hair. When she finally entered the stall next to mine, I dashed out.

The crowd had thinned considerably, but the band played on. Back at our table sat Tad, smooching with Marie as if nothing had happened. Charlotte was gone and so were the two girls who had sat at the other end of the table and the young soldier with the cane. Only the other soldier remained, sitting alone and drinking a beer. His eyes were bloodshot and he stared up at me with a strange expression.

Tad tried to mask his relief at seeing me. "Jesus, Gerd, what'd you do, get lost in the ladies' room?" he joked. He couldn't know how bad a joke it was. "Those bastards took two truckloads of girls out of here, like they have nothing better to do."

"They didn't get you?" I asked Marie, feeling suddenly dizzy.

"I really am eighteen, my birthday was two months ago," she said smugly. "But Charlotte was arrested – hey, where were you?"

"I know, I tried to help her," I stammered. "I tried to reason with those apes, but they don't listen, they just follow orders!"

"Well, don't worry about Charlotte," Marie said. "She'll be out before you know it. Her father's a biggie in the party, he has a lot of pull."

"So where the hell were you?" Tad hissed at me.

"Diarrhea," I said weakly. "Must have been the beer."

I sat slumped in my seat for at least another hour. The music had changed to an atonal jazz, and the few remaining couples swayed slowly, drunkenly, in each other's arms. The lonely soldier still sat a few feet away from me, lost in his beer and his private thoughts.

At about one in the morning, when I finally got up to leave, I checked my pants pocket. Somewhere in the confusion, I had dropped my key to Opa's apartment. I started back to the ladies' room to look for it, but one of the waitresses was leaning against the wall next to the door smoking a cigarette. I could not very well return to Opa's in the predawn hours and bang on the door until the old geezer heard me. It was too dangerous. "Lotharchen," I said to myself, "this is not your day." And the day was still not over.

It was surprisingly balmy outside for late November. I walked through the deserted streets with no clue as to where I was going. I was so emotionally and physically drained that I could hardly drag my feet along. I hadn't spent a single night on the streets since going underground, and the thought of it, the insecurity of sleeping out in the open with so many policemen and soldiers around, scared me to death. But tonight I didn't seem to have a choice.

The Janowitz Bridge loomed up ahead. I climbed down the abutment toward the river. Its bank was covered with garbage, broken bottles, and old cartons. Among the weeds I spied a large, flat rock that looked as if it could accommodate me. Even Moses, I reminded myself, had slept on a rock in the wilderness. I lowered myself onto the slimy stone, wrapping my jacket around me, and curled into the fetal position.

Suddenly, I heard the crunch of footsteps just behind me and, before I could move, I felt the cold muzzle of a gun pressed against the back of my neck. When I turned my head, I was blinded by a flashlight.

I couldn't see his face. "Hands up on the wall and spread your legs," he said tersely. "Any sudden moves, and I'll shoot."

I started to stagger to my feet, my heart thumping so loudly I could barely hear my own voice. "Forgot my keys," I stammered, "got to get ready for school – Technische Hochschule – I have papers ..."

"Bullshit," he snarled. "Legitimate people don't sleep on the streets."

"A bombing," I gasped, grasping at straws. "Our apartment ..."

"Plenty of shelters for our German folk in need. Put your wrists together. I'm cuffing you and taking you in."

"Please! Let me show you my papers ..."

"You can show them at the station. I'm sick and tired of cleaning you vermin out from under this bridge, all you Jews, and gypsies and deserters."

I could hear him fumbling for the handcuffs. For a second he lowered the gun. That was all I needed.

I whirled around and kicked at him with all my strength. He went over backwards and hit his head on the rock. I snatched up the flashlight and trained it on him. It was the soldier who had shared our table. I didn't think he was seriously injured, but he seemed dazed and blood poured from a gash on his temple. He pushed himself up to his knees and felt around the ground for his gun which had been knocked from his hand and had slid somewhere down the river bank.

I took out my pistol and saw his eyes go wild with terror. His head shook in a silent plea; his mouth opened and his jaws moved but no sounds emerged. So this was the power they loved, the power to dominate, to reduce a human being to a groveling, bleating animal – the power to kill.

He lay there, mute, terrified that I would finish him off. But I didn't. I couldn't. I just turned and climbed up the side of the bridge and hurried across it.

For several blocks I walked as fast as my legs would carry me. One of the streets I came to seemed to have been hit particularly badly in an air raid. Gingerly, I made my way through a maze of shattered bricks and broken glass. To my amazement, a ripped up sofa stood in the street before me, nestled inside some sort of an enclosure. I didn't know exactly where I was, and at that moment I didn't care; I threw myself on it, drawing my coat around me and assuming the fetal position once more.

The soldier's face kept coming back to me, the long moment when his eyes met mine, those eyes beseeching me without words, "Let me live! Let me live!" It wouldn't be too long before someone found him; Berlin was filled with wounded, disoriented people, corpses waiting to be identified. If it weren't he it would have been me. I tried to capture what had happened, and slowly realized I felt nothing. There was only numbness. I could think about these events, but could not feel them. I remembered what I had seen in Erika when she had first called out to me in the street, a robot rooted in pain and fear and loss. It was beginning to happen to me, only my numbness was rooted also in shame.

And then I put it all out of my mind, the shame and the fear and the emptiness, and I slept. It was the first time I had had to sleep on the streets of Berlin. It was like all the other trials underground: you feared it, you loathed it, and then, once forced to do it, it turned out to be nothing because you were still alive, which was all you cared about.

I awoke just before dawn to the purring of a stray cat rubbing against me and licking my face. A train station was several hundred yards away. Adjusting my eyes to the gathering light, I saw the couch I had stumbled upon was surrounded by other pieces of broken furniture, chairs, tables, and lamps. Behind me and on two sides were the remnants of fiber-board walls. I had been sleeping in what remained of the window display of a bombed-out furniture showroom.

It was barely seven o'clock when I went into a phone booth and dialed the number of Hans Scheidt. He was glad to hear from me. "Gerhard, good morning! I was just about to leave for school. I'm so glad you caught me! To what do I owe the pleasure of such an early call?"

"Well, my winter vacation is coming, and I wondered if I could spend a few days with you, you know, we talked about it."

"Excellent!" said Hans heartily. "Let's just be sure that our schools are on the same holiday schedule. What are the dates again?"

Suddenly my mind went blank. I, who had always had a glib answer for everything, could not think straight or even speak. Then I realized that I was crying, that great tears were streaming down my cheeks, that I could not go on.

"Gerhard, are you there?"

"Hans, I ... I need help," I sobbed.

There was a pause. Silence. And then he said, in the voice of a school teacher: "Be at my place at four o'clock this afternoon. Whatever it is, we will take care of it."

"Yes," I said.

"Do you hear me, Gerhard?" he said pointedly. "*Whatever* it is!"

"I hear you," I said.

Opa was sitting at the kitchen table in his underwear when I came in. He stared at my disheveled appearance, but asked me no questions. When he saw me heading toward the bathroom carrying a change of clothes, he barked, "Forget bathing, goddamn water's been turned off again!" I threw my few possessions in a bag, and told Opa that I was going to stay with Hans for a couple of weeks. He was surprisingly agreeable. Perhaps he had grown as tired of me as I had of him.

On Fridays I usually stopped in to see my mother. But on this day I felt too distraught, too tired to lie, and too ashamed to tell the truth. She would say that my narrow escapes could have all been avoided, and I knew she was right. But in my head I also heard Tad's voice: "This might be our only chance, our last chance to live!" I resolved that I would call my mother the next day, from Charlottenburg, after I had an opportunity to talk with Hans.

The train ride to the suburb of Charlottenburg showed a war-torn city with pockets of great beauty. On its outskirts, Berlin was still lovely and bucolic. Somehow people's lives went on. The children played in the parks, the storekeepers sold what they had, the bus drivers transported their passengers. Judenrein. All the Jews were gone, swept away, as if in a dream.

Hans welcomed me with outstretched arms. With a puzzled look he surveyed my grimy face and hands. "I have a nice liverwurst and some homemade dill pickles for us," he said gently. "Or, if you prefer to wash up before we eat, the shower is the second door on the left."

I hadn't had a real shower or bath in weeks. Before Opa's water had given out entirely, it had dwindled down to an ice-cold, mustard-colored brine. Here, Hans's porcelain tub sparkled. The shower curtain and thick terrycloth towels, all in yellow, were embroidered with a large Roman "S." An unused bar of Tosca soap lay in a yellow ceramic soap dish that was in the shape of a seashell. Everything matched. Everything was in order, and cared for. This was not the home of any ordinary janitor.

Under Hans's steaming shower, using his perfumed soap, I tried once more to wash it all away – the soldier under the bridge, the Vier Jahreszeiten, Opa, the oversized Eva, even the rich feel against my neck of the safari jacket I had stolen from the father of the Nazi maidens of Dahlem Dorf. I tried to wash it away, but the ugliness of it all had seeped inside my skin.

When I got out of the shower, the mirror was covered with steam. I wiped it with my hand. The face I saw was my face. I don't know why I was surprised, but I was. I remembered something my father used to say to me, when I was a child and would stand next to him in the bathroom, fascinated, as he shaved. And there he would often declare: "Lotharchen, when you get up in the morning you need to look at yourself in the mirror, and say quietly to yourself, and to yourself alone, 'I am precious, for God has created me in His own image, and I must love and respect myself!' When you do that, my son, the world will also respect you."

"I am precious, for God has created me in His own image, and I must love and respect myself!" I whispered the words fiercely before Hans Scheidt's steamed-up bathroom mirror. And I tried to believe them; I knew I had to believe them.

The food was ready on the table. Hans watched me eat. I said very little, and he did not press me. After we ate, he took out a deck of cards, and the two of us played wordlessly for about an hour. It was barely nine o'clock when Hans handed me a heavy quilt from a wooden chest of drawers in his living room. "You are tired," he said. "Tomorrow we will talk." A thick featherbed covered the mattress in the guest room. I felt as though I were sinking into a cradle. There were no dreams, no nightmares, just deep, blessed sleep, the kind of sleep I had not had in a long time.

I awoke the next morning to find I was alone in the apartment. On the kitchen table sat a basket of fresh rolls, butter and marmalade, ham and bacon, sliced onions, and four uncooked eggs in a small pot covered with cold water. The smell of fresh coffee filled the room. Hans had left me a note; he was out to get the morning paper and a few groceries, and he would be back shortly. What a fine man he was. No wonder my thoughts had turned to my father; I was with someone who could be a father figure, someone decent, protective, wise.

Hans returned just as I was finishing breakfast. It was much colder today, with the hint of an early frost. He came into the kitchen rubbing his hands to warm them, his face red from the cold. "Gerhard, good morning! I got some very fine herring in wine sauce at Reichelt's, and also my fifty allotted grams of coffee, so tomorrow there will be another good breakfast after church," he said cheerfully. "Well, how did you sleep, young fellow, your first night in a strange bed?"

Little did Hans know of all the strange beds I had slept in. "It was great, the best sleep I have had in a long time."

"You look better today," he said.

"I feel better."

"Would you like to go to the zoo?" he said earnestly. "Or I promised you the museum?"

"Thank you, Hans," I said, "but you don't have to entertain me, your hospitality is more than enough. Besides, isn't it a little cold for you?" Hans rubbed his neck and shoulder and nodded ruefully. "Well, the truth is, my rheumatism does act up in this weather." Then, eyeing me closely, he said: "You know, Gerhard, I have spent my life among young people. Tell me, how did you become such a considerate and thoughtful young man?"

I felt a surge of guilt as Hans beamed at me affectionately, and I didn't know what to say. Finally, it came out.

"In the past few years, I have come to appreciate kindness," I heard myself say. "Didn't Schiller say in *William Tell: 'Der beste kann selbst nicht in Frieden leben, wenn es dem boesen Nachbarn nicht gefaellt'* (The best can't live in peace if the bad neighbor won't let him)?"

"Schiller," he said. "Wait until you see my collection. Is he your favorite?"

I shook my head. "No. Heine and Goethe. Here's Goethe: *'Oh seelig, oh seelig ein Kind noch zu sein'* (Oh how precious, how precious to still be a child)," I said hoarsely and with a sound of yearning. He looked at me with concern. I was trying to control my expression, to wear my usual mask of nonchalance, but he must have read the anguish inside me.

"What is it, Gerhard? For God's sake, what is it?"

By now we were standing in the living room. I pushed him gently down onto the couch, so he would be sitting.

"I'm a Jew. I'm a Jew." I heard myself say the words, words I had not been able to say in years. "My bag is still packed if you want me to leave." Hans looked at me. He sat as though unable to move. He said not a word. "It's all right, you're a wonderful person," I stammered. "I'm sorry, I'll go now." I went to the bedroom to pick up my bag.

When I came back, Hans had risen to his feet. He put his two hands on my shoulders with surprising strength. I wondered if I would have to push him aside to leave. "You are going nowhere, Gerhard," he said. "This is your place now." I stared at him, dumbly. "Emmi's grandmother was Jewish. She would have been the first to say, 'Hans, we help the boy!'" He threw his arms around me. "I'm sorry, I'm sorry," he wept.

"For what?" I asked. "You've been so kind ..."

"It's our fault! This avalanche, it cannot be stopped, but maybe, if I can save one life ..." his voice trailed off.

We did not leave the apartment and talked late into the night. Hans sat quietly as I told him about my father, being taken, deported, and returned in the striped urn from Sachsenhausen. I told him about the Christmas eve escape with my mother. I told him about Tad and about Erika, about Kitty's brothel and about the billiard hall, but not the crooked card games in which he had been one of my victims. He gasped when I showed him my false papers from the Technische Hochschule. I even showed him my gun. He listened to it all raptly, sometimes with wonder, sometimes distress, and often with tears in his eyes. That night, as I slid into bed, I felt a sense of peace, of wholeness, that I had not felt in many months.

Just before I drifted off to sleep, Hans knocked lightly on the bedroom door.

"I wanted to say goodnight," he said. "And also, I realized in all this there was one thing ..."

"Yes?"

"Your name, what is your real name?"

I had found him and now he had found me.

"I am Lothar," I said, with a pride I could barely remember, "I am Lothar Orbach."

Chapter 11

Hauling Coal, Lifting Cash

There was a quiet beauty in the snowfalls that blanketed Berlin and its suburbs during December of 1943. A pristine white cover obscured the rubble and decay of the bombed-out buildings, creating an illusion of serenity though chaos still reigned.

Rarely a day went by that Hans did not tell me how glad he was to have me living with him, and I knew he meant it. Yet my conscience nagged, because he did not look well. He appeared to be losing weight, and barely picked at his already modest meals. My appetite was enormous as usual, and I was afraid I was taking his food. But Hans firmly denied that he was depriving himself on my account, and alluded to a medical condition. Then he always steered the conversation to another topic.

Advent season was under way, and the stores were decorated for Christmas, but on a much smaller scale than before, as most of the window glass in the city had been shattered by the steady bombing. All over the city, Hitler Youth and Bund Deutscher Maedel girls were shaking Winterhelp cans in the streets, collecting funds for a vast array of Nazi charities. The usual Nativity scenes were erected in the parks and town squares, but few citizens were in the holiday spirit.

One frigid night, a large shelter run by the Mutter und Kind welfare organization in the bowels of the Alexanderplatz subway station was hit by British bombers. For days afterwards, rescue teams dug through the rubble, extricating the bodies of hundreds of women and children. Like many others, I raced there in the morning when I heard the news. I stood behind police lines, stunned and sickened at the sight of hundreds of corpses laid out amidst the wreckage of the once beautiful plaza. I had seen bodies of bombing victims, but never so many in one place. They were stacked in rows covering the entire city block that had been leveled, many broken in postures no human could assume while alive, many missing limbs, and many charred with blackened masks for faces.

Surrounded by a phalanx of officers stood Goebbels, wearing his trademark black leather trenchcoat. There stood the symbol of death among the deaths he had evoked, the innocent dead. Why did wars always kill the innocent first, the guilty last or never? I began to feel a new ambivalence about the bombs I had so effortlessly avoided and which I had assumed were killing Nazis; it was one thing to welcome the destruction of the Third Reich, but quite another to watch the destruction of a civilization and its innocent people.

One Sunday morning, Hans was later than usual coming home from church. When he finally returned he was pale and panting, and lugging a medium-sized sack filled with coal. These briquettes were burned in tile stoves to provide heat to homes and businesses throughout Berlin. They were usually delivered in crates of a hundred, but for some reason the deliveryman had not come to Hans's apartment earlier as expected. The coal supply had run out and, as it was a Sunday, Hans decided to pay a visit to Herr Schelonka, the coal dealer, to pick up some briquettes to tide us over.

Hans sat on the sofa for several minutes, breathing heavily. Once he had regained his breath, he told me Schelonka's deliveryman had been in some kind of accident, and the company was in desperate need of an able-bodied young man to deliver coal and ice in the area. He had recommended me for the job.

"I told them that my second cousin from Pomerania was staying with me while attending school in Berlin, and could use some extra pocket money for Christmas," he said. "What do you think? I'm getting pretty good at all this lying, aren't I?" I nodded, thinking how ironic it was that this man, who had always prided himself on honesty and integrity, was now cultivating the art of deception.

"This Schelonka fellow, is he the suspicious type?"

"I doubt it. He and his wife, who runs the business with him, are very simple folk. I've known them for years," said Hans. "They won't even care that you have no working papers. That way they pay you cash under the table and don't have to deal with insurance and all those, uh, details."

All of my other sources of income had dried up; it seemed worth a try. When I was a little boy, I loved watching the sweaty coal carriers trudging up three and four flights of stairs with huge, hundred-pound bags and crates on their backs. I even tried to carry one once, just to see if I could do it, during my brief tenure in a sandblasting shop. I could manage the weight but I straightened my back too much, and most of the briquettes tumbled to the ground and broke. My boss cursed me and made me pick up every last piece.

Hans brought me over to the coal dealers' office the next morning. Frau Schelonka seemed quite harried but greeted me warmly. A plump, red-cheeked woman of about my mother's age, she kept the books and took all the orders from customers over the telephone. She said that her husband was out delivering ice to restaurants in the area; refrigerators were still quite rare, and the restaurants and larger families needed blocks of ice to keep food cold in their iceboxes. Herr Schelonka drove a specially insulated truck that kept the ice frozen. He used an ice pick to break off chunks of the desired size, and charged his customers accordingly.

Dutifully I displayed my identity card to Frau Schelonka and outlined my school schedule, but she hardly paid any attention. She was too busy fielding phone calls from irate customers whose coal deliveries had been delayed. "When can you start, dear boy?" was all she asked me. Hans gave me a thumbs-up from the corner of the room. He was beaming. I told her that I was ready to begin immediately, but that I needed a few pointers on how to carry the crates holding the briquettes. I didn't want to draw attention to myself by dumping a mound of dirty briquettes in the lobby of someone's building.

"Don't worry, it's nothing, you'll do just fine. If you meet my husband here at the end of the day he can answer all your questions," Frau Schelonka assured me. Then she looked up at me with a pleading expression. "But in the meantime, I have three customers right here in the neighborhood who need their deliveries right away. We'll pay you fifty pfennig for every bag, and of course you get tips." I glanced over at Hans. He gave me an encouraging nod. He believed I could do anything I put my mind to.

"Good! Let's get moving, then! " said Frau Schelonka briskly, not even waiting for my reply. "The most important thing is, don't forget to collect the coal stamps.

Without them, you mustn't deliver anything. They see a new man coming, they might try to hold onto the stamps."

She took me downstairs to a large, musty basement, where the charcoal stood already weighed and packed in burlap sacks, waiting to be carried up the stairs and piled onto the delivery wagon. Frau Schelonka watched approvingly as I carried the sacks upstairs and lifted them into the cart. She helped me put a strong leather belt around my shoulders. "You're a natural, young man!" she called out. "And one more thing, they have to give you an empty sack for every full one delivered, or you have to charge them an additional mark."

My first foray went a lot better than I expected. Maneuvering the cart through the streets, wielding the bulky sacks, was more a matter of concentration and balance than brute strength. The customers must have let out all their annoyance on Frau Schelonka over the telephone, because they could not have been nicer to me. They were clearly relieved to have heat for the cold night ahead. I even got some good tips. The superintendent of one building tried to engage me in a long conversation, but I shied away. I remembered how the superintendent of our old apartment complex on Greifswalder Strasse had betrayed us after knowing us for so many years, taking our money and keeping the back exit locked so we could not escape.

Herr Schelonka was at the office when I returned. Weatherbeaten, stocky, and barely taller than his wife, he shook my hand so heartily I winced. His palm was as rough as stone. The coal was so imbedded in and around his fingernails that no soap could remove it. He seemed tired after the long day, but insisted on teaching me the basics of coal carrying. He gave me a leather protector to wear over my back and shoulders, a sleeveless vest with a belt that crisscrossed in the front. He showed me how I should walk, with a slightly forward bent, so the coal wouldn't spill out of the crates. By the next morning, I had a new career: coal carrier and heating expert.

Most of the apartments I delivered to had some kind of sticker on their doors, declaring: "We gave to Kraft durch Freude," or to "Arbeitsfront," Nazi welfare organizations that relied on private donations. Whenever I entered any of these homes, I greeted its occupants with a resounding "Heil Hitler!" This way I did not have to get into any explanations about why I wasn't in uniform. Everyone assumed I was a loyal German youth moonlighting to help my family.

The Christmas spirit seemed to prevail among the customers. One of them, Frau Grueger the baker, was especially kind. Seeing that my hands were filthy from coal, she insisted on stuffing a large hunk of streusselcake, still warm from the oven, directly into my mouth. I told her how delicious it was, and bemoaned the fact that I had no stamps with me so I could get a piece for my mother.

"God bless you. A young man today who thinks about his mother! I will tell Schelonka what a treasure he has in you!" she said, filling a small bag with cake and rolls, and handing it to me over the counter. "You will never need stamps in this establishment. When you make your deliveries, there is always a treat from Frau Grueger. And say hello to your dear mother from me."

I thanked her profusely, and was about to leave with my usual "Heil Hitler," when my eyes became locked with hers and she looked back into mine. Something told me that this would not be the appropriate farewell for Frau Grueger. Her magnanimity toward me seemed to go beyond mere holiday friendliness. I sensed she was a kindred spirit – certainly not a Nazi, perhaps even another who harbored a secret.

One day Frau Schelonka told me to carry two one-hundred-pound crates down to a customer's basement, remove twenty-five briquettes from one of the crates, and then deliver them to a second-floor apartment. She said that the middle-aged couple who lived there, the Dietrichs, were good tippers, and would make the extra effort worth my while. I did as I was told, and rang the couple's bell. A tall, trim man in a gleaming white Naval officer's uniform opened the door.

"Heil Hitler!" I declared in a self-assured voice. "I have already brought the bulk of your delivery to the basement, as ordered, and here, sir, is the rest."

"Very good, young man," said the officer, looking me up and down. "Please come in while I get my stamps."

I waited in the vestibule, where I could see and smell his lunch, cooked and ready on the dining room table. It wasn't a fancy meal, but it was one of my favorites – hot dogs and potato salad. He must have noticed me eyeing it intently when he walked back into the room.

"Hungry?" he said.

"Yes, I'm about to stop for lunch myself. It's been a long morning, sir. Everyone is stocking up on coal before the holidays."

"What, if you don't mind my asking, has caused a well-spoken young fellow like you to work at such a hard and common job?"

"Money, sir. I am an engineering student and my mother is ill, so every little bit I can earn is useful. But when I graduate, I would like to join the Navy, just like you, sir."

He nodded appreciatively. "Young man, forgive me for sounding boastful, but I have what is called *Menschen*

Kenntnis, good judgment about people," he said. "I could see immediately that you are not a typical coal carrier."

"Really, sir?"

"That's right. I only wish my son were as ambitious and hard working as you. He volunteered to go into the Waffen SS, but beyond that he has no idea of what to do with his life."

"Why doesn't he follow in your footsteps? You are a commander, aren't you, sir?" I said, flattering him shamelessly. I had to admit, the uniform was impressive, so clean it sparkled, ironed with knifelike precision and adorned with a colorful array of medals and stripes.

"I am a commander indeed. And when you are ready to join the Navy, you call me. We need enterprising young men like you. I will give you an excellent recommendation." No, you won't, I thought, but for the moment I'll be happy with a decent tip.

To my astonishment, he pressed five marks into my hand, and said, "I am giving you a little extra, because I'll be away for awhile, and I would like you to make sure that my wife does not run out of coal. She tends to be forgetful about such things." I bowed to him and clicked my heels. He asked me what my name was, and I told him. His next question surprised me.

"Well then, Gerhard, how would you like to stay for lunch? I cooked entirely too much, and I need to stay in shape for my next voyage. Please say you'll share all these calories with me."

"Thank you, Herr Kommandant. I can only take a short break, but I accept your offer, to ensure the success of your next voyage!" We both laughed, and he hurried into the kitchen to get more hot dogs from a pot on the stove, and an extra place setting. Being waited on by a

Nazi Kommandant! My mother would have been aghast, but I loved every minute of it.

Over lunch I asked Kommandant Dietrich many questions about the Navy, as was befitting of a future seaman. He regaled me with long-winded answers and I could tell he was eager to groom me as his next recruit. He asked for my home telephone number to continue our discussion, but I explained that our address was only temporary, and he could reach me through the Schelonkas. The more we talked, the more loose lipped the ebullient commander became.

"Look here, Gerhard, I look forward to a long association between us, but as I mentioned, I will not be here during your next few deliveries," he said, lowering his voice. "In several days I will be leaving for an extended period, bound for South America – but that is classified information, so please do not reveal it to anyone."

"South America!" I exclaimed. "Very exciting!"

"Well, I'll let you in on a little secret: up until recently we had the oceans pretty much to ourselves, but now the Allies are getting much tougher on us. Their convoys are bigger than ever and much more difficult to penetrate."

"But Herr Kommandant, I hear on the radio that we are sinking a lot of their freighters, even destroyers and other warships. How long can they keep it up, losing so many ships and men? Admiral Doenitz recently said that our Navy and our U-boats are the masters of the Atlantic." I knew this was Nazi baloney, but it was the right thing to say, and I awaited his reaction with venomous glee.

"Oh yes, my boy," he said quickly, "you heard it right, we are giving them a lot of problems, but it seems the more losses the Americans have, the more ships they build. They have more money than they know what to do with, those Americans! Have you ever seen a newsreel of their stock-market headquarters? It's a madhouse!"

"Why is that, sir?"

The commander laughed and shrugged his shoulders. "Who knows, maybe we should have kept some of our shrewd, money-grubbing Jews around, the way they have. But don't you worry, we have plenty of secret weapons still to come. By the time you join the Kriegs Marine, we will have brought Mr. Roosevelt and Mr. Churchill to their knees."

"Oh, we must!" I said fervently. "We cannot lose to the American, English, and Jewish enemies!" He stood up, eyes glistening, clicked his heels, and extended his arm in salute. "Heil Hitler!" he intoned. I mimicked his every move. "Heil Hitler, Herr Kommandant, I wish you a good trip!" Then, silently: "Yes, a good trip right to the bottom, you bastard!"

As I stood at the door, the commander handed me another two marks. "Do remember to come back to check the coal supply and introduce yourself to Frau Dietrich."

"I'm sorry I did not meet her today."

The commander sighed. "She is out Christmas shopping, feeling quite chipper as a matter of fact, but she does suffer from depression from time to time. She is alone so much, you know." I promised him I would return after the holidays, and again Heil Hitlered eagerly as I backed away.

Hans had been invited to spend Christmas week with old friends in Treptow, a suburb about an hour or so from Charlottenburg. He went with some misgivings, as the couple had lost their only son at Stalingrad, and their son-in-law was a prisoner of war captured in Tunis by the Americans. Hans often said to me that he was now glad that he and his wife had not been able to have any children; it was too terrible to think of them in the horrors of war.

The Schelonkas gave me some time off because they too were going out of town. I couldn't wait to return to my old haunts in the center of the city, and to spend time with my mother. Christmas had no religious significance for me, but I found it an emotional time. Seeing the decorations, hearing the familiar music, and exchanging greetings with people on the street was a painful reminder of bygone days, when my parents, my brothers, and I brought gifts to our Christian friends and neighbors, and rejoiced with them. And, of course, Christmas eve marked a year since my mother and I had slipped from the Gestapo's grasp and gone underground. And I recognized that we were alive, at least in part, because of some gentiles who had not been diverted from their Christian virtues by the rhetoric of madmen.

With that in mind, I bought some inexpensive picture frames for Hans, Kitty, Anne, and Sylvia. I knew that Anne frowned on religious traditions, but even she softened up a bit around this time of year. At the last minute, I picked up a little gift for Opa, too, some cotton handkerchiefs, since I didn't think he would have a picture of anyone to put inside a frame. Even though I didn't consider Opa's impulses the least bit altruistic, I still took free lodging under his roof whenever I needed it, and it was important to me to show my gratitude.

I decided to drop in on Opa first on Christmas eve, as I was sure the old curmudgeon would be completely alone. Sure enough, he sat there in almost the same position in which I had left him several weeks earlier – in his underwear at the kitchen table, marking up his damned cards. He had no Christmas tree and pooh-poohed the notion of a special meal, reviving my long-standing suspicion that he was a Jew, a suspicion that I could never confirm.

Not long after my arrival, there began an air raid, which was so fierce that I decided not to venture out again. Opa's building shook so hard that I knew the bombs were falling very close by. For once, I was glad not to be enacting my usual charade as a phony air-raid official, barking orders at frightened citizens, and ending up alone on some roof. But Opa did not flinch at the onslaught of sound and light. All he did was cackle, over and over, "Silent night, holy night, the assholes! Ha-ha-ha! Ha-ha-ha!" Sure enough, when I went out onto the street the next morning, it looked as though it had been hit by an earthquake. I could barely hold back the tears as I watched my city burning. Yes, it was still my city.

I rushed over to the Choriner Strasse and was relieved to see that my mother's new home, the apartment building of Tante Hedel Pauli, remained intact. When my mother saw me at the door, she flung her arms around me and did not let go for several minutes. When she looked up at me and I saw the suffering in her eyes, those intensely bright eyes, I remembered Hans's words: "So much pain, to love a child trapped in war, almost too much pain to bear!" Hans was right, but he could not know the joy of reunions. Tante Hedel, too, awaited me with hugs and kisses. I handed her a Stollen that Frau Grueger had given me the day before. It was obvious that Tante Hedel had made every effort to make my mother feel comfortable in her home. On Mama's bedroom door was a handpainted sign declaring *Herzlich Willkommen* (A Hearty Welcome). There was a small green plant, tied up with a red ribbon, on her nightstand. And in the living room, to my surprise and delight, there was Sylvia. Another hug, quite a different one this time, and more kisses.

"I thought you had to spend the day with your cousin, what's-his-name," I said, unable to honor the Nazi Michael with a name.

"I do, unfortunately. I just came to say hello and to drop off the last of your mother's things. I also brought over a carrot cake."

"Still baking?" I asked her, burrowing my face in the silky knot of hair on her neck. "Carrot cake, sounds delicious."

"Believe me, it's not. Carrots are about the only sweet thing we can get with our food stamps nowadays."

In honor of the holiday, Tante Hedel brewed a pot of real coffee. The four of us sat around her kitchen table, drinking and eating and laughing and talking for hours, as though nothing were wrong. We reminisced about the good old days, we talked of books and movies and recipes, of everything but present reality. Under the table, my mother had found my hand and gripped it tightly. On the other side, Sylvia had slipped her tiny palm inside my grasp. I felt wrapped in a blanket of love, held aloft on the wings of my two angels.

After Sylvia left, Tante Hedel announced that she was tired and went off to her room, but I knew that she just wanted to leave me and my mother alone. The two of us lay down on her double bed. She was eager to hear all about Hans and about my job with the Schelonkas. It comforted her to know that I was safe under the roof of a kindly schoolteacher, and earning my keep honestly. To go into any more details about how and where I spent my time seemed unnecessary.

And yet tears began to flow. She had been thinking of my brothers in America. Were they all right? Had they given us up for dead? Would we ever see them again? I squeezed her hand, the hand that still clutched mine, but

I had no comforting answers. I tried not to think too often about Heinz and Manfred, about how close we had once been. The truth was, I was jealous that they had managed to flee Germany under the wire, while I had to stay behind with our parents. My brothers used to tease me about my unusually close relationship with our mother, saying that the umbilical cord had never been cut. There was definitely some truth to it.

After a day of relaxing and playing cards, I decided I would stay the night. Before we fell asleep, I could hear Tante Hedel's radio playing the sounds of Christmas softly in the next room. "When is Chanukah this year?" I asked my mother.

"I have no Jewish calendar," she replied. "Maybe it has already passed, or maybe it is right now, who knows?"

"Or maybe there will never be another Chanukah."

"Don't you ever say such a thing! Your father would have swatted you if he had heard you!" Indeed he would have. So I apologized to my mother, and, together, barely louder than a whisper, we sang the "Maoz Tzur," Rock of Ages, the stirring hymn of Chanukah. This night was as good as any to celebrate, though we had no menorah and no candles to light.

The next day I convinced my mother, Tante Hedel, and Sylvia that we should all go to see *Jud Suess,* a virulently anti-Semitic film that was all the rage. It depicted the slimy machinations of Suess Oppenheimer, a court Jew who was chief financial advisor to the Herzog Karl Alexander von Wuerttemberg. It was directed by Goebbels's bosom friend, Veit Harlan, and starred the popular actor Werner Krauss and two of the Fuehrer's most loyal consorts, Heinrich George and Kristina Soederbaum. Later, back in Tante Hedel's apartment, we had a heated debate about the movie. The ladies were outraged by its racist stereotypes, and were angry with me for cajoling them into spending their money on such garbage. But this movie was tame compared with our reality. Once again it became time for me to say good-bye to my mother. When we embraced, I saw it in her eyes again: she was asking herself, will I ever see him again?

Erika and I had planned to be together on New Year's Eve. Opa was off visiting his brother for a few days, so we would have his apartment, disgusting as it was, all to ourselves. Our plans changed at the last minute, however, when I learned that Hans had returned home early from his friends' house in Treptow. The family was so distraught after the loss of their son that Hans had cut short his stay. When I learned that he would be home alone on New Year's, I asked Erika if we might postpone our date until the following evening, and she agreed.

So Hans and I rang in 1944 together, singing folk songs, eating jelly donuts and toasting each other with schnapps. Hans's spirits were greatly lifted by my company, though he was looking worse than ever after his vacation. He had been deeply affected by the anguish of his hosts. The irony of it was not lost on me: a good, patriotic German family spent Christmas submerged in grief over the loss of their son, while I, Gerhard, the Jewish diver, rejoiced in the company of my mother and friends.

Before we went to sleep that night, Hans went to a cupboard and took out a coffee can in which he stored his modest earnings. He pressed a few bills in my hand and told me to take Erika to the movies. When I protested, he said, "I was saving this money for a rainy day. You have brought me sunshine instead. I beg you, give me the joy of sharing with you."

So thanks to Hans's largesse, the following evening I took Erika to a theater on the Frankfurter Allee to see

Baron von Muenchhausen, which starred one of Germany's most beloved actors, Hans Albers. It was rumored that Albers's wife, Hansi Burg, was Jewish, and hiding somewhere in England. We thoroughly enjoyed the story of the infamous hoaxster, and no one could have identified with his elaborate machinations more than we. During the movie, I occasionally stole a look at Erika's perfect Aryan profile, at her platinum braids that practically glowed in the dark. If I had to bet on any of us getting through this war alive, it was Erika. She seemed to be made of steel.

After the movie, we went to Opa's empty apartment. We spent hours dancing and singing to music on the radio. The setting was far from romantic, but we were content to be alone together. The one thing we hadn't thought about was food. Opa had left nothing more than a few slices of stale bread, some margarine, and a half-empty jar of prune jam. When that was gone, we began to do what all hungry people do during wartime – we fantasized about all the wonderful meals we would eat when it was all over.

Erika lay in my arms and started cooking: "A huge platter of smoked goose breast!" she squealed.

"Lamb shanks with green beans, one of my mother's specialties, and for dessert, *Schwartzwaelder Kirschtorte* (Black Forest cake)!" I rejoined.

"Ooooh, and what about my mother's goose with cauliflower in cream sauce!"

Suddenly Erika sat upright and covered her face with her hands. First there was silence and then she exploded into wrenching sobs. "Oh, God, why me? Why did this happen? They are all gone, everything is gone! My little brother would have been sixteen tomorrow. Only sixteen!"

I had no words to comfort her, she who was so much stronger than I. So I put my arm around her shoulder, and just let her cry. And she cried and cried, for all the months that she had kept silent, her mouth etched into that thin, straight line.

"We could have gone to Argentina," she gasped. "My Tante Paula even sent us the llamadas. But, no, only to America, my father insisted, only to America!"

"Erika, we are going to get through this, you'll see!"

"What difference does it make? I have nothing and no one."

"Don't say that! That's what they want, for you to lose your will, to give up! There is everything still to live for, everything!"

She turned to me with an icy expression. "Lothar, you are still a child," she said brusquely. "You have a mother." From then on I kept silent. I knew what she had said was true.

We stayed together at Opa's for two nights and two days. I had planned to stop in at the billiard hall, to see how Tad was doing, but we never left the apartment. These were two of the most glorious days of my life. We laughed and soaped each other in Opa's tiny bathtub – the water was cold and brown, of course, but at least there was water. I managed to get a rabbit from Frau Schreiner the butcher, and roasted it in Opa's oven using a little margarine, an onion, and the spices from Opa's cupboard that were so old that they all smelled alike. We played chess and read poetry aloud, and over and over we made love on the lumpy sofa. It was as though the world did not exist – except for the bedbugs, which cannibalized poor Erika with a bite on each buttock, and the air raids – the Brits, this time – which made the entire building tremble. Even so, we were not afraid, because we knew the bombs were not meant for us. I don't know how, but we just knew it.

And Erika never cried again, not during those two days, and not in all the time I knew her.

The Monday morning after New Year's, I was scheduled to return to my job at the coal bin. I was late, and by the time I got there the wagon was all packed up and ready to go. The Schelonkas looked relieved to see me, as though they questioned whether or not I would really return after the holidays. On that first day back at work I finally met Frau Dietrich, wife of the Navy commander. As arranged, I delivered 175 pounds of coal to the basement, and brought the remaining twenty-five pounds of briquettes up to her apartment. Frau Dietrich insisted that I call her Ingrid, and greeted me more like a long-lost relative than a delivery boy. Her husband, she said, had been terribly impressed with me, and had told her all about our meeting. She insisted I join her for coffee and cake in the dining room. I still had two deliveries left that afternoon, but food was something I never refused.

Ingrid Dietrich was a well-built blond who appeared to be in her late forties. She had fluttery mannerisms and an anxious expression. "Thank the Lord you came when you did!" she said melodramatically. "I only had four pieces of coal left to heat this big old apartment, and look at me, I have come down with a terrible cold!"

Indeed, her eyes were bleary and her nose was red, and she held a lace handkerchief over her mouth while coughing loudly. I looked around the elegant dining room, and noticed on one wall a large map of the world, with colored push-pins stuck all over the European continent. Oversized maps hung prominently in many German households at the beginning of the war, but now that German forces had begun to retreat on most fronts, more and more of the maps were being retired to back rooms, or removed from display altogether.

"Well, it is turning out to be a cold winter, but we are a lot better off than our poor guys in Russia. And what have you heard from the men in your life, your son and the Kommandant?"

"Oh, I don't want to burden you with my troubles," she said. Her eyes filled with tears and she bit her lower lip.

"Has something happened? Are they all right?"

"Oh, I suppose so, I would have heard some official word if they weren't," she sighed. "Let's just say that my son and I don't see eye to eye about things, and Walter — he's away six months at a time, and almost never writes."

"It must be very hard. But then, there's the honor of commanding a U-boat?"

"Do you have a girlfriend, Gerhard?"

"Well, yes and no ..."

"If you intend to join up as you told my husband, have any future bride of yours talk to me first," she said, dabbing at her eyes with her handkerchief. "I will tell her what it's like to be married to a Navy man."

I really didn't want to get into her problems, as I had problems of my own and two more deliveries, but Frau Ingrid did not let go easily. She brought me second and third helpings of a tasty coffee cake to distract me, while asking me questions about myself, which I answered with my usual lies, and talking nonstop about her dreary volunteer work. The lady was starved for conversation.

Before I left, she asked if she could pay me to do some food shopping for her, as she was feeling too sick to go out in the cold. Remembering what Herr Schelonka had said about the Dietrichs being generous tippers, I told her I would be glad to. She handed me a shopping list, her ration card with food stamps, and thirty marks. Reichelt's

Kaffee Geschaefte, on the Wilmersdorfer Strasse, Charlottenburg's main shopping street, was where she told me
to go. They still had a fair selection of goods, she said.

I had heard about Reichelt's from Hans, who stopped
in there on rare occasions to splurge on a delicacy. I was
happy to have an excuse to see the place for myself, but
not simply to admire its wares. Over New Year's, Erika
had begun to persuade me to think of some sort of a
break-in. She said that the Tauchers staying at Kitty's were
down to their last pocket change, business had fallen off
at the brothel, and Kitty could no longer afford to subsi-
dize her or the boys camped out in the back room.

Although Tad was still living with Ilse, a bomb had
ripped through her beauty salon and she faced weeks
without income while repairs were being made. I was
grateful for my luck in finding a job where my employers
cared not a whit about my background, but without
Hans's generosity I could never have survived on my
meager earnings alone. And it had been months since I
had been able to provide my mother or her benefactors
with anything beyond a bag of fresh rolls or pastries from
Frau Grueger. When I returned to the office at the end of
the workday and tallied my tips, I was shocked to see that
they amounted to barely half of what I had made per day
before the holidays. I mentioned it to Herr Schelonka, and
asked if any of the customers had complained about my
work. Not at all, he said. My previous tips had been so
good because it was Christmas. Now, after the holidays,
people were back to counting every pfennig.

So it was with distinctly ulterior motives that I went
to Reichelt's emporium that evening. It was a new experience for me to go shopping with a legitimate ration card.
While the clerk scurried around to fill Frau Dietrich's
order – clearly she was a valued customer – I carefully

examined the store's layout. The front windows were all boarded up to prevent the glass from shattering during a bombing raid; barely a square foot of glass showed around the front door. No stores had burglar alarms working anymore; the systems had either been disabled or destroyed by bombs. Strict laws were the only deterrents for would-be thieves: anyone caught committing a robbery during a blackout would be executed.

The liquor was stored on the top shelves, with dry goods underneath. Butter, eggs, and cheese were in a refrigerated case to the right of the glass-topped display case that also served as the check-out counter. Chocolate was kept inside the display case. Coffee, I decided, was probably tucked away behind it.

The ration stamps were piled in a drawer inside the cash register. I wondered if they were kept there overnight. Certainly there was slim hope of getting away with any cash. Every evening after closing time, store owners put the day's receipts in night deposit boxes at their banks. That was what my parents had done when they owned their store, and now, for security reasons, the practice was universal.

When I brought the groceries over to Frau Dietrich's apartment, I saw that she had set the dining room table for two. Not only was she eager to give me a tip, but she had prepared supper for me as well. Hot dogs. It seems the commander had told her I liked them. She was as grateful for the company as I was for the food. Frau Dietrich, Ingrid, though she was obviously troubled, seemed quite harmless. She was scared to death of the air raids, she said. She almost never went out of the house except to attend meetings of Mutter und Kind or Winterhilfe. But the women she met there were nosy and competitive, she said – whose son won the most medals, whose husband had the highest rank. She suspected that some of them were even government spies. Most of all, she was desperately lonely. She tortured herself with the tales of sailors having the proverbial girl in every port, and confessed to worrying about "those camps filled with Jew girls and gypsies."

I tried to make her feel better by telling her that she was a very attractive woman, and that her husband had expressed affection and concern for her, but she grimly shook her head. "My husband has but one love, and that is his boat," she declared. "I am of no importance in his life. My son, too, has only contempt for me. Perhaps because I had to raise him alone, with no real father figure, no authority."

And then we heard the familiar, piercing wail of the siren, and all the windows began to rattle. I opened the shades and watched searchlights crisscross in the darkness. The sky was red from fires close by. The commander's wife clutched the table. Her knuckles were white and she seemed unable to move.

"Frau Ingrid, why don't I just take my chances up here while you go down to the shelter?" I said nervously. "Your neighbors might get the wrong idea if we show up together." Of course, I was lying. I avoided air-raid shelters for fear of being caught.

"You are very sweet to consider my reputation. But the neighbors know I live a solitary life. For all my complaining, I have stayed true to my husband."

"That's very admirable, Frau Ingrid, something to be proud of in these crazy times." But I still wasn't going into that shelter.

"You're probably right, though. This unholy war has brought all the gossips and liars out of the woodwork like cockroaches. Why don't we both stay up here?"

"If you're sure."

"Yes. But one thing, Gerhard. Maybe you'll spend the night here? In my son's room of course. It would be so dangerous for you to go home in all this, and for me to be alone."

She was right. It was safer for me to stay. She showed me to a room with a narrow twin bed. The bedspread had a nautical motif. Model ships covered shelves from floor to ceiling. And there was a picture of the smiling commander, resplendent in the uniform of the white knight. How proud the son seemed to have been of him, the father he scarcely knew. This was the first of several nights I slept that winter in the comfortable bed of a young fellow my age whom I had never met, a patriotic German youth who was off fighting in the Waffen SS.

Herr Schelonka taught me how to deliver ice to local restaurants and grocery stores. I became an expert with the ice pick, cracking off pieces of exactly the right size from the massive block. In every store, I kept my eyes peeled for the possibility of a break-in, surreptitiously studying the layout and the merchandise. At one green grocer's, I made small talk with the manager and asked what they did with the stamps at night during those terrible air raids. He gave me a very dismaying reply: the proprietor took them home. I hoped that the manager of Reichelt's didn't go to such lengths. It wasn't worth risking life and limb simply for a few armloads of groceries, but it might be worth it for several month's worth of food stamps.

One evening, the five of us – Erika, Tad, Philippe, Jacques, and I – gathered at Kitty's to set our plan into motion. They listened intently to my description of Reichelt's, and agreed that a busy store like that was our best bet. Philippe had already spent a great deal of time planning this heist. His main concern was how we would break in through the pressboard, a material thicker and stronger than wood, that encased most retail establishments during the war. Whatever our mode of entry, it must not knock the merchandise on the window display behind the pressboard off the shelves and make a crash.

"We can't just smash through the board or push it in," said Philippe. "Somehow we have to cut a hole in it, and then pull it out with a hook."

We agreed that the robbery should take place in the middle of the night, when there was the least likelihood of people or patrols on the street. It would be best, too, during a snowfall, so that the weather would obscure our activities. There was only one thing we disagreed on: Philippe didn't think this was a job for a female. He obviously didn't know Erika Weissman very well.

"Pardon me," she snapped at him, "but your friend here can hardly walk. It's Jacques who should stay behind. I will stand guard for you. While you and Gerhard are in the store, Tad and I will wait outside. We'll act like lovebirds, you know, kissing or something, to distract anyone who comes by."

"Fine by me," Tad grinned.

"She's right, Philippe," I said. "Jacques will still get his share. Let him rest so he can get his health back." It was obvious to everyone that Jacques would never get his health back, but the two friends looked at each other and slowly nodded.

The answer to how we would penetrate the pressboard covering Reichelt's window came from an unexpected source – Hans Scheidt. One afternoon I arrived home to find him with his left arm bandaged and in a sling. He explained that he had burned himself in school that day while trying to remove paint and rust from an old metal desk using a solution of sulfuric acid. The acid had spilled onto Hans's forearm, and it had eaten through the skin. The school nurse treated it immediately but told him that the severe chemical burn would take at least a month to heal. Later that evening, I helped Hans change the dressing; I gasped when I saw the raw flesh underneath.

Sulfuric acid, that would probably do it. Now the question was how to get some. It was not readily available, and I didn't have enough money to pay for it. I hated lying to Hans. The honesty and trust between us was the cornerstone of our relationship. But the next evening, while we were changing his dressing, I said to him casually, "Hans, Tante Hedel mentioned to me that she has an old metal headboard that needs some scraping and cleaning. Do you think you could get me some of that acid so I could help her out? I can pay you something for it."

"No problem. They have a couple of extra bottles at school, mostly for the chemistry classes. I'll just fill out an appropriation slip and bring some of it home. Just be careful, you don't want to end up with your arm in a sling like me!"

"Oh, I'll be careful," I assured him. I could end up a lot worse.

A couple of days later, Hans handed me a brown bottle with a skull and crossbones, and big black letters on the label: "Sulfuric Acid: Caution Poison!" He also gave me a pair of rubber gloves and warned me once more to be careful.

Now we were ready to go. We decided on Saturday night, January 22nd, which happened to be my mother's birthday. It was an old family joke that each year on her birthday it invariably snowed.

The evening began innocently enough. Erika took the train to Charlottenburg, and I introduced her to Hans. He greeted her with the delight a father might greet a future daughter-in-law. Once again he took me into the kitchen to press a few marks into my hand, and urged me to take Erika out to a movie. It was a good idea, as we had hours to kill before meeting Tad and Philippe at the Charlottenburg Station.

In a theater on the Ku-Damm, we watched a light-hearted farce called *Kleider Machen Leute* – Clothes Make People. I tried to laugh, but found it hard to forget the sulfuric acid in one pants pocket, my gun in another, and a six-inch knife, rubber gloves, and a flashlight inside my jacket. My friends and I were about to commit a serious criminal offense for which we could be exterminated like the underground rats we had become.

It was nearly ten o'clock when the show ended. When we came back out onto the street, it was snowing! The other moviegoers headed home or to nearby cafés. We walked to the Wilmersdorfer Strasse, which, as we expected, was deserted because all the stores were closed. While Erika stood watch, I scratched a half-meter square into the pressboard with my knife. It barely dented the material. I put on the rubber gloves Hans had given me, poured the acid onto a cotton rag, and rubbed it over the lines of the square. I did this several times. Then the two of us left to meet Tad and Philippe at the station. Philippe, who was extremely lanky and thin, looked almost rotund under his threadbare winter coat. He was carrying a large selection of tools borrowed from Etienne.

An hour had passed by the time we returned to Reichelt's. The chemical process had softened the board considerably, but it still could not be penetrated. I rubbed in more acid, and again we left. We went back to the station and pretended we were waiting for a friend to arrive on a late train.

It took until almost two o'clock in the morning for the acid to create a hole with a circumference of about one inch, and to weaken a large section around the hole. With my knife I was finally able to saw completely through the softened material. Philippe used the hook he had brought to pull out the large square of loosened pressboard. Within seconds we had a hole large enough so that we could wriggle, one after the other, into the store.

Tad and Erika fell into each other's arms, staring intently in opposite directions down the street. In the faint glow of moonlight, with snowflakes in their hair, they looked like any pair of young lovers on a Saturday night, enjoying an intimate moment on a deserted street.

I pointed my flashlight into the store and snaked my way in head first, careful not to disturb any of the display items. Once I was inside and on my feet, Philippe reached in the hole and handed me two empty sacks. His own entry was a good deal more awkward; skinny as he was, Philippe was extremely tall, nearly six foot four, and needed a lot of landing space. Sliding in, he ended up knocking over two cans of soup. We winced as they clanked and rolled around the tile floor, but there wasn't a soul around to hear it. For a moment we just stood there, adrenaline surging, grinning at each other, enveloped by the smell of coffee and chocolate. We felt like the youthful conquerors of Berlin!

The cash register stood wide open. It was empty but for a few coins, and there were no food stamps. Philippe looked as though he were about to cry. I told him I had noticed several locked drawers inside the display cabinet beneath the register. While he tried to jimmy those open with a crowbar, I made my way through the store, shoving everything I could into the two sacks – a ten-pound bag of coffee, about fifty chocolate bars, nougat and marzipan, a small barrel containing twenty-five pounds of fresh Danish butter, and seven or eight bottles of liquor. I took the time to wrap each of the bottles in sheets of paper that were kept on the counter for that purpose, so nothing would be broken on the way out.

"Dear God!" Philippe gasped. I sprinted over to the counter and peered inside the opened drawers. The first contained an unlocked cashbox filled with about 1,000 marks. The second held the treasure we had come for — food stamps, thousands of them. Reichelt's must have had a good week.

I grabbed a paper bag and dumped everything inside. In a surge of giddiness I became a salesclerk: "Here, sir, are the food stamps that the government has owed you and your mother and your friends all these months! Will that be all, sir? May I get you anything else? Some coffee, perhaps? How about a few marks to tide you over, since you are all unemployable? Enjoy them, sir! And thank you for shopping at Reichelt's!"

It was time to get out of there. As Philippe and I approached the door, out of the corner of my eye I spotted a bottle of Cherry Heering brandy, Trudy's favorite, the one she had served out of a blue crystal decanter. I lunged for the bottle and tried to stuff it in my bag, but it wouldn't fit.

"Damn, I really want this," I hissed to Philippe.

"Greedy bastard!" he chortled. He used his Swiss army knife to open the bottle on the spot and handed it to me. I poured the stuff down my throat and passed it to Philippe, who guzzled some more.

"L'Chaim!" I said to him.

"Ja, L'Chaim," he answered, his voice catching. It had been a long time since either of us had spoken a word out loud in Hebrew.

L'Chaim — to life. The traditional Jewish toast in a most untraditional setting. But never had it been more appropriate, for the robbery could help us all stay alive another few months. By that time, the war might be over.

Tad and Erika were amazed when they saw me emerge from the hole with the open bottle between my teeth. Tad laughed as he took it from me and both he and Erika, shaking from the cold, drank deeply from it. By the time Philippe crawled out of the hole, the bottle was almost empty. He put it inside the display window and then pushed the piece of pressboard neatly back in its place so that early morning passersby would not notice that Reichelt's had been robbed. We hopped on the train to go back to the Neue Weber Strasse. It was three o'clock but, at Kitty's place, night was day and day was night.

Jacques lay sleeping in the back bedroom. Philippe knelt down next to him and whispered something in his ear. Jacques nodded feebly. He reached up to pat Philippe on the back, and drifted back to sleep. Etienne, the consummate hustler, could hardly wait to see what all the commotion was about. He gave a long, slow whistle as we emptied out the sacks. As we expected, he was the expert on how we could maximize the profits from our haul. He said that we should each keep some of the stamps and he would help us sell the rest, splitting the take. Ditto for the coffee, which always fetched an unbelievably high price on the black market. The butter, another precious commodity, was to be repackaged in small quantities and sold right away before it went rancid. Fortunately, because it was wintertime, perishables could safely spend a night or two on the windowsill. We all felt confident leaving the details of these transactions to Etienne. He had been dealing in the black market for years, and he had always been square with us. Before giving him most of the stamps to sell, we each took a handful, enough to share with our various benefactors – Kitty, Hans, the Dudacys, Tante Hedel, and Tad's Ilse.

Tad, Erika, Philippe, and I, still in our clothes, curled up for a few hours of sleep on the floor of Kitty's living room. By the time we woke up, Kitty had already been to the grocer's with some stamps from Etienne. The grocer knew that Kitty routinely entertained large groups, so he was not suspicious when she left with two dozen eggs, two loaves of fresh bread, a dozen rolls, a half pound of bacon, milk, and a large spongecake. It was our victory brunch. In one sitting I had five eggs, half a loaf of bread drenched in butter, several strips of bacon, and two cups of coffee. We all stuffed ourselves – except for Jacques, whose digestion was shot.

Because we had made other plans, I had not been able to see my mother on her birthday. When I showed up at Tante Hedel's later that morning, I was loaded with gifts – a wad of food stamps, some of the coffee, and a birthday cake from an exclusive Ku-Damm bakery. I had the clerk write "Nelly" in blue icing on the top, and decorate it with pink and white roses and curlicues. Later, I realized I had made a serious mistake: my mother, of course, had been living as "Ida" for more than a year.

"My goodness, Santa Claus has finally arrived!" Tante Hedel chortled after I spread everything out on the kitchen table. My mother was a good deal more suspicious. "Where did you get all this, Lothar?" she demanded. "What have you done?" If I had told her the truth, she would never have slept again.

"The cake is from Frau Grueger," I mumbled. "And everything else I won in a billiard game."

"She is such a wonderful woman, that baker!" said Tante Hedel. "I will definitely shop there the next time I am in Charlottenburg."

"Well, I don't believe in Santa Claus," said my mother gruffly. As upset as she was at me, she still clung to my hand. It wasn't because she was worried that I had done something illegal, for those days were long gone; she was terrified that I had put myself in danger.

"Look, remember you got mad when I said there would never be another Chanukah? Well, let this be our Chanukah. And we'll have many more of them, I promise, with Heinz and Manfred, and with wives and children. You'll see." She nodded, teary eyed. And the next week, when I brought her several hundred marks from my share of the robbery, she did not question it.

As spring approached, my work as a coal carrier brought in even less money. We committed five more robberies that season, none of them as lucrative as the first, and became accustomed to reading about our "crime spree" in the newspapers. We were never caught.

Chapter 12

Vice Squad

Though the weather had already turned balmy, and the commander's wife had accumulated enough coal to last her through two Arctic winters, she kept calling Schelonka for more. I think she was becoming agoraphobic. She ceased virtually all her volunteer activities, and had me do most of the shopping. Her skin developed an unhealthy pallor and her hands began to shake. Her conversation was increasingly morbid and irrational, though sometimes she tried to act cheerful and ask me about school, just to make sure I would always come back.

What made me keep coming back, of course, was the food. It is impossible for anyone who has never been truly hungry to understand how powerful a magnet a meal can be. Each time I set foot in her apartment, bag of briquettes in hand, the table was always set for me, and something bubbled on the stove. It pleased her that I appreciated her cooking, and she watched me finish every last bite. I always made sure that hers was my last delivery of the day, so I would have time to eat a complete supper.

At first it really wasn't much of an effort to humor the lady and listen to her endless litany of sorrows. She had been filled with romantic illusions when she married the handsome young Navy officer. She was determined to be the perfect Hausfrau, dedicating herself to the German wife's triple "K" credo of "*Kinder, Kueche, Kirche*" – children, kitchen, and church. She was pretty and well-groomed and, she confided, a willing sex partner, but her husband, during his brief periods at home, always seemed to prefer locking himself away in his study with his maps and charts.

About her son she spoke very little. She had probably smothered him, too, and he had escaped by enlisting at the earliest opportunity. She said that he had been given a new post, as a guard in a concentration camp. Every so often, she insisted I take some of his clothes; they were much too small for me, but she did not seem to notice. I passed them along to Hans, who had lost so much weight that his pants were sliding down his hips.

I had a feeling I knew where all this was leading. I still spent nights in young Dietrich's boyhood room undisturbed, but I began to worry that one night Frau Ingrid would make her move. It wasn't that the notion of having sex with her was altogether unappealing. Despite her age, she really was quite attractive. But her neurotic intensity frightened me. I could not afford an entanglement with someone who needed something I could not give. She began to wear a great deal of makeup, and dress up for me in provocative outfits. Whenever I happened to be there during an air raid, she would snuggle close to me in the darkness, her body trembling. Sometimes during the blackouts, if she could control her shaking, she played the piano, Mozart's "Eine Kleine Nachtmusik" or Haydn's "Minuet", or my favorite, "Fuer Elise."

Once, while she serenaded me, I drifted off to sleep on the sofa and had a dream:

I was back in our apartment on the Greifswalder Strasse, sleeping in my own bed, when I heard the strains of a piano. I got out of bed and opened the door, and surrounding me was a distorted maze of twisting corridors and oddly shaped rooms. I entered one room, and there sat my father, reading a newspaper. "Not yet, Lotharchen," he said pleasantly, lowering the paper. "Come back later, all right?" And then he raised the paper, hiding his face behind it. Behind the next door, I found Heinz and Manfred sprawled on the floor, playing cards. "Not yet, little brother, get out of here!" they said. Heinz stretched out his leg, and kicked the door shut in my face. I followed the music down the hallway, which seemed to get longer with every step I took, until finally I saw her. From the back, she was exactly as I remembered her from that moment of my adolescence – the tragic Ilona Anker, her jet-black hair cascading to her waist, naked, achingly beautiful, playing "Fuer Elise." I crawled under the piano to look at her from the front, to see her face, her breasts, the place between her legs. But when I peered up at her, I saw to my horror that she had been destroyed! Her face was torn, blackened by fire, blood dripped from her mouth – she looked like one of the corpses I had seen after the bombing in the Alexanderplatz, burned beyond recognition!

I woke up screaming "No! No! No!" Ingrid had covered me with a light blanket, but I was bathed in sweat and kicked it to the floor. She came running into the living room in her negligee. I told her I had had a nightmare. She put her arms around me and stroked my hair until I calmed down. Her touch became more insistent. I felt as though I couldn't get enough air.

"I'm sorry, forgive me," I said, pushing her away from me. "I have to get out of here." Her whole body flinched, as if she had been struck, but she lowered her eyes and said nothing.

It was after midnight when I left her apartment. The planes still dropped their bombs overhead and the sirens roared. But I was Lothar the Invincible with the nine lives of a cat. Nothing could hurt me.

I let myself quietly into Hans's apartment. I looked in on him before I went to my room. His breathing was labored, his face so gaunt it was almost skeletal. I did not know how much longer he had to live. He had finally admitted to me that he suffered from cancer of the colon. He had been diagnosed days before I moved into his apartment, but did not want to burden me with his troubles. The doctors said that with surgery and treatment, he might have a chance, but he had refused. His wife was gone. His civilization had collapsed around him. Hans had put himself in God's hands and He would take him when He would.

But it was all he could do to go to work each day. He came home in the afternoon and could barely make it to his bed. When I was there, I would massage his back and feet, and try to take his mind off the pain by playing cards or chess with him. He loved to hear me read aloud, and seemed to be comforted by the familiar words of the poets. What sustained him most of all, however, was his faith. Each Sunday, he walked the two blocks to his church. I had asked him once if he was praying for a cure. No, he had said, and he was smiling, for he was bound for a better place; he prayed for me and for my mother, and for Jesus Christ to forgive the sins of the German people, and to return them to the path of righteousness through His teachings.

That night as I looked at his sunken face, I could feel tears welling up in my eyes. But Lothar the Invincible could not afford to get too emotional about anything, or too attached to anyone. I shut his door and went to bed.

And all night long I tossed and turned – I, who usually slept like a rock. I was worried about Hans, and about Ingrid's advances, but most of all, I could not stop thinking about my dream. To see my father's face again, to burst in on my two brothers – they had all looked so real! But the dream was also filled with gruesome images that terrified me. Perhaps I was not as invincible as I thought.

The next day I told Herr Schelonka that I did not want to deliver to Frau Dietrich anymore because she was making overtures toward me. He said he understood completely, and would take over her deliveries from then on. That would surely put an end to her constant phone calls. But it didn't. She stopped the charade of requesting more coal, and just asked to speak to me. Most of the time I wasn't in the office when she called, but even when I was, my employers would lie.

One day she called, crying hysterically, and said it was a matter of life or death that I contact her immediately. I happened to be there and took the phone from Frau Schelonka. "What is it you want, Ingrid?" I asked her brusquely.

"I thought we were friends!" she sobbed. "Right now I need a friend!"

"What is it?"

"I can't tell you over the phone, it's too awful!"

"What's going on?"

"It's the Kommandant! I can't say any more! Oh, please, Gerhard, I need you!" I told her I would come over after work. She did seem genuinely distraught. But all day I tried to think of ways to avoid a situation. I did not want to have to fight her off again; if she were truly vindictive, she could tell the authorities I tried to rape or rob her. That would be curtains. I decided to call Tad and ask him to go with me. That would force her to behave herself. Or maybe she would go for him, and leave me alone.

When we arrived she was clad only in a black slip. Her eyes were red and puffy, and, for the first time since I had known her, I smelled liquor on her breath. She stared at Tad with open contempt. "Who is he? Why the hell is he here?"

"He's my best friend. We planned to spend the evening together before you called."

"You bastards are all alike! How dare you bring your 'friend' into my home? How dare you do this to me?"

"Ingrid, I'm sorry ..." She began pacing around the apartment, muttering to herself. Tad looked at me in consternation. "Look, Gerhard, maybe I'll just go," he said.

"Oh, don't leave!" she shrieked sarcastically. "Stay, and let me watch! Maybe I'll learn something!"

"What are you talking about?" I asked her. "This isn't making sense."

"Well, I mean, look at him! He is prettier than I am, I'll give him that! Maybe Walter's boyfriend is that pretty, too – irresistible, during all those lonely months at sea!"

Through her hysterical tears, I finally made out what was going on. She had heard from one of the other U-boat wives in the Mutter und Kind group that Walter was involved with a young sailor on board. It wasn't the first time, either, the woman told Ingrid. The Kommandant was notorious for his penchant for tender new recruits.

"He used to call them 'my glorious boys,'" she sobbed. "He was always so proud of them. Sometimes he'd even bring one home to stay with us on leave! Oh, God, I've been such a fool, my whole life has been a lie!"

I didn't know what to say or do. I tried to put my arm around her, but she recoiled from my touch. "Don't pity me! I hate your pity! I want love, not pity!"

"Ingrid, you're a good lady, you deserve love, you really do," I said honestly. "But I can't give it to you."

"Then get out! Just leave me alone, you and your friend the homo! Go and screw each other! I hate you!"

We got out of there as fast as we could, leaving her in a sobbing heap on the floor. Either she switched coal carriers, or more likely, she was able to make do with the coal she had accumulated, because she never called Schelonka again.

I missed the meals, and though I was relieved to be rid of her, I could not forget her. Like Ingrid Dietrich, I lived each day with the anguish, the helplessness, the rage of betrayal. I had been a faithful German, as she had been a faithful wife. We were both betrayed.

* * * * * * *

Officially, homosexuality was punishable by death, according to the doctrine of the Third Reich, but clandestine homosexual behavior like Kommandant Dietrich's pervaded all levels of German society, including, it was widely rumored, the very highest echelons of the Nazi elite. Known homosexuals were ultimately arrested and sent to a concentration camp for extermination. As a result, most of them were quite secretive about their activities.

In the slang of the day, they were called "*Warme Brueder*," warm brothers. My friends and I, when we were younger, had made our share of smutty jokes about them, but as the situation in Germany grew ever more ugly, there was not much fun in mocking another "undesirable." Our attitude was "live and let live."

Except for one day. It was a gorgeous Sunday afternoon in April 1944, the only time that Tad and I ever knowingly victimized another victim. Even with his share of the take from our robberies, Tad remained desperate for a source of income. The building that housed Ilse's beauty salon had been hit by a second bomb, and she had been forced to close her business. He was such a legend in the billiard hall that no one would play, or bet, against him anymore. I was not in much better shape than he, as the coal deliveries were now few and far between. For weeks he had hinted that he was developing a new money-making scheme, but he refused to tell me anything about it until he felt he had worked out the details.

That Sunday, while Hans was at church, Tad called and asked me to meet him at the Bahnhof am Zoo. He said, mysteriously, that he wanted to show me something. When I got there he was already waiting for me, dressed impeccably as always, in a pair of dark gold worsted pants, and a cotton shirt of the same color. I did not know where Tad got his clothes, or how he managed to keep them looking so nice. Ilse probably had something to do with it.

He did not waste any time with small talk. "Gerhard, answer me one question. How badly do you want to get through this?"

"You know how badly."

"Would you say, then, that anything we have to do to survive, to make it through another couple of weeks of this shit, is permissible?"

"Of course."

"Even if sometimes innocent human beings must suffer?" He folded his arms and waited for my answer. I wasn't sure what he was driving at. "Look, Tad, I don't want to kill anyone, I don't even want to break anyone's legs!"

"No, Gerhard, no killing," he replied quickly. "The only thing you might end up breaking is some poor bastard's heart. Come, I want to show you something."

And with that, Tad propelled me toward Joachimsthaler Strasse. The busy promenade was filled with strolling pedestrians enjoying the spring day. Few vehicles were on the road, but, thanks to the ingenuity of Germany's engineers, those that were had miniaturized wood-burning ovens attached to their hoods; wood power was now being used to propel the engines, as gasoline was hard to come by.

Many of the neighborhoods were still digging out from the devastation of the air strikes. Debris was piled high on the sidewalks, with cleaning crews slated to haul it away during the work week. In the meantime, the citizens of Berlin, notoriously compulsive about neatness and order, took the cleanup into their own hands. For much of Sunday, they used their brooms on the streets and sidewalks, trying to sweep away all the signs of death and destruction.

Tad pointed to the *pissoir*, the men's public lavatory in the center of the square. "I showed you this place before, Gerhard, remember? A lot of these guys are male prostitutes. This place is the same for picking up men as the Mulack Strasse is for picking up women. On Sundays, the military and the police usually look the other way, so there's more action than usual."

"Still, these guys are taking big chances," I observed. "The army won't take them, and I've heard that most of them end up in concentration camps."

Tad pulled me into a doorway, and gripped my shoulders. "What I am suggesting to you isn't pretty, but it's easy as pie, a sure thing," he began.

I thought I understood what Tad meant. "Not a chance, friend!" I interrupted. "I have nothing against these people, but I don't know how you could think I would do such a thing, no matter how bad things are getting, I'm not about to get into this."

"Hold it, hold it, are you crazy? I wouldn't go for that shit if there was a gun to my head! Listen," he said, "do you still carry around that police badge you stole a year ago in Dahlem Dorf?" I nodded. I tried never to set foot outside without my police badge, my air-raid warden's armband, and my gun.

Tad said that he would pose as a prostitute, proposition a prosperous looking fellow and go back to his house. I was to tail the two of them, and burst in on them as a badge-carrying member of the Berlin Vice Squad, but a corrupt one, whose silence could be bought. As he spelled out the details, I realized that, once again, Tad had thought of everything. And as I watched the men across the street furtively making their transactions and saw the naked fear in their eyes as they huddled nervously on the corners, I knew his plan would work.

"So I'm supposed to follow you to the guy's place?" I interjected. "What if I lose track of you, then what?"

"You won't. You were a member of the Pathfinder Scouts when you were a kid, right?" Tad pulled a crumpled piece of newspaper out of his pocket and tore off a corner. He squeezed it into a tiny ball and dropped it onto the sidewalk. "You remember how we used to leave those trails, one little piece of paper after another? That is what I will do for you."

Just then a handsome man in his fifties, wearing an elegant tweed suit and carrying a burnished leather attaché case, walked quickly by us, his eyes lowered. At his side was a skinny youth in rumpled, threadbare clothing, a wide-brimmed hat pulled low over his face. "Wow, that old guy looked like my father," I muttered, shaking my head.

"Well, my boy, you'd be surprised how many men are homos, just like your friend the commander, all married and proper and patriotic," said Tad in his world-weary way, continuing, as he spoke, to crumple the little paper balls and stuff them back into his pants pocket. "The human race is strange and wonderful, and these people are part of it. The Nazis have laws against everything, and most of them are probably homos themselves anyway – Lutze, Roehm, and who knows who else – maybe Hitler himself! Maybe the bastard has a secret room where he keeps a captured Jewish boy!"

"How much do you think we could make?"

"A lot," he replied. "Let's only hope he stashes a lot of cash at home, otherwise we'll go for jewelry, anything that's available. So what do you say?" He stretched out his hand expectantly, eager for me to seal the deal with a handshake. I glumly placed my hand in his. He gave me a fiendish leer and shook it vigorously; then he planted a noisy, wet kiss on my neck. "Oooh, Gerhard, or is it Gertrude?" he murmured. "I think I'm falling in love!"

"All right, all right, enough!" I said. "And when, pray tell, do we do this dirty deed?"

"Right now," said Tad.

"You're crazy!" I heatedly replied. "I haven't even had time to think about it."

"That's right, that's just the point! I've done all the thinking for both of us. Now it's time to act. The pickings are good, the weather's good, let's seize the moment!" Without another word, Tad sauntered slowly across the street in the direction of the pissoir. Immediately I could see half a dozen men craning their necks to admire him. He was handsomer than any hustler on the street, and new blood besides. He once told me he had been fending off homosexuals since he was a little boy. I was sure it would not take him long to captivate some unsuspecting soul. But when Tad emerged from the latrine barely five minutes later on the heels of a well-dressed, middle-aged man, my heart sank. I knew my friend was a fast worker, but now I would have to be one, too.

Tad walked about a dozen steps behind the man as they approached, and then crossed, the Ku-Damm. I followed about fifty meters behind Tad. Several times the man turned around to make sure that Tad was still with him. Amazingly, my view of them was unobstructed, a rarity on Berlin's busiest shopping boulevard.

Suddenly they both turned left into the Uhlandstrasse and disappeared from view. Everything had happened so fast that I became flustered and worried that I had lost them. I was seized with the fear that the guy had noticed me tailing them, and decided to ditch or hurt Tad. I rushed to the corner of Uhlandstrasse and squinted down at the ground. And there they were, the balled-up scraps of paper forming a jagged trail up the tree-lined, residential block. The trail stopped in front of the last house on the far corner, a gray brick apartment building with neatly trimmed shrubs and vines.

Tad and I had agreed that I would wait outside for five or ten minutes, and as I stood there, nauseated with dread, I toyed with the idea of bolting, or at least of making Tad sweat while waiting for my entrance, so that he would never suggest such a loathsome enterprise again. But I knew my friend was counting on me, that if we were to survive we could not let each other down.

The front door was left unlocked, as Tad had promised, and the vestibule was quiet; people seemed to be taking their Sunday afternoon naps. As I tiptoed up the building's winding staircase, the stained-glass windows that illuminated each landing transformed the hallways into a glinting kaleidoscope of color. I was surprised that the artistic windows had not yet been shattered by the constant bombings.

First floor, second floor, and still no sign of Tad. Once again I began to fear that the man had caught on, and that Tad was in danger. But in front of an apartment door on the third floor, shining like a tiny diamond in a beam of blue-white light, was the last of Tad's paper trail.

I dug into my breast pocket for the badge, and took my gun out of my back pocket. I had never liked the feel of the pistol and hadn't touched it since the Janowitz Bridge; for all my bravado, I was scared silly just to hold it in my hand. Even if there were no violence and the damned gun just went off accidentally, it would alert the entire building and they would be after us in seconds. I stared at the ornate brass door knocker in the shape of a lion's head, knowing that when I touched it there would be no turning back.

I rapped at the door with the brass ring.

"Yes, who is there?" a man's voice called.

I spoke in a low voice, lest the neighbors were listening. "Open the door immediately!" I growled. "Sitten Polizei!" For nearly a minute, there was silence.

Then I heard Tad's voice: "Shit, you'd better open up, mate! These guys know me, they must have followed me, but I'd rather go with them than with the Gestapo."

A key turned in the lock, and the distinguished-looking gentleman in a starched white shirt and gray slacks swung open the door.

"Can I help you, sir? What is it you want?" His voice was even and polite, but as he stared wide-eyed at my drawn pistol, his face went white and he struggled to control the trembling of his hands.

I stepped into the foyer of his apartment. A quick glance around told me that this man had money; the foyer was covered with a heavily flocked fleur-de-lis wallpaper in pale blue and gold, and a gold Persian rug lay on the gleaming wood floor. I flashed the stolen badge at him, and quickly stuffed it back into my pocket. "I am with the Berlin Morals Squad. You were seen entering this building with a known male prostitute, and it is my duty to search your apartment."

"Do you have a warrant, Officer?" he began bravely, but his voice broke before he finished. Before I could answer, Tad came out of the bedroom holding up his trousers with his belt unbuckled and fly opened.

I turned to him sternly, waved the pistol in his direction, and shouted: "Well, well, so we meet again, Karl! This time your luck has run out, this time you will not be released so quickly! I will see to it that you are taught a lesson you will never forget! Now come with me! I'm taking the both of you in!"

"Oh, my God, Detective Peters!" pleaded Tad, catching me off guard by using my real alias. "Have mercy on us! I don't want to be sent to a camp, and this man hasn't done anything! Please, today is Sunday, and just a week before Easter. Have a heart, please, I swear this will never happen again!"

I glanced at the man who now cowered behind Tad. His rounded shoulders shook as he buried his face in his hands and wept convulsively. I felt dirty and cheap, but by now the thing had to play itself out.

"You're damned right, this will never happen again," I said pointedly, glaring at Tad to make it clear that I meant it in more ways than one. "Now let's get going, the both of you!" But the man stood mute and frozen to the spot, wide-eyed as a hunted deer. Every few seconds, he would steal a terrified look at my pistol, and begin to cry again.

"Detective Peters, sir, may I go into the other room and talk to my friend privately for a moment?" said Tad. "You know you don't have to worry about me, you know I carry no weapon, and I swear to you I will not try to run away. I certainly can't jump from the third floor."

"Very well," I replied. "I'll give the two of you exactly three minutes, and, if you are not back by then, I'm coming in after you, and it will not be pleasant, believe me!"

Tad ushered the frightened man into the bedroom. In a short while they returned to the foyer, the man still looking shocked and sad while Tad grinned and winked at me over his shoulder. "Detective Peters," Tad declared, "I make the following proposal not just for myself, but to protect the reputation of this good citizen. Yes, I have chosen to be a prostitute, but he, he can't help himself. Would several thousand marks possibly persuade you to let both of us go? I only have two hundred, but I'll ask my friend here for the rest. Would five thousand be enough?"

"Five thousand!" the man cried, turning to Tad in desperation. "Wait a minute, when you said to offer this fellow something, some, ah, incentive, I never imagined you meant that much! I haven't got that kind of money in the house! I've never been in prison, I am a church-going man, a member in good standing of my community, a taxpayer, how can this be happening?"

I acted insulted and quite above this whole talk of bribery. "This is the last straw, you two! I have heard quite enough. Get moving, the car is waiting downstairs."

Tad trained his intense gaze on the trembling man. "Look, mister, how much money *do* you have?" he said urgently. "Maybe he'll still let us go! Here's my two hundred marks – quick, give him whatever you can, maybe some good jewelry, anything, before it's too late!"

"I have, I have a couple of thousand marks in the house. I would give it gladly if this incident won't be publicized," said the man in a choked voice. "This would ruin my reputation, my career, all I have worked for my whole life. Please, please, I will go to the wall safe in my bedroom, oh, my God!"

Tad gave me a triumphant look and, without waiting for my reply, solicitously put his arm around the man and steered him into the bedroom. His frightened sobs continued unabated.

As I waited in the foyer, I tried to block out what was happening by focusing my attention on a lace-covered shelf of knickknacks that hung at eye level on the wall. There were several glass globes with Christmas scenes inside, the kind that swirled with snow when you shook them. There was a Chinese lacquered box in the shape of an apple, and an ornate ceramic sleigh, with strips of real leather for the reins of the horses. And in the center, in a gilded frame propped up on a miniature easel, stood a sepia-toned photograph of a curly haired little boy in short pants and suspenders, smiling a shy, nervous smile, and carrying a Zuckertuete – the huge paper cornucopia brimming with sweets. For decades, every German schoolchild, including me, had been photographed in the identical pose. It was the ritual of the first day of kindergarten. Who was the boy? Was he the man moaning in anguish only a few feet away because of what Tad and I had done?

I had no time to ponder it. They returned to the foyer, and Tad pressed a fat wad of bills into my hand. "Here, Detective Peters, take it, take it!" he said melodramatically. "I'll never forget you, for you are the best of all the Nazis

I have ever known! God bless you for sparing us, for giving us another chance!"

I grabbed Tad brusquely by the arm. "Not so fast, you son of a bitch! Your friend here, it is his first offense, but you I am taking in regardless of any money! That money – I don't even want to touch it – will go immediately to our department's benevolent fund for the families of fallen officers! Sir, I will give you a receipt for this contribution."

"Oh my God, no, no, please! I just want to forget this whole nightmare! I'll never do this again!" the man cried. "Please, just go now, don't make any noise, and please, Officer, don't handcuff this young man, just take him. I don't want any of the neighbors to see," he pleaded, exhausted.

"All right, since you say you have learned your lesson, I will oblige you," I agreed. Then I gave Tad a look of disgust before yanking him out of the man's apartment and into the hallway. "Hey, you, the cow stall remains ajar!" I said with contempt, motioning toward his still-open fly. He barely managed to button up before the man slammed the door in our faces, and the chambers of its lock clicked loudly. It was over.

Tad and I walked back across town to Hans's house and barely spoke a word to each other. It was a relief to have the money; it was a huge sum, one that would buy us all more time. But I felt deeply ashamed. Tad whistled tunelessly as he walked. He was much more sophisticated than I, in some respects much harder. Suddenly he let out a wrenching groan.

"Jesus, how could we have stooped so low?" he blurted out, his eyes downcast, his face contorted. "He actually seemed like a nice guy. Maybe he was a good German, the kind who would help us if he knew the truth about us."

Thank God for Tad. He had said what I was feeling but hadn't been able to say. And he had closed what would have become an empty chasm between us if he hadn't said it. Tad, the cool-headed con man without a conscience, turned out to be the man I had hoped, and knew, he really was.

Neither Tad nor I ever told a soul what we had done. We buried our secret inside ourselves, and we never did it again.

Chapter 13

A Pause for Passover

A week or two later, Hitler's birthday rolled around again. The mood was more somber than in earlier years, but schools and businesses were closed, the Brown Shirts, the Hitler Youth, and the Bund Deutscher Maedel girls marched through the streets, the flags and banners waved. But this year, on this day, I decided to celebrate the holiday I had missed the year before, when Tad and I were frolicking with the two sisters in Dahlem Dorf. To everyone else in Berlin, April 20, 1944, was the exalted Fuehrer's birthday; for me, it was Passover, the festival of freedom.

Hans was at a church gathering, so I invited Tad to come and spend the evening with me in Charlottenburg. He thought we were going to play chess and listen to records, as usual. When I told him that I wanted him to participate in my makeshift Passover ceremony, he blanched. "Why don't you visit your mother and say your little prayers with her?" he said stiffly.

"I can't," I explained. "Hedel and Anne are very antireligious, and I don't want to offend them."

I knew instantly I had said the wrong thing. Tad was no less an atheist than they. Although he had been christened a Catholic as an infant, he had later shunned any religious training or affiliation.

"So offend *me*, right? When will you get it through your egghead that God is only a fairy tale, a bedtime story to make you fall asleep? If there were a God, he should have helped you long ago!"

I could not fault his logic. Maybe Tad was right, maybe religion was a crutch, a straw at which I grasped, a comforting memory of my childhood. But I needed that crutch, that fragile connection to my past, my people, and to whatever the future might bring.

"You don't have to do anything," I said quietly. "Just join me at the table. Please." He rolled his eyes and made a great show of his exasperation. But he did as I asked.

"It's not much of a Seder," I said ruefully, "but under the circumstances ..."

"What's a Seder?" asked Tad.

"The family banquet each year when we repeat the story of our exodus from Egypt with parables and symbols. For example, the egg here is a symbol of life, of its sanctity."

"Like at Easter."

"Right. And we dip it in salt water for the tears of our enslaved forefathers. We eat bitter herbs to remember their plight. Usually it's horseradish, but I took a little mustard from Hans's cupboard. And there's supposed to be Charoseth, a mixture of nuts and apples that reminds us of the mortar used by the Hebrew slaves in building cities, but I couldn't find a substitute for that. Or for the matzoh, the unleavened bread, the bread of affliction, that the Jews baked in haste as they fled."

Tad stared at the kitchen table, which was bare but for the mustard, a single egg and a half-finished bottle of vermouth left over from our first heist. "You're right, it's not much of a family banquet," he laughed, "with no family and no banquet!"

"That's not true. It is a Mitzvah, a sacred obligation, to invite a stranger to partake in the ceremony. So, by sharing this table, we become a family. And by praying over these few morsels they become a banquet."

I took the Hagaddah, the Passover prayer book that I had liberated from Dahlem Dorf, and began by reciting the Kiddush, the sanctification of the first of the four traditional cups of wine. My mother had always concocted a raisin wine for my brothers and me to drink during the Seder. This year's vermouth was stronger than wine, and Tad and I would welcome its anesthetizing warmth.

"In every generation each individual is bound to regard himself as if he had gone personally forth from Egypt, as it is said, 'And thou shalt relate to thy son on that day saying, this is on account of what the Eternal did for me, when I went forth from Egypt.' Thus it was not our ancestors alone, whom the Most Holy, blessed be He, then redeemed, but us also did He redeem with them, so that He might give us that land that He swore unto our ancestors."

As I turned the book's gilded pages, I was amazed that I remembered every word, every melody, every ritual act. My father would have been proud, and, I was sure, quite surprised.

"The Eternal hath remembered us, He will bless us, He will bless the house of Israel, He will bless the house of Aaron! He will bless those who revere Him, the small as well as the great. May the Eternal increase you more and more, you and your children. Ye are blessed of the Lord, maker of heaven and earth, Hallelujah!"

The house of Aaron, the High Priest, from whom I, Eliezer the son of Aaron, was actually descended. Would God remember me, would He find me worthy, after all my transgressions, of His blessing?

"Blessed be He whose Torah speaketh of four
children: the wise one, the wicked one, the simple one,
and the one who hath not the capacity to inquire."

Which child was I? The wise one, who had followed
the path of righteousness by cleaving to his parents? Or
the one labeled wicked, who had fallen to stealing, lying,
and fornication? Was I the simple soul dutifully staying
behind after my brothers had fled this God-forsaken land?
Or was I the one too stupid to read the writing on the wall,
to sense what had happened, what would happen?

"These are the ten plagues which the Most Holy,
blessed be He, brought upon the Egyptians in Egypt:
blood, frogs, vermin, flies, murrain, boils, hail, locusts,
darkness – the slaying of the firstborn."

I soon forgot that Tad was there. I became lost in the
hypnotic, black and white terrain of the Hebrew lettering,
in the rise and fall of the ancient melodies. My eyes closed,
my body began automatically to rock forward and back,
mimicking unconsciously the rapturous sway of the rabbis
at prayer, the movement they call *"shuckeling."* My brothers
and I and our friends had always been amused by the
fervent shuckeling of the pasty-faced young rabbinical
students who shushed and glowered at us during our
infrequent trips to the synagogue. I did not understand
how this instinctive rhythm had suddenly found its way
inside my body after so many years. Or maybe it was there
all along, lying in wait for my soul to be awakened.

"Fear the Eternal, ye his saints, for there is no
want to those who fear Him! The young lions do lack
and suffer hunger, but those who seek the Lord shall
not be deprived of sustenance. Praise the Eternal, for
He is good and His mercy endureth forever!"

Tad typically shunned emotional displays and was
always ready with a sarcastic comment. But not this time.

He sat at the table staring at me and barely moving a muscle, mesmerized, it seemed. I wasn't putting on a show for him, and I certainly wasn't trying to convert him. I wanted to go home, and all I had left of "home" was inside the pages of this book.

"All this business about Egypt, it's very real to you, isn't it?" Tad asked after a long silence.

I nodded. "It's the only thing that is real anymore."

"You're very lucky, then, to have something left, something that's real."

He slumped low in his chair. It was true that his church had abandoned him and my synagogue lay in ruins. But that night, Taddeus Vronski saw that in spite of everything God could live on inside the human heart.

We were both quite drunk by the time I came to one of my father's favorite parts of the Hagaddah, among its closing prayers.

"L'Shana Habah b'Yerushalayim!" I sang. "Next Year in Jerusalem!" Over and over I crooned the words, so many times that it became a mantra, and I could feel my father beside me, inside me, enveloping me. Tad began to clap and stomp his feet, lost in a reverie of his own. Together we rose from the table and linked arms in an impromptu dance.

Next Year in Jerusalem! What a beautiful prayer, what an exquisite hope, for a youth hiding underground. I did not know that next year, instead of Jerusalem, I would be in Auschwitz.

Chapter 14

Learning to Swim

The midday sun always flooded Hans Scheidt's little kitchen with light. On the days that there was no work for me at the Schelonkas', I had taken to sitting there by an open window so that the first rays of summer, with the aid of peroxide, would turn my hair a pale yellow. Hans often joined me, and the two of us played chess. He was an excellent player, and I beat him only once in all the time I lived with him. It was the only activity, besides going to church, for which he could summon any energy.

At the close of the academic year, Hans had told the school's officials that he would not be returning in the fall. They finally agreed to give him a tiny pension, a far cry from the substantial one he had earned after decades as a master teacher. He often said he wished he could transfer his pension over to me after his death. We both knew it was impossible. It would be too risky for both of us should anyone, except the Schelonkas, discover our connection while he was alive; that was one reason why he shunned doctors and hospitals. After his death, for my own safety, I would have to steer clear of people like bank officers and funeral directors.

I hated it when Hans talked about dying. I could not imagine life without him. Each day he seemed a little weaker, his skin more yellow. Even with his belt fastened on its tightest notch, his pants hung loosely from his hips. Yet he never seemed angry or morose. On the days that we were home together, in addition to playing chess, we would pour over his collection of German literature and poetry. He was delighted that I could still recite so well the verses I had learned years before, when I really was a student. He encouraged me to write poems of my own, in the diary I was keeping. He always said I was his last student, and his best.

It broke my heart to see him pick at his food like a bird, while I devoured every morsel placed in front of me. At times I felt that the stress I had put on him by revealing the secret of my identity had ruined his health. I agonized about staying on in his apartment, and kept offering to leave, but Hans insisted that I was his only reason for living. At dawn one morning in June, I awoke with him standing over me and shaking my shoulders.

"Hans, what's happened?" I asked, bolting upright. "Are you all right?"

"Yes, yes, it's wonderful! The Allies have landed in Normandy! They must have been successful, or the *Deutschlandsender* would never have made the announcement so fast. It's over, I'm telling you, it's all over!" I was by nature an optimist, but too many disappointments had inured me against premature celebrations. It had been years – I could no longer remember how many – since my mother had first declared: "Don't worry Lotharchen, this will all be over in six months."

I patted my friend's bony hand. "It's great news, Hans, but don't forget what happened in Dunkirk and Dieppe. Maybe we shouldn't celebrate just yet." I rose and followed him into the living room, where the radio was on. We heard of places we had never known before, Carentan, the rivers Vire and Orne. The names Eisenhower and Montgomery were added to the roster of Germany's mortal enemies. Incredibly, the *Deutschlandsender's* insane fantasies continued unabated: "The fighting men of the great German nation were successful in their heroic stand against hordes of Americans and British! Massive numbers of the enemy were thrown into battle, but the courageous German Army rebuffed all onslaughts, showing that they will triumph!"

From the unusually overblown bombast, there was no question that the invasion had been a success. It took several days for the German Army to concede that the Allied invasion forces had established a beachhead, and that the British and American armies were now pushing south and east into the French countryside. The casualties on all sides were tremendous. It occurred to me that my brothers, wearing the uniform of their adopted country, could have been among those who landed in Normandy. Maybe Nelly Orbach had already lost one of her sons. But if Heinz or Manfred were to die, they would die as free men.

Sudden air raids now ripped through Berlin during daylight hours as well as at night, but I no longer reveled in the sound and fury from a rooftop. A bad experience several weeks earlier, just after my twentieth birthday, had finally cured me of this folly.

I had just emerged from the Charlottenburg train station after visiting my mother at Tante Hedel's when I heard the alarm. As usual, I slapped on my air-raid warden's armband, and headed for the nearest apartment building. I sprinted to the top floor, where I lit a match and burned some newspaper to create a smoky odor. Then I opened the door to the laundry room. A woman who stood folding her clothes looked up at me with a startled expression.

"By order of the warden, you must go down into the shelter immediately!" I shouted, wrinkling up my nose. "Don't you smell it, a possible firebomb?" I helped her toss her clothes inside her basket, and off she ran.

From the laundry room, it was only a few steps to the roof, where the clotheslines were stretched. The hum came closer and the heavens turned black. A huge fleet of planes blanketed the entire sky, the big bombers, the four-motored Fortresses in the center surrounded by scores of fighter planes. The bombs began to fall all around me; how awesome, how thrilling, for the youth who loved to dance on the edge of the volcano! Then I heard a loud thud and saw something rolling in my direction. I had never seen anything like it in my life; it resembled a big, fat pencil, almost two feet long, and three inches in diameter. I heard a crackling sound, and the fire bomb ignited, practically at my feet. There was no time to think. I grabbed the burning stick by the end that was still dry and hurled it with all my strength from the roof of the building, as far away as I could. And then I got the hell out of there. I could hardly breathe as I raced down the stairwell. Lothar Orbach, the diver, had saved the building and, under other circumstances, I might have been a hero. But Jews were never heroes.

In mid-June I was delivering ice to a restaurant when, once again, I heard the signal and the roar of the motors overhead. I left the hand truck in the middle of the street and ran to Hans's apartment, which was just a block away. The bombing lasted for hours; even inside my enclosed room, I could feel the smoke in my lungs. I later read that more than 1,500 planes flew in those formations.

After the all-clear signal, I went back to get Schelonka's hand truck. The entire block was in flames. Firemen battled the inferno, ambulances sped away the wounded, and police loaded charred bodies onto wagons. All the phone lines were down. I knew I would not be able to get through to my mother to make sure that she was all right. Much of the public transportation was suspended as well. Two days later I was able to make the connection by train. As it turned out, most of the damage had been to munitions plants on the outskirts of Berlin. I hoped the bombs had leveled the factory in Borsigwalde, where Tad and I had been assigned before we had gone underground.

With public transportation from her neighborhood completely suspended, Anne Dudacy had walked half-way across town to look in on her sister and my mother. I greeted her with a grateful hug. The dark circles under-neath her eyes were more pronounced, but other than that, Anne had never looked better. Anne was a political animal, and the turn of the tide against the Nazis had placed a new spring in her step. Her absentee husband was now a prisoner of war in England, but, according to his infrequent letters, he was waiting out the war there quite contentedly. Hedel had confided to my mother that Anne had a new boyfriend, a hotheaded Communist leader at least ten years younger than she. And Sylvia had a boyfriend now, too, a French foreign worker, suppos-edly a very nice fellow. I felt a pang of jealousy when I heard that Sylvia was involved with someone. But what did I have to offer her, or any other girl, for that matter?

As the four of us sat around the kitchen table, Hedel and Anne discussed their plans to visit Hella, another one of their sisters, in Silesia at the end of the month. This gave me the perfect opportunity to present to my mother an idea I had been toying with for weeks. Tad had recently re-established contact with an elderly aunt of his, Selma Weska, who lived alone in Rahnsdorf, a lakeside community about an hour and a half outside Berlin. He had gone to visit her several times, and she had invited him to bring his friends during the summer. I was going stir-crazy in the city. And I had a fantasy: I wanted to learn to swim. Several times when I was young, my father had tossed me into the water in order to teach me, but I was so terrified that I began choking and sputtering, and one of my brothers always had to pull me out. When I got older, Jews were barred from the public pools and beaches. But now I dreamed of wading into the water by myself, unpressured and unsupervised, and teaching myself to swim.

My mother looked at me dubiously. "A vacation, now? At the home of a stranger?"

"If Tad says she can be trusted, I trust her. Besides, don't you think Tante Hedel could use a little breather from you?"

"Nonsense, young man!" said Hedel sharply. "I would be lost without your mother. It is those beach patrols you should be concerned about. You could still be arrested in your bathing trunks, you know!"

"Hedel, my dear, it does no good to try and reason with my bull-headed son," said my mother. "If he wants to go to Rahnsdorf so he can swim in the Mueggelsee, that is what he will do, whether you and I like it or not. All right, Lotharchen," she sighed. "Make the arrangements with your friend and his aunt. We will go in two weeks, while Hedel and Anne are out of town."

I couldn't wait to leave for the lake with my mother and Tad. I fantasized about a summer idyll, feeling the sun on my body, luxuriating on the sandy beach, eating Langnese ice-cream pops like the ones I used to buy in the schoolyard during recess.

My childlike glee was dampened, however, by the downfall of Philippe and Jacques. The two of them had left Berlin in the late spring, bound for the suburb of Falkenberg where it was easier to find odd jobs than in the city. Both men still posed as French laborers; they told the locals that they were looking for work as handymen during the daytime to supplement their night shifts at a factory. There were several bungalow colonies in the area, and they found a deserted, rundown shack and lived there as squatters. They also found the country an easier place to scrounge for food. There were many farms, and the trees were heavy with fruit during harvest season. I remembered riding my bicycle on the Falkenberger Chaussee, and filling my knapsack with fallen apples.

Jacques's weakened state made it difficult for him to work, and he came back to Berlin to rest for a week and to stay with Kitty. It was probably the security guard at the bungalow colony who put the Gestapo on Philippe's trail that week; nobody knew for sure, but by the time Jacques got back to Falkenberg, his friend was gone. When Jacques called Kitty with the news, she begged him to return immediately to Berlin. But he said he wanted to spend several more days in Falkenberg, just in case Philippe was unexpectedly released.

Nobody ever heard from Jacques again. But a few weeks later, an article in the *Morgenpost* said that the decomposed body of a homeless man had been found in a wooded area of Falkenberg. They said that the corpse was of a "Jewish male criminal," and described it in graphic detail. All of us agreed, it must have been Jacques. Tad, Erika, and I met at Kitty's place, and lit a candle in his memory. The mood was subdued; we were each wondering, with two divers down, who would be next?

I was saddened by Jacques's death, but not surprised. He had been sick from the day I met him in the billiard hall. I had never really grown close to him; perhaps because of his illness, he was extremely quiet and kept to himself. His only bond was with Philippe, who had been his closest friend since childhood. It was Philippe's arrest that really shook me. He was always a bit of a loose cannon, but the two of us had developed a camaraderie after executing all those robberies together. I couldn't believe they had finally closed in on him. I wondered if he would make it, if I would ever see him again.

The week before I was to leave for Rahnsdorf, Hans was invited to spend several days at the home of a former student in the suburb of Lichterfelde. The young man had to have a leg amputated because of the frostbite he had suffered during the winter on the Russian front. Hans said that his student had been a proud Nazi at one time, but his recent letters had revealed a profound disillusionment. After they lose a leg, Hans commented, they're not such good followers anymore.

Hans said I could invite Erika to stay with me while he was away. The two of us hadn't been together in a long while, and we luxuriated in the privacy and tranquility of Hans's comfortable home. The testiness that had once characterized our relationship was gone. I had completely accepted Erika as her own person. She slept with me, but she would not commit herself to me; she lived in a whorehouse, but she would not become a whore. My romantic yearning for her had turned into friendship and respect.

Erika had taken up drawing and painting to pass the time at Kitty's. Although her art supplies were crude, she managed to create the most exquisitely detailed still lifes. Erika loved to sketch fruits and flowers, and occasionally animals, but never people. She said she could no longer find the beauty in them. While she sat before her drawing pad, I wrote in my diary. Fortunately, she never asked to read it. Mostly I wrote sentimental paeans to her gleaming hair and glowing skin. I, at least, had not lost the ability to see beauty in the human form, Erika's especially. We talked and talked about ideas, as all young people do, about peace and freedom, justice and equality. We talked about books and music and movies; we wondered if we would ever get to see another movie, for by now most of the city's theaters had been bombed out. And we talked about yesterday, the old school, the old friends, all the fun we had. About tomorrow, we never said a word.

After my weekend with Erika, I stopped by the Schelonkas to tell them that I would be away for a while. I knew there would be no problem, as there was little work for me anyway. Most of my funds, for the past several months, had come from the occasional robbery or foray into the billiard hall. And every few weeks, I checked in with Opa. He always knew of a card game somewhere, and was only too happy when I agreed to participate.

Passing by Frau Grueger's bakery, I waved to her, and she beckoned me to come in. She scurried from behind the counter carrying a large cake box. "I have a new assistant who burnt everything to a crisp this morning," she whispered. "I can't sell these for ration cards. Here, dear, take them to Mother." When I left the store, I looked inside the box. Crammed inside were rolls and pastries that were barely singed around the edges. As I walked down the Sybelstrasse, many of my coal and ice customers greeted me cordially from the windows of their businesses. Charlottenburg was a nice place to live, and I enjoyed feeling like a member of the community, but I did not delude myself: with the exceptions of Frau Grueger and the Schelonkas, any of these pleasant people might turn me in to the Gestapo if they suspected my true identity.

Hans seemed more frail than ever after returning from Lichterfelde. He insisted that he just needed to be back in his own bed, and that after a few days of rest he would come to himself again. I hated leaving him this way and offered to cancel my trip to Rahnsdorf, but he would not hear of it.

"Live, my boy, live!" he declared, grinning, though his eyes were filled with tears. "As long as you are young and healthy, live!" I put my arms around him, and kissed him good-bye. I was shocked by how shrunken his body had become, by the boniness of his bent form. "May the Lord bless you and keep you," he breathed into my neck.

I remembered another blessing from the distant past, one only the priests could confer upon the children of Israel: "May the Lord bless you and keep you; may He shine His loving countenance upon you and be gracious unto you; may the Lord lift up his spirit unto you and grant you peace." In the synagogue, the entire congregation would avert their eyes, fathers clutched their children underneath their prayer shawls, so as not to look upon the holy light that was said to emanate from the Kohanim, the priests, who intoned this solemn prayer with arms raised high, fingers splayed in a special configuration that only the priests were permitted to perform.

"Be careful," said Hans. "They patrol those beaches, you know, if anything were to happen to you ..."

I couldn't bear to meet his eyes. What a wonderful man he was to worry about me when his own life was so precarious. I bounded out the door. My few belongings were in my satchel, slung over my shoulder. I left nothing behind.

Tad accompanied us to Rahnsdorf, but said that he could stay only one night. He had promised Ilse he would be back for her birthday, which was two days hence. I was grateful that he could at least help us find our way to his aunt's place; people who did not know where they were going, who seemed out of place in certain neighborhoods, often drew the attention of police.

The resort village of Rahnsdorf was as charming as a picture postcard. The quaint homes and gardens were immaculately tended, with sculpted shrubbery and flower gardens in a riot of color. Vacationers in straw hats strolled to the beach, dogs barking and bounding around them. In Berlin, very few dogs remained. It was too hard to keep them fed, and some homeless people had nothing else to eat. Birds chirped and soared overhead. It was hard to believe that war engulfed the land.

Selma Weska was a head taller than my mother, and had a weather-beaten face and a booming voice. She greeted Mama and me with a delighted smile and solid handshake. Then she squealed and lunged at Tad, covered him with kisses, and let loose a torrent of Polish. When she was finished, Tad turned to me with an embarrassed smile. "Auntie doesn't get too many visitors," he whispered. I couldn't imagine why. Her rustic cottage looked small from the outside, but inside it was spacious and inviting. The decor was restful, and in keeping with the natural setting – sisal rugs on the floor, ceilings crisscrossed by antique wooden beams, the walls covered with paintings of the forest and the sea.

"What a lovely home you have!" exclaimed my mother. "Everything so spotless!"

"There's no one around to get it dirty," Selma Weska sighed. "My Karl is dead, and our three children are all grown, God bless them, all of them far away."

"I know what you mean," said my mother. "I also have three children."

"Oh, you, too? Remember when they were little, how you hated all the mess!"

"I remember," said my mother. And then she grew very quiet. Selma Weska patted her hand. "Look here, dear lady. Why don't you go and rest for a few hours? My Taddie will bring you to your room. After that we will have an early supper." My mother nodded. I could tell she was fighting back tears. I sometimes forgot that I was not the only child my mother prayed and worried for.

Bunk beds! The room Tad showed us to had bunk beds, my most cherished dream as a boy. Finally I would get the chance to clamber up the ladder and sleep in the top bunk.

I knew what my mother was thinking as she stretched out on the lower bed. Where were her other boys? "Lotharchen?" Her voice was tiny from below. "I hope one day I can give you a better life, the life that you deserve."

"It's OK, Ma, it's not your fault."

"You are the best son, the best in all the world."

"Don't, Ma, I am not as good as you say. Sometimes I am pretty bad." Sedated by the country air, both of us drifted off to sleep.

The next morning, Selma Weska offered me her late husband's bicycle to ride to the beach. It was a top brand, Semper, barely used, complete with chain and lock. My mother said she preferred to stay at home with Selma and putter around in the garden. Her limp made it difficult for her to walk in the sand.

I pedaled around the countryside for about half an hour, and then followed the sunburned tourists to the Mueggelsee, an enormous inland lake that was one of Berlin's premiere vacation spots. As I approached the beach area, I saw dozens of bikes already parked in the racks, and I locked mine inside one of the few empty slots.

Underneath my shorts I wore a pair of bathing trunks I had borrowed from Selma Weska. I peeled off my shoes and clothing, and while I was putting them neatly on my towel, an oversized beach ball whizzed over my head. I ran a few steps to retrieve it, and went to return it to a family ensconced on my left, a harried-looking older woman surrounded by four platinum blond children, two of whom were wailing loudly. She grabbed the ball from me and thrust it at one of the squalling youngsters.

"Here, here, you little monsters! Stop your crying or I will have to speak to your mother when she returns!" She turned to me with an apologetic smile. "Thank you, young man. I'm grateful I didn't have to chase that cursed ball into the lake!"

"It's all right. You certainly have your hands full. Are they all brothers and sisters?"

"Four of them, under the age of five," she sighed. "A kindergartner, a set of twins, and the baby."

"And you are the grandmother?"

"Good heavens, no, I'm the nanny. I'm from Belgium!" she said, with a laugh. "But I wouldn't mind being the grandmother, I'm telling you!"

"Why's that?"

She winked at me and lowered her voice. "Money, money, money!" she hissed. "So much they don't know what to do with it! Talk about living the good life."

I looked more closely at the children now happily playing with their ball. They sat atop oversized velour bath towels, and were shaded by two yellow-and-white-striped beach umbrellas. Under one umbrella were two large coolers and a water jug. A fancy cordovan pram, edged in mahogany and covered by mosquito netting, stood beneath the other.

I asked the nanny if she would keep an eye on my belongings while I went into the water. She said she would be glad to if I would move my things a little closer, next to one of their umbrellas. As I did so, it occurred to me that it would be a good idea to hook up with this noisy little clan. For as I scanned the crowded beach, I saw many women, children, and retirees, but almost no males my age. There were a few young husbands playing in the water with their children, but nobody else alone like me. Looking as if I belonged with the gaggle of blond children would help me blend better into the family atmosphere.

I entered the lake slowly. The temperature was perfect. About fifty yards from shore there was a large float on which a group of young teenagers was sunbathing. Every few minutes, I watched them get up and jump into the water, then paddle back and climb back up onto the float. I made up my mind: I was going to do that!

I waded into the water until it was up to my neck. And then I looked around at the experienced swimmers, some of them little children, and concentrated on imitating the way they moved and breathed. Time after time, I was unsuccessful; I kept sinking and I swallowed a ton of water. My limbs began to ache, but I knew myself well enough to know that I would not return to shore before I had jumped off that float at least once. Finally, finally, I was able to coordinate my arms and legs to achieve some sort of crawling motion. It wasn't exactly swimming, but I was staying on top of the water.

I hoisted myself onto the float. The teens looked at me with amusement, and whispered behind their hands. I realized that I had been entertaining them for over an hour with my ungainly attempts at mastering a skill they had had all their lives. But their parents were permitted to take them swimming. Mine were not. I leapt off the dock into the crystal-clear waters of the Mueggelsee. It was wonderful! I did it again and again and again. And each time, I thought: "Look out, kids! Here comes the Jewish diver, uh-oh, polluting your lake!"

I was exhausted by the time I staggered back onto shore. I saw that the nanny had managed to get all four children corralled underneath one of the umbrellas. They sat there munching salami sandwiches and grabbing fistfuls of cherries and grapes from a large bowl. I dropped onto the towel on my stomach, and covered my head with my shirt. The sun dried me almost immediately and lulled me into a delicious drowsiness. I don't know how long I slept. I only know it wasn't long enough. This time, the beach ball landed on my back.

"Sorry about that, but you're practically on top of us, you know." The voice was German, and the tone one of dry amusement. It definitely wasn't the nanny who had urged me to move my things there in the first place. I pulled my shirt off my face and squinted up at her. All I could make out in the intense light was a halo of blond curls.

"Look at you, you're burning. You had better put more lotion on. Your back is all red. Lucky your face was covered."

I knew nothing about lotion. I had never sunned on a beach before. "I must have forgotten my lotion."

"Wait here. I'll get my Nivea." I watched her saunter over to the farther of the two umbrellas, squat beneath it, and rummage through a large totebag. I realized that she was the mother of all those children. She seemed to be in her late twenties or early thirties, and she had a good figure for the mother of so many children. From the cut of her bronze two-piece bathing suit, made of a shiny moire fabric, and the way she walked, I could tell that she knew just how good her figure was. She also knew I was watching her. She walked back slowly in my direction.

"Hold still," she said, and crouched down over me. She scooped a big blob of cream out of the jar, and began massaging it vigorously onto my back and shoulders.

"Thanks," I said. "I guess it's good the ball woke me, or I would have really broiled." She continued rubbing in upward strokes, her fingers caressing the back of my neck. "Well, what can you do? They're annoying, but they're children, they have to play."

"You are their mother, then?"

"Well, I certainly wouldn't put up with all this ruckus if I weren't. I would be stretched out in a much more secluded spot, with an ice-cold beer and a fat romantic novel."

"You have so many of them – children, I mean."

"Well, don't we all, for the Fuehrer? There, your back is finished. Should I do your front?"

Was this a blatant come on, or was it just wishful thinking on my part? I really couldn't tell, but whatever she thought she was doing, she was certainly arousing me.

"It's OK," I said uneasily. "I can do my front."

"Oh, come on, everybody needs someone to do their front," she laughed.

I decided to meet her bold approach. "So who does your front?"

"Now that's a personal question. You don't even know my name."

"What's your name, then?"

"Brigitte. And yours?"

"Gerhard."

I turned onto my side and leaned on my elbow to get a better view. She stretched out facing me in the identical position, a few respectable feet away. Behind her I could see the red-faced nanny, huffing and puffing as she chased the children and the beach ball.

Brigitte offered me one of the children's leftover sandwiches and some lemonade, which I accepted. She said that she had eaten lunch earlier, back at the family's summer home a block from the beach, and it became obvious that she had also had several of those ice-cold beers.

Once Brigitte started talking, there was no stopping her. She held back only one detail, her last name. It was the same old story: she was another lonely wife of a high-ranking Nazi, showered with material perks and starved for attention. But Brigitte was absolutely venomous toward her husband, whose name she said I would recognize if she told it to me. He and his cronies, members of Hitler's inner circle, were so full of themselves that they considered it their duty to impregnate every young secretary who set foot in the War Department. For the Fuehrer, of course.

"Excuse me, Madame," croaked the nanny. She looked as if she were about to pass out from heatstroke. "I think the children have had enough sun. Shall I take them back to the house now, and get them bathed and ready for their naps?"

"That's fine. What time is it?"

"After two o'clock, Madame."

"Thank you, Ernestine. That will be all."

The nanny led the children down the beach, struggling to push the pram across the hot sand. Suddenly Brigitte rose unsteadily to her feet. "Damn, I was supposed to call my husband at two! He's sending a car for us to return to Berlin tomorrow, and I need to let him know what time!"

"Well, I guess you should go home, then, and make your call."

She furrowed her brow and I could see the wheels turning. "There's a public phone next to the boathouse further down the beach. We keep a rowboat there. Why don't you come with me, and then we'll go out on the lake for a bit."

"What about your umbrellas, all your things?"

"Who cares?" she snorted. "No one will take them. And if they do, we'll buy new ones." We made our way across the beach, stepping carefully around people's blankets, until we reached the boathouse. Brigitte pulled a few marks out of the top of her bathing suit and handed them to the attendant. She asked him to have her rowboat ready next to the pier when we returned.

Behind the boathouse was a cylindrically shaped phone booth, one of the modern kind, with a door that slid shut on a track. The glass was opaque, and laced with wire. From the outside, it was possible to see whether or not the booth was occupied, but only the general contour of its occupant was visible.

We had to wait several minutes for someone to finish a call. After a young woman came out, it was Brigitte's turn. She entered the phone booth, leaving the door slightly ajar. I could hear the coins dropping into the slot. She gave me a strange look while she dialed the number, and then she reached out to grab my arm and deftly pulled me inside the booth, fastening the door behind me. There was no room for two in the tiny space. That was the whole idea.

"Hallo, Marta? This is Brigitte. How are you?" Her voice was cheery but her face was filled with loathing. "May I speak with my husband, please?"

While she waited for him to come to the phone, she kissed me wetly on the mouth, and yanked down both of our bathing suits. I couldn't believe what was happening. When her husband got on the line, she told him how much she missed him, and in very explicit language described all the things she would do to him when he came back. All the while, she was doing those things to me.

When it was over, the receiver flew out of her hands. It took a contortionist to pick it up, but I managed it. "Hallo? Hallo? What happened?" I heard him shout. I handed the phone back to Brigitte. "Nothing," she said. "Look, I've got to go. There are people waiting." For a moment she listened intently, nodding her head and trying to pull up the bottom of her bathing suit at the same time. "Noon tomorrow, then. OK. I love you too. Bye."

The boat, as she had requested, was waiting at the pier. Two large towels lay on one of the seats. Brigitte climbed in, pulled me aboard, and began rowing expertly. She said rowing was her favorite form of exercise, that was how she kept her stomach so taut after her pregnancies.

When she got the boat out to the middle of the lake, she hung the oars out on their chains, spread the towels on the floor of the boat, and began again what she had done in the phone booth, only horizontally this time. I had to be careful to angle my body so she did not see me in the bright sunlight. I cannot say it was without pleasure, though it was certainly without love or even affection. Revenge, it was clear, was Brigitte's motive. She said very little as she rowed us back to shore, but what she did say was chilling. She began with a bitter laugh.

"Let's see if you're a stud like my husband."

"What do you mean?"

"He gets everybody pregnant on the first shot."

"What are you talking about?" I gasped. It had never occurred to me that a woman would knowingly put herself in the position of getting pregnant by a man other than her husband.

"Don't look so shocked. Why should only the men in this society have their way with women? Why can't it be the other way around? Besides, my husband wouldn't know the difference. He's like you, blond, with a medium complexion."

I didn't know whether to laugh or cry. So later that night, back in Selma Weska's cottage, I did a little bit of both, as I tossed and turned in the top bunk while my mother slept soundly below. There was some poetic justice to it, really. Adolf, Joseph, and Hermann, those bastards, might hope or even believe that they had succeeded in killing off every last one of us, but they were wrong. In fact, I realized, the Aryan nation would carry Jewish genes, perhaps even a few of mine, for the rest of eternity. It was an exhilarating thought.

I went back to the beach every day for the next week. I learned to swim like an expert, but I never saw Brigitte or her family again.

* * * * * * *

My mother and I returned to Berlin tanned and rested, and I promised I would stay with her until Tante Hedel returned so she would not be alone in the apartment. The first thing I did when we got back to the city was to telephone Hans. I became very worried when he did not answer calls at different hours of the day. Maybe he was in the hospital. If that were the case, there was nothing I could do to help him; all I would do would be to cause trouble for him. I had to burn all the bridges that led to Hans, including my job at the Schelonkas.

After several days of calling, I finally got an operator who told me that the number had been disconnected. There was no question in my mind that Hans was dead, and that he had willed himself to die while I was away, to spare me the pain and the potential danger. His decency and generosity had spanned from this world to the next. I prayed that his heaven would be everything he dreamed it would be.

For days I walked around in a fog. The despair was crushing, as though I had lost my father and my home a second time. But I could not afford to wallow in my grief; Tante Hedel had returned to the apartment, and I needed to find another place to live. There was always that oasis of last resort: Opa, king of the cards, lord of the bedbugs.

Chapter 15

Betrayal

Opa gloated over my reluctant return, as if I were a prodigal son who had finally come home where he belonged. But the filthy apartment on the Lange Strasse was not where I belonged. After living with Hans, I was even more aware of its disgusting conditions. They had gotten worse in my absence. Opa stank, and so did his apartment. He washed and changed his clothes only before he went out to a card game.

Most of the big games now took place in Gesundbrunnen, a working-class section of north-central Berlin. Nearly all of the players were semi-retired tradesmen in their sixties or seventies. These guys were built like bulls, with massive hands, powerful as sledgehammers, and I would not have liked to tangle with any one of them. They had plenty of money to gamble with; not only did they receive pensions, but also many of them, at the government's request, had re-entered the workforce to help the war effort. The games were held in a run-down social club on the Brunnenstrasse, Gesundbrunnen's main street. There was lots of drinking, and noisy fights frequently erupted. I was positive that somebody was paying the police to look the other way. This was too big an operation to go unnoticed.

I was always the youngest at the table, Opa's wayward nephew who had been born, as he confided to the other players, "with a silver spoon in his mouth." I played my part to the hilt, and effortlessly read Opa's most subtle gestures. Our biggest win in one night was over 2,400 marks.

In mid-August – by my estimate, almost a month after Hans's death – I decided to go to Charlottenburg and drop by the Schelonkas' office. I wondered if they knew any of the details about his death, but I could not come right out and ask them, since it was I who was supposed to be his kin, not they. They were very happy to see me, but the first thing they did was question me about Hans. They had heard only that he had died.

I was devastated that I would probably never know what his last days were like, or where he was buried. I hoped he had made arrangements to be buried next to his wife, and that someone had bothered to search for the necessary papers. So many of the cemeteries had been destroyed by the bombings, though, it might have all been for naught. Hans was again "alone like a stone," I thought. I vowed that if I survived the war, I would search for his grave, and visit it so he would not be so alone.

The Schelonkas did have one bit of news about another of their customers, the great Kommandant Dietrich. He and his entire crew had gone down with their U-boat, all of them missing in action. Frau Dietrich had called several times to speak to me before leaving Berlin to move in with her sister's family somewhere in the country. She had left a telephone number, said Herr Schelonka, but I shook my head. As far as I was concerned, both Dietrichs were better off missing in action.

Schelonka said that business had gotten so busy in recent weeks that, when he didn't hear from me, he gave my job to a young Polish foreign worker. Apparently there had been a sudden surge in requests for coal, highly unusual during the sweltering month of August, because serious shortages and higher prices were forecast for the coming cold season, so people were stocking up early. This seemed to me a prudent idea, and when I returned from Charlottenburg I mentioned it to Opa, Anne, Tante Hedel, and Kitty. Since I had plenty of time on my hands, I suggested that they all give me their coal ration cards so I could periodically pick up briquettes for them at a local dealer over the coming weeks. Each of them readily agreed; they were happy to have someone haul their coal for them; they saved money on the tips, and it was one less thing to worry about for the winter ahead. We should have known that having their ration cards in my pocket could deliver them to the Gestapo.

With Philippe gone, Tad, Erika, and I were hesitant to stage any more robberies. Some store owners, aware of the growing desperation of the populace, began to use watchdogs, while others hired armed guards. We agreed to call it quits after a newly installed alarm went off when we tried to break into a grocery store.

Philippe and Jacques were not the only ones to be caught that summer. The most brazen one of all, Horst Atlass, who had strutted openly around Berlin in a stolen SS uniform, was cornered by the Gestapo, along with his stepfather, in the eastern part of the city after an intensive manhunt. This was the second time Horst had been arrested; several months earlier, he had escaped after wresting a gun from the Gestapo man and shooting him right up the ass. He had become something of a legend in Taucher circles. I had met Horst years earlier, just before the war, when our parents signed us both up for an upholstery course so we would have a useful trade if we ever emigrated. I would run into Horst from time to time in the billiard hall, but I always found myself backing away from him. I would hear my mother's voice in my head: "Steer clear of him, Lotharchen, he is too much of a daredevil." Indeed he was. But he was also a good friend and clever, incredibly clever.

* * * * * * *

By now, the Allied armies were closing in on all fronts; in Italy, the end was in sight, the Russians had taken Poland and the Baltic countries and were thrashing the once victorious Germany Army without mercy, and, on the Western front, the British and Americans were scoring one victory after another. The German generals were begging Hitler to negotiate a surrender with honor, but the madman insisted that they defend to the last man, and anyone who surrendered would be shot.

Then, on July 20, the generals tried to kill him by planting a bomb under his table. By a satanic miracle, Hitler escaped serious injury. The leading general, Count von Stauffenberg, and scores of other good German patriots suffered vicious executions. Those who had been the cream of Germany's past and the hope of her future perished at the hands of the wicked and deranged. Hitler, by now completely crazed, went on the radio at one a.m. the next morning to thank his God for saving his life for the sake of the German people who supported him. Germany's Axis allies, the Japanese and Italians, and many satellite diplomats, of course, congratulated him on his miraculous survival, but we were astonished to learn that they were joined by the Vatican's representative, Monsignore Orsenigo, who was one of the first to sign the Visitor's Book at the *Reichs-Kanzlei.*

The new secret weapon, the *V-1*, was hitting London day and night and the propaganda accounts reveled in the number of British citizens being killed by the *Wunderwaffe*. The "V" of these weapons came to stand for *Vergeltung*, vengeance, and there was talk of other new weapons, bigger and with greater accuracy, for the destruction of all of England. And the worst was still to come: heavy water, stored in Norway, would be used to make an "atom bomb." As the war became uglier with each passing day, the mood in Berlin darkened with it.

* * * * * * *

Tad and I were back to spending several days a week in the billiard hall. It was still a place where Berlin's fringe types mingled with lonely pensioners and drunken soldiers on furlough. Interestingly, the billiard hall was the only place where I actually saw leaflets exhorting the citizens of Germany to rebel against the Nazi leadership. The authors of these subversive documents were the leaders of Germany's Communist cells, people like Anne's boyfriend. Just having such a paper in one's possession was grounds for arrest.

But most of the dissent in the billiard hall was personal, not political. Living in a war zone had shortened everybody's fuse and exacerbated the personality problems that they all had to begin with. A dangerous antagonism was festering between Opa and the volatile Martin, whose past as a violent criminal appeared to be more than just a rumor. I didn't know exactly what was at the root of their conflict, but knowing Opa, he had scammed Martin in some way, and Martin, though he couldn't prove a thing, was out for blood. Several times the two of them had to be separated after coming to blows, which was ludicrous because Martin was twice Opa's size and half his age.

Talking to Opa about the situation had gotten me nowhere; the old man was totally irrational. Martin had always made me nervous and generally I tried to stay out of his way. However, seeing that things were getting out of hand, I tried to approach him as a friend. I even played a game of billiards against him and lost on purpose. I told him that Opa was a senile old jackass and he should just forget the whole thing, that his menacing outbursts were endangering everyone at the billiard hall.

It was like talking to a brick wall. Now I became Martin's enemy, too. He owed me sixty marks from several previous games, and whenever I asked him for the money, he cursed me at the top of his lungs and stalked off. I was so unnerved by this maniac that I would not have made an issue over the money if I had not needed it desperately.

One afternoon I went to the billiard hall in a driving rainstorm, wearing a full-length raincoat that belonged to Anne's husband. When I entered the vestibule of the poolroom, which was always rather dark, someone came at me from behind, lifted my open coat over my head, and began to choke me. I was thrown to the floor, stomped on and kicked, totally unable to defend myself. I was dazed, but I caught a glimpse of the man's silhouette as he ran away. I was positive it was Martin.

I brushed myself off and went upstairs. At first I didn't say anything about the incident, but later that evening, I warned Opa that he needed to stay out of Martin's way. The old man would not have been able to pick himself up as easily after such an ambush.

Two days later, I decided to give Martin a taste of his own poison. I waited for him in the same dark hallway where he had assaulted me. Only I didn't creep up on him from behind. Looking him straight in the eye, I grabbed him by the throat with both hands and slammed my knee into his groin; when his head lurched forward, I punched him with a straight left and then a right uppercut. He crumpled to the floor and that was where I left him. I went upstairs to the billiard hall and wondered if he would soon follow, but he didn't, that day or several thereafter.

When I told Tad what I had done, he slapped me on the back. "Congratulations! Finally, somebody gave that son of a bitch what he deserves! He owes me over a hundred, did you know that?"

"I didn't do it just for the money."

"I know. He needed to be put in his place."

"So why didn't you go after him?"

Tad gave me a laconic grin as he chalked up his cue. "Oh, Gerhard, all that messy punching and kicking. You know that's not my style!"

I burst out laughing. That was Tad. Europe was in ruins, but his hair still looked great. Twenty years later, he would have been accurately described as the essence of "cool." I knew he was itching to get out from under Ilse, that he was convinced that life held more in store for him than all this squalor. He was intelligent, charismatic, and amazingly adaptable. He could be anything in the world he set out to be. I only hoped he would have the chance.

Friday, the twenty-fifth of August, 1944, began like any other day in the underground. I spent the morning at Opa's, going over the signals for that evening's card game. At lunchtime I went to the Glocke, the café down the street from the billiard hall, and had their Stammgericht – that day, a gelatinous potato soup spiked with lard, oregano, and some rubbery chunks of meat. It tasted awful, but I took a second helping when they offered it.

I went to the billiard hall and played several rounds of Ping-Pong against a couple of soldiers, guys about my own age. Between games, Tad wandered in and told me he had run into Trudy the previous evening. Dear, sweet, Trudy. It seemed like such a long time ago. But her name still sent a shiver through me. Tad said she and her husband were still together, and more miserable than ever. He had seriously injured his arm in an accident at his military base, and was home on permanent disability. Apparently he sat around the apartment all day and barked the orders at her he could no longer bark at his men. Fortunately for Tad, Trudy's husband disliked Ilse, and never ventured inside her apartment, but Trudy fled there every chance she got.

"She's still mooning over you, pal," said Tad, laughing. "You must have been pretty good for a virgin."

"Who's a virgin?" one of the soldiers called out.

"Gerhard, here!" Tad said, poking at me. "Look at him, he's pretty hard up!" A lot of laughter and jostling ensued.

Over Tad's shoulder, I saw Martin coming toward me. He had not set foot inside the poolroom since I had roughed him up in the vestibule. He reached into his breast pocket and handed me fifty marks. "Good day, Gerhard, how are you?" he said with a smirk. He didn't wait for an answer, just turned on his heels and walked away. He walked over to Tad and did the same thing, and then he turned around and walked out the door.

We couldn't believe it. Johann the proprietor and several of the regulars came over to shake my hand. "I guess the rough stuff did the trick," I said. Tad nodded. "Sometimes it's better to face up to guys like that than to pull in your tail."

Tad hadn't eaten yet that day, so he decided to go to the Glocke and have some of the potato soup that I had described to him in gory detail. From the large second-floor window, I saw him saunter down the street; Tad, for whom life was so easy and yet so empty, Tad, my best friend, to whom I owed so much of my life of the past two years. I never saw him again.

As I watched Tad, I noticed three men standing on the other side of the boulevard. One of them had his arm in a sling and, with the other arm, was gesturing in the direction of the billiard hall. I couldn't get a good look at him from such a distance, but I thought he looked vaguely familiar. I didn't think a thing of it, and got involved in a game of caramboulage with my new "buddy," one of the young soldiers. Tad had taught me well and within a few minutes I was well ahead of my opponent. And then everything happened very fast.

I was bent over the table holding my cue stick, engrossed in the game, when someone came at me from behind, grabbing me around the waist and spinning me around. Another man stood directly in front of me and pointed a pistol at my head.

"Lothar Orbach? Game's over!" said the one with the pistol. "You're under arrest!"

I had always wondered what I would do if this moment ever came. There were no swashbuckling heroics, no brilliant diversions. The men were in plain clothes, which was why Johann hadn't sounded the warning. I was caught off guard, and they overwhelmed me with ease.

My first thought was of my mother: what had I done? I should have had the sense to stay out of this place as she said. The goddamn war was almost over, the Nazis were losing on all fronts, and *now* I got caught!

My friends in the billiard hall stood transfixed. I kept my head low, didn't dare make eye contact with any of them for their own safety. The taller of the two men grabbed my right wrist and handcuffed it. He placed the other cuff on his own wrist. There was no escaping. His partner frisked me once, twice, and then a third time. He seemed bewildered that there was no gun – I had left it at Opa's that day – as though someone had forewarned him that I would be armed. My captors questioned no one else, just pulled me out of the building and into the street. They had obviously gotten what they had come for.

They began walking me west on the Grosse Frankfurter Strasse, in the direction of the Alexanderplatz.

"Where are we going?"

"On a pleasant little excursion, don't concern yourself," said the taller one. The shorter one laughed. "So Lothar, now you will have no more worries. You'll get your food and you'll have a place to sleep. It will be much better than what you've been doing until now."

"That's right, Lothar," the other one said. "How the hell did you manage to hide for so long? A lot of people must have helped you. You must be a very popular fellow. Tell us about all your nice friends." I said nothing, just matched their strides on the sidewalk. They had placed a jacket over the handcuffs, so passersby would not see that a prisoner was being taken.

"And what about your mother? She isn't registered with us either. Wouldn't you like to go with her to a place where you'll both be safe from all this bombing, hmmm?"

"I wish I knew where she was. I don't think she's alive. She told me when we separated that she would commit suicide, jump into the Spree or maybe the Havel. I haven't heard from her since I left home."

The tall man suddenly yanked his wrist so that the cuff dug into my flesh. "Come now, Lothar, don't give us this shit! Your old friend told us everything. We know Frau

Nelly Orbach is out there too. Don't wait until the interrogators go after you. They are not nearly as nice as we are."

I dug my left fist into my left pocket, and nearly stopped dead in my tracks. My God! I was still carrying all the coal ration cards, complete with addresses, of Anne, Tante Hedel, Kitty, and Opa! If the police found them, they would be the death warrants of all my friends – and of my mother.

"Maybe one of you guys has a cigarette for me? I could really use a smoke, I've got a match in here somewhere." I kept my hand inside the pocket and crumpled the ration cards into a little ball.

The short one sneered at me. "We don't smoke, Lothar, and neither should you. Didn't anyone ever tell you it's bad for your lungs?" The two of them started laughing again.

I slowed my pace and started to act agitated. "Hey, I'm really dying for a cigarette. Maybe there's an old butt somewhere here on the street."

I squatted and cursed and pretended to scrounge in the gutter, next to a leaky fire hydrant. One of the men cursed. "Christ, you're disgusting! Get up, Schwein!" They grabbed me underneath the armpits and hoisted me back to a standing position, but not before I had managed to deposit the ration cards into the garbage-strewn gutter.

They took me by underground train to the Alexanderplatz Prison, and from there, by police wagon, to the former Jewish Hospital, a small institution on the Iranische Strasse that had been converted to a collection depot for Tauchers. It was known as the last stop before Auschwitz. As I entered the hospital complex through the courtyard, wedged between the two goons, I noticed a young woman leaning out of a window. It was Friedel Weinberg, the older sister of one of my childhood friends.

She still worked as a nurse at the hospital; there were still some Jewish patients left to be dealt with before their deportations. I saw her gesture in my direction.

"Lothar, it was Goldstein!" she yelled. "Siegfried Goldstein!" And then she quickly ducked back inside and slammed the window shut.

It only took a moment to put all the pieces together. Siegfried Goldstein, that was the fellow with his arm in a sling who had been pointing at the billiard hall. He had been enrolled in the upholstery course with me and Horst Atlass. The nurse, who had known us all since childhood, was letting me know that it was Goldstein who had turned us both in to the Gestapo. And somehow, I didn't know exactly how, the vengeful Martin must have helped him track me down. I remembered then that when I had last talked to Horst, he had mentioned that our mutual acquaintance Goldstein, son of a Christian mother and a Jewish father, had been involved in a traffic accident with an unlicensed motorcycle. Horst said there was a rumor that Goldstein had cut a deal with the authorities to suspend his sentence if he would work as an informer.

We came through the main door of the building and they steered me toward a stairwell. "Now where?" I asked my captors.

"The perfect place for you," said the tall one in a chipper voice. "The morgue. That's where we keep garbage like you until we're ready to ship you out."

Downstairs, the place was like a fortress, crawling with guards. They took the handcuff off me and thrust me into a small, filthy cell with two other men and bolted the door.

Slumped over on the floor, ashen faced, was none other than Horst Atlass. The other man, who stood cowering in the corner, was his stepfather Leopold Arendt. Although they had been arrested more than a week earlier, both of them were being detained until the Gestapo rounded up enough Jews to send a full transport to the south. In the earlier days of the war, these transports ran continuously. By the summer of 1944, traffic was down to a trickle. There were very few of us left.

Horst told me that he was being beaten severely – the Gestapo knew he had a wide network of friends in the underground – but he wasn't talking. They had not broken his spirit. In fact, he was obsessed with escaping and said that the two of us should come up with a plan. None of the other prisoners had the guts, he said, they were all older men, like his stepfather Arendt. At first I hesitated. And then I thought: if they catch me in an escape attempt, they will probably kill me, and if they send me to Auschwitz, they will probably kill me, too. What did I have to lose?

For three nights, under cover of darkness, Horst and I used a sharpened teaspoon to chip away at the brick wall of our prison. Digging slowly through the mortar between the stones, we managed to remove six bricks, quickly replacing them whenever we heard one of the guards or dogs approaching. By the fourth night, we could feel the outside air. We prayed we still had a few more days before the transport, so we could make the hole large enough to crawl through.

Horst had warned me that I, too, would be interrogated before I would be permitted to board any transport. On the fifth day of my incarceration, they came for me. They placed my arms and legs in shackles. They took me to the office of Kommissar Dubberke, director of the so-called Jewish Department. This was where spies like Siegfried Goldstein and Stella Goldschlag made their deals with the devil. Sitting at a desk in the reception area outside Dubberke's office, I saw a man who looked familiar. I said a name aloud, and was stunned when he actually glanced up at me.

"Rektor Reschke? Is that Rektor Reschke?" He was the former principal of the Jewish Grammar School on Kaiserstrasse. Could it be true that he was now collaborating with the Gestapo, trying to save his own skin by destroying the children he had taught? He kept shuffling his papers. When they dragged me past him, he tried to look right through me. I leaned over and spat in his face. He said nothing, just wiped the saliva with his sleeve. Didn't he know they were going to kill him anyway?

Dubberke was quite cordial at the start. He began reading off a list of names and closely following my facial expression to see if I recognized any of them. There were many Tauchers whose names I knew, and many I didn't. From the inscrutable Opa, I had learned the art of conveying nothing.

"Erika Weissman." He mentioned many other names – Max Hirsch, Henry Atlass, Wolfgang Neumann – some I knew, most of them I'd never heard of. Nothing.

"Nelly Orbach."

"She's dead. A suicide, in the Havel." Maybe it would be true. She said her life would be over without me.

"Filthy liar!" bellowed Dubberke. He walked around his desk to my chair, and kicked me several times in the leg.

Dubberke went through the list again. This time, by the end, his three henchmen were punching my face and chest. Then one of them took out a heavy, braided electrical cord and began to beat me with it, raising thick welts all over my body.

Nothing. It was getting easier and easier to say nothing. Did they know that their torture was lulling me into a dazed and incoherent state? I really didn't remember, I really didn't know. The beating continued unabated for almost two hours. It was a blessing to be thrown back into my cell in the morgue. I could not sit or stand for days.

Meanwhile, Horst had managed to loosen two more bricks. We were now ready to scrape the outer cement layer off the wall. Early the next morning, the cell door suddenly swung wide open, and two policemen with barking dogs invaded our cell, guns drawn. They yanked us off the floor where we slept and made us back up against the wall with our hands in the air. One of the policemen stalked around the cell, cursing and kicking the walls. Someone had told them about our escape plan. There was only one other person who knew, besides Horst and me: our cellmate, his scared stepfather. He must have gotten cold feet. Maybe they had threatened him with the electrical cord. Again we were beaten severely. They put us in separate cells, and from then on, both Horst and I were kept shackled and in handcuffs at all times.

I did not see Horst again until the night of September 6, when a large truck pulled up to the hospital in the darkness. Thirty-five Jewish prisoners were loaded inside, each one handcuffed to another to lessen the possibility of escape. They cuffed me to Horst's stepfather. He trembled so hard at my side that the chains rattled. He appeared to be as terrified of me as he was of the Gestapo.

We were taken to an industrial railroad station. It was so dark that I could not make out the station or the neighborhood. Then we were loaded into an old wooden freight car with no windows. We could barely breathe. There were only a few gaps between the slats that we could peer out of, sucking in air and trying to guess our location.

We were each given a tiny ration of bread and water, too little food to sustain us but enough to prevent us from dying before reaching our destination. After a raw, cold night and a dark day aboard the boxcar, the guards finally unbolted the doors. We were bathed in an evening breeze, and gratefully we gulped the fresh air. I squinted at the station sign and realized that we were in the town of Koenigshuette, in Upper Silesia, home of Hella, the sister of Anne and Hedel. Her sisters had risked their lives for us; she would help me, too, I was sure of it.

I noticed that the guards had changed. Perhaps the new ones had not been warned that I had tried to escape. I looked at the grizzled old man still handcuffed to me. He whimpered and shook and gasped for breath. If only I could get rid of him.

Two by two, the prisoners were being allowed to jump from the train to relieve themselves on the banks of dirt alongside the tracks. Those who had to defecate had nothing but their bare hands to clean themselves with. I was loath to re-enter that car, dreading the stench that would soon pervade it.

"Make it fast, now!" barked one of the guards, gesturing at us. We sat down together in the doorway and jumped off at the same time so as not to injure each other's wrists or arms. The area closest to the train was already covered in feces, so I pulled him further down the track. We stood there and urinated.

And then I said to him, tersely: "You want to live?"

"Sure, who doesn't want to live?"

"OK. I have a friend in this town. She'll help us, both of us. She'll hide us until the war is over."

"What are you saying?"

"We're getting out of here. If you say or do anything, I'll kill you. Do you hear me? I'll kill you. Or they'll kill you."

His jaw dropped. No words came from him. A freight train was approaching on an adjacent track. I sped him over in its direction, and we were able to hide behind it. He was going through with it! We would make it!

Suddenly, the old man screamed. He covered his face with his free hand, and hurled himself to the ground, pulling me down with him and slamming my head against the rail. The guards came running with their rifles ready to smash or shoot.

"You bastard, you bastard," I moaned, "this was our only chance!"

He sobbed, his face pushed in the dirt. Dazed and bloodied from the fall, I told the guards that the old man had become disoriented and was pulling me off the path, and I had lost my way in the darkness. I don't know why they didn't kill both of us on the spot. Perhaps they didn't want to let us off that easily.

The next stop was Auschwitz.

Chapter 16

Vignettes of Hell

It was the middle of the night, I think, when our train pulled up to Auschwitz, but the spotlights were so powerful that it was brighter than daylight. Our captors wasted no time. They removed the handcuffs from about a dozen of us, only the youngest, and led us from the train to an open boxcar. Horst Atlass made his way to my side. They ordered us to climb up into the boxcar and unload its contents onto trucks that were parked alongside. In terror, we scaled up on all four sides as a dozen new guards boosted us higher, ramming their rifle butts into our backs. I was pushed so hard by two carbines that I toppled into the car, finding myself, in utter horror, sprawled on top of hundreds of twisted corpses still dressed in striped prison cloth.

The stench was indescribable. My stomach and lungs rebelled, and I could do nothing before standing as high as I could to catch my next breath over the side of the car. A voice yelled at us: "You will work in teams of two and throw them over the side onto the trucks! And get moving! This had better be finished by dawn!"

Together, Horst and I struggled to lift the hands and feet of one of the bodies. Gingerly and carefully we slid it – him – over the side. I will never forget the "thud" of this corpse as it hit the hard bed of the empty truck. I can hear it today. That thud, that terrible sound. It was the sound of finality, of the end of hope. I had heard and seen a fair amount of despair and death, but nothing I had heard had been as chilling as the one terrible sound of that body hitting the bed of the truck.

After the first one, it became much easier. Later, with each body falling on the others, the thud softened and slowly lost significance in the larger context of what had happened to these human beings. When dawn broke and we were nearly done, I took my first good look at one of them. He was very young, probably my own age, his hands and face ingrained with black soot. He and his fellow prisoners had probably toiled and died digging coal for Germany in the mines of Silesia. When we were finished, they took Horst away from our group. I learned later that he and his stepfather were executed within minutes because Horst had shot a Gestapo man.

When we reached the "sauna," the area into which all prisoners were herded on arrival, they took my only possession from me, a picture of my family. We were stripped naked and led to the showers, men and women together, and our heads, our bodies, and our pubic areas were shaved. The razors were applied brutally, leaving nicks and open cuts all over us. Immediately after we were shaved, they sprayed us with pesticide, and the air filled with screams of pain as the chemicals penetrated our razor burns and wounds. Then I was led to a prisoner sitting on a bench. Gently, he took my left arm and asked me to sit beside him. Using a fine needle dipped in blue indelible ink, he began to tattoo me. He worked so skillfully I assumed that in his previous life he had been an artist. I became prisoner B.9761, a number I still carry today.

* * * * * * *

*That tatoo buried all that had been before, and
began my transformation into a nameless, sub-human
creature whose identity had been branded as a number
on its hide. If there are words to describe the consum-
mation by the utter darkness, the antithesis of humanity
that was Auschwitz, I do not know them. For me,
Auschwitz remains unspeakable, a nightmare beyond
my ability to describe, for I still cannot believe it myself.
Even after fifty years, I can summon only incoherent
fragments of memory, except for the vignettes of those
moments that enabled me to survive.*

* * * * * * *

I had arrived in Birkenau, the death wing of Auschwitz where the exterminations would take place, among
thousands of other prisoners, but still very much alone –
no family, no friends, and too young to live with only my
memories. For some idiotic reason I began to hum a tune,
some German folk song that came into my mind, a song
of no importance, just a pretty melody to lift my dejected
spirits. Suddenly, a firm grip on my shoulder twisted me
around.

"Nu, Yekkeh," said a voice using the Yiddish slang for
a German Jew, "Why do you sing in a place like this?" An
older, Polish Jew, weather beaten and thin but still strong
looking, had heard my humming and stared at me with
contempt. I was startled by his unexpected intrusion upon
my inner world, and although I had never learned nor
spoken any Yiddish, I understood his question. Like many
other elitist German Jews, I had harbored a disdain for this
language, considering it a bastardization of my mellifluous

mother tongue, the language of my beloved poets. And we Yekkehs felt disdain, too, for the Yiddish speakers, whom we saw as scruffy, stooped-over rabbis in shapeless black coats, religious fanatics completely lacking in culture and sophistication. But here, in Auschwitz, the fact that I had been a patriotic defender of the German language and culture was a bad joke, and Yiddish now had a new tone, one of kinship.

"Why shouldn't I sing?" I replied, feeling feisty.

He took me again by the shoulders, though gently this time, and spun me around. "Turn around, Yekkeh. You see the smokestacks of the crematorium, how they are smoking, smelling, and burning? Tomorrow you, too, will be in there!"

Again I replied swiftly and bluntly: "So, my friend, if this is all true and I'll be there tomorrow, at least let me keep singing today."

He put his arms around me, his dark eyes brimming with love and sorrow, as if for a foolish son."Oy, oy, Yekkeh!" he lamented in a choking voice. Silently we walked arm in arm for a short while, each determined to deal with this horror in his own way. Then our paths separated and I would never see him again.

* * * * * * *

My chief assets were my youth and health, which I had kept up with the food I had received from so many benefactors while in the Berlin underground. I was grateful to them all – to Sylvia, Anne, Hedel, to Frau Schreiner, Frau Grueger, to Hans, Opa, and to Trudy – to all those who had fed Gerhard the Aryan, Gerhard the Taucher, Lothar the Jew. At first I was assigned to the kitchen to peel potatoes, and I stole as many as I could. Once they caught me with eight potatoes in my pants pockets, and a Kapo gave me as many lashes as the potatoes I had stolen. I bled profusely, and couldn't sit or sleep on my back for several days. Later on I became the head man of the *Scheisskommando*, the tank wagon that carted off the contents of the latrines. In this august position, I steered the tongue of the wagon, while a dozen others pulled the wagon with ropes. The tongue was heavy and hard to steer, and it was a job nobody else wanted, but surrounded by those pulling the wagon I was protected from the SS German shepherds that nipped at the heels of my fellow prisoners. As we hauled our human waste, I recalled the pictures from the Haggadah of our forefathers in bondage, hoisting the heavy blocks to erect the pyramids of Egypt. And what we mined from the latrines was sold as fertilizer to the neighboring farmers.

* * * * * * *

At least once a week we stood in line to face selection to live or die, a selection often conducted by the notorious Dr. Josef Mengele and his learned assistants. He looked us up and down, coolly appraising us only for our ability to work. As long as I remained healthy and able to work, I would be waved to the right, which meant at least a few more days of life. And that all depended on how much food I could find or steal.

While in this line, I met Ossip, a Russian political officer. The German High Command had decided to treat these prisoners like the Jews and other undesirables. Ossip was a rugged young fellow who spoke German pretty well, and he had managed to smuggle a miniature "stick" chess game into the camp, a real coup. One night, by moonlight in our cellblock, we played chess, our bodies nearly wedged together by prisoners on either side in the crowded bunk.

At one point, Ossip moved his piece and then whispered: "Frankly, I can't understand you Jews. Here you all are, being annihilated by the millions, and you still cleave to your almighty God. How can you still believe you have a savior?"

I didn't know what to answer. I knew only that I was not ready to give up hope, not yet, and that hope relied implicitly on faith, not only the blind faith of youth, but also on a sort of corollary of faith — a refusal to believe my world, my life, would end, could end, like this. I didn't know where God fit into this picture, but I wasn't going to rule Him out yet, not by a long shot. To be without faith, even my kind of faith, would be to give up hope, to be orphaned completely, to hear only that unearthly "thud."

I looked out at the full moon, calm, perfect, eternal. It was the same moon that had shined on me as a boy, when I went on overnight camping trips with my youth group. It was the same moon that had shined on me one glorious night when I had stolen a kiss from Sylvia, on our way back from the movies. It was the same moon that shined on everyone, even in those few places where there was no war.

"I don't know, Ossip. They can take everything from us, but they can't take away our God any more than they can take this moon or the sun or the sky." In another time, in another place, we could have continued this discussion, but in Auschwitz words like these rang hollow. We continued our game in silence.

* * * * * * *

Just before the High Holy Days, Rosh Hashanah and Yom Kippur, we heard that a machsor, a special prayer book for these holidays, had been smuggled into the camp, and word spread that there would be a prayer service. On Rosh Hashanah, the Jewish New Year, only a few participated, because most were too frightened. But on Yom Kippur, the holiest day of the Jewish year, hundreds of the inmates stole away to join in. For a brief time, the air of Auschwitz was filled with muted cries and fervent supplication: "Aneinu, Hashem, Aneinu! Answer us, our God, answer us! Answer us, our Father, answer us! Answer us, our Creator, answer us! Answer us, our Redeemer, answer us!"

And then they came, wielding water hoses, clubs, and rifles, screaming orders and obscenities. They used trucks and carts to haul literally thousands away to their deaths. The day after Yom Kippur, the population count posted in the kitchen workroom where I peeled potatoes was under 1,000; the day before, it had topped 15,000. Later, it was worse; when the crematoriums with a capacity of only 4,000 bodies a day failed to keep up with the requirements, they dug long furrows in the ground, ten by fifty meters and filled with pitch, in which they burned thousands more, many while still alive. By October 1944, in Birkenau, as many as 17,000 people per day were cremated to meet the Nazis' schedules. We breathed the air of hell.

* * * * * * *

One night in the middle of winter, as we lay sleeping in our bunks, an elderly Jew alongside me suffered a terrible hemorrhage, and as he lay dying his blood poured onto my shirtsleeve. The next morning, we were scheduled for one of Dr. Mengele's selections. Despite the freezing temperature, I tore the sleeve off of my shirt rather than be seen with blood on my clothing, which could suggest a wound or sickness that would make me unfit for work, and that would have sent me to the "*F-Lager*," the *Vernichtungs-Lager*, the gas chamber. By now, we were all sick, desperately thin and wasted, and we were all constantly cold.

* * * * * * *

Then, one morning, there was an announcement at the Appell Platz, the parade grounds, that 142 workers were urgently needed at one of the aircraft factories, a labor camp under the administration of Buchenwald. I had a little experience from the arms factory in Borsigwalde, and was among the first to volunteer by raising my hand. I exaggerated my abilities and experience, and was selected for what would be a new lease on life. We were ordered to be ready for immediate departure.

It was an enormous stroke of luck to have a ticket out of Auschwitz at this moment, for I was fast becoming a candidate for the gas chamber. My once sturdy physique had shriveled, I must have lost nearly half my original weight, and I had begun suffering intense gallbladder attacks that made me spend long stretches of time in the latrine, feigning the need to relieve myself when I was actually doubled over in spasms of pain. Both my ankles were distended with puss from lice and infection. My selection was the kind of luck that had come so often at critical points in the past four years. It was this kind of luck, divine or otherwise, that had kept up my hope and faith, and it was this faith and hope, I believe, that had kept me in place for the next stroke of luck.

Almost immediately after my new designation as a lathe operator, my gallbladder began acting up, and I stole away to the latrine, where I writhed in agony. Moments later, Rudy Jacobsohn, a fellow Yekkeh Taucher who arrived on the same transport with me from Berlin, came rushing in.

"Orbach, come on!" he gasped. "They've begun the count, they're leaving in a few minutes, hurry!" I ran for the line of men that snaked around the parade ground.

"One hundred forty-one," the Kapo counted the man in front of me, and he squinted at me as I hurtled to the end of the line. "Here's the last one, 142! That's it, forward march!"

Rudolf Jacobsohn, who had apparently tarried to use the latrine after warning me to run, came running up just behind me, but was waved off the departing column. He never made it; he died in Auschwitz. By saving my life, he paid with his own. Again, it was fate: one man's bread meant another's starvation, one man's survival meant another's demise. Twice, in that one short morning, fate had chosen me to live.

* * * * * * *

Upon our arrival at Niederorschel, a forced labor camp next to the airplane factory, it was obvious to the local Kapos that virtually every member of our sorry-looking detachment was too debilitated to perform a full day's work, though not one of us would have ever admitted it. They created a makeshift hospital where our infections were treated and we were fed creamy soups, horse salami, and good German bread. After a week off my feet, my sores were almost cured, and I had filled out a bit. I was now ready to produce – and try to sabotage – wings of Focke Wulfes for the Luftwaffe.

We were still prisoners, of course, but all this was heaven compared with Auschwitz. Because our work was vital to the war effort, we were protected from the worst of the SS interference and brutality. As the weeks continued, however, things went downhill rapidly. The decent rations came to an abrupt halt, and in a camp that was so small, compared with Auschwitz, there was nothing left to steal. But the dog belonging to the camp commander, a poor little dachshund, disappeared one night and helped sustain a group of us.

At the factory, I made friends with a German foreman named Herman Kruse, a civilian engineer who consented to smuggle out a letter to Angela Ciupka, a sister of Anne and Tante Hedel, who in turn contacted my mother with the news that I was still alive. Through Kruse, my mother was able to send me two letters and a package, again via Angela Ciupka, that helped me through many rough days and weeks. Inside it was a warm football shirt and long underpants, which, under my striped prison uniform, helped keep out the cold. And the clothes reminded me that my mother was still alive and with me – my best reason to cling to life.

* * * * * * *

By spring, we could hear the bombs coming closer, and the air raids were getting heavier both day and night. The Americans were closing in. On the first of April, it was announced that we were to leave the place that had saved us from imminent starvation and death in Auschwitz. We were each given two pieces of bread and a pat of margarine. It would be the last food, as it turned out, that I would receive from the Nazi authorities. We knew we would have to make do with these rations for as long as our journey lasted, but we did not know where this trip would lead us. We were embarking on a death march which few would survive and, as we found out later, our destination was Buchenwald.

* * * * * * *

After several days of walking, and nights sleeping in haylofts, silos, or the open air, we ran out of our bread. Only those too weak to eat had anything left. We began to chew on all kinds of plants, including *Sauerampfer*, a spinach-like leaf that caused severe diarrhea, but the smell and the cramps were preferable to gnawing starvation.

I stayed close to Antonius, a prisoner from Saloniki whom I had befriended at the factory. He had developed the classic features of a *Musselman*, a candidate for imminent death by starvation, that were by now so familiar to all of us – his body was skeletal, his cheeks were swollen, and his sunken eyes were surrounded by very dark rings. The fact that he still had most of his bread hidden inside his shirt was something only I knew. He no longer had the strength to eat it. I watched him closely day and night, helping him during the waking hours, and watching him while he slept, like a jackal guarding a crippled wildebeest. When he took his final, rattling breath I went for his bread.

* * * * * * *

When the end came, it came suddenly, simply, silently; like a car that had run out of gas, I just stopped trying and caring. It was a week later, April 9, and we had still not reached Buchenwald, nor had we had anything more to eat.

Now I was barely alive. I was losing feeling and sight. I walked mechanically, stumbling, not knowing or caring what went on about me. Now it was no longer a question of faith or hope, for I had slowly lost physical contact with life and its normal functions, and could no longer connect to memories of the past, events of the present, much less any concept of a future. I could no longer think or feel rationally; I could no longer feel or think at all. I was no longer awake or asleep, but always floating in a void. My memory of what happened that day is no more than the fragments still embedded in my unwilling senses, like a dream reconstructed days later.

We were marching, endlessly, to Buchenwald when I stopped and sat down by the road. Nothing mattered any longer; I was giving up. Our guards were now *Heim-wehr*, elderly Germans who replaced the younger SS who had all been taken to the front. One of these pedaled his bicycle in my direction.

"You there, get with your column!" he shouted at me. "What are you doing so far behind?"

"I don't care anymore, I am too goddamned sick," I said feebly. "Soon it will all be over anyway, either we will be dead or we will be free, and I just don't give a damn anymore."

The guard jumped off his bicycle. "You're a Berliner, right? I can hear it. I am from Spandau." I just nodded. He bent over and whispered loudly in my ear. "Come on, boy, take the bicycle and catch up to the rest of the column. It's only a matter of days, maybe even hours, until it's all over, so snap out of it!"

I stood up and got on the bicycle, and with every ounce that was left of my strength, began pedaling in the opposite direction.

"Hey, goddammit, what are you doing, stealing my bike? Get back here!" the old man yelled. I didn't turn around, I just kept pumping my matchstick legs. My instinctive reaction was to flee. For several minutes more, the bicycle seemed to move of its own accord. I was delirious, yet my legs continued to jerk. An air-raid siren sounded, and American planes roared overhead, fighter bombers, flying so low I could see the pilots, some of them looking down at me. Then, alongside a small overpass near a brook, I noticed a large open pipe about two yards in diameter. I let the bike drop, crawled inside, and collapsed.

* * * * * * *

I don't know how long I lay curled inside the pipe – minutes, hours – before several irate citizens stumbled upon me. One of them reached in and poked me with a stick. "Wake up, what are you doing here? You must be one of the prisoners who just marched by! Where did you steal this bicycle? You won't get away with it!"

They loaded my limp body into a horse cart, and after almost an hour's ride they deposited me back with my column. While I had lain barely conscious in the cart, many of my fellow prisoners, unable to march any longer, had fallen and died by the side of the road.

It was shortly before midnight when we arrived in Buchenwald. Starvation, diarrhea, lice, gallbladder disease, and typhoid fever racked my body. As I staggered inside the gates, thousands of other unlucky prisoners were being led away. I have never learned why we were led into Buchenwald, while at the same time so many others were being marched out to other camps only to be exterminated en route – all on the eve of liberation.

The next day, April 11, 1945, prisoners with hand-made guns, made secretly by those working in the local factories next to the camp, freed themselves and us from our camp guards. I learned this later, for at the time I was too weak even to know what was happening. Hours later, a black American soldier driving a life-giving water-filled tank truck opened the gates of Buchenwald. All I can remember from that day is the expression on his face and the horror in his eyes. We could tell he had never seen human beings that looked like us.

Chapter 17

Picking Up the Pieces

On April 12, 1945, about a month before my twenty-first birthday, I was six feet tall and weighed barely eighty pounds. I watched the gates of Buchenwald swing open, as if in a dream. The GIs poured into the camp, pressing food and water on the dazed and the dying. More than a few unfortunate souls died when their shut-down digestive systems could not accommodate entire K rations, chocolate bars, and raw fruit by the handful. The water system in the camp had been poisoned by the Nazis before they had fled, but, thanks to fast action by the Americans, we now had enough water.

All day long, our liberators shuttled truckload after truckload of German citizens into the camp, all those good neighbors who had seen and heard nothing. We were made to parade before them, to make them see the true Buchenwald, the one that contrasted so vividly with the motto on its wrought iron portals, *"Arbeit Macht Frei,"* "Work Will Make You Free." They stared at us, the zombies, the walking dead, and they gasped in horror. Soon I would see a new look on the faces of Germans when they saw me, the look of fear.

Some of the GIs were just my own age, and their military training had not prepared them for what they would find at Buchenwald. One minute they laughed, exhilarated and proud that they had snatched us from the jaws of death; the next minute they sobbed, overcome by what they saw. They also grieved for the loss of President Roosevelt who had died that morning. During an impromptu memorial service on the parade grounds, I fainted. It was typhus; I had a fever of 106 degrees and was quarantined for three weeks.

I could not wait to leave the hospital so I could search for my mother, who I feared would be lost somewhere in the rubble of Berlin. When I was well enough to travel, the Americans stuffed a satchel with K rations and other canned meats for the road ahead. I took a freight train, in an open boxcar, first to Dresden, and then on to Berlin. There were dozens of people crammed inside the car.

I wore the dark blue Eisenhower jacket the Americans had given me on which I had sewn my number, B.9761, and my yellow prison triangle on the lapel pocket so that any Nazis I might meet could appreciate the dramatic reversal in our relationship. Now it was they on whom the wearers of the yellow stars could spit. The other travelers tried to avert their eyes from me, but they could not. Beyond the trauma of defeat, they were now compelled to confront the living reminder of the monstrous horror they had so long ignored, or from which they had at least managed to blind themselves.

As the train chugged on under the night sky, a drunken Russian soldier raped a young German girl in full view of everyone. No one raised a hand to help her; there was no sound but her screams. So much for the Master Race who, in Auschwitz, I had watched slam the head of a Jewish baby into the wall of a shower room. The baby had died instantly, his brain protruding and his blood spurting; they had laughed, full of triumph and swagger. Now they were too meek even to protect one of their own children. Nor did I intervene; these were people who had set me apart, told me I could not be one of them.

As I sat, eating my American rations, they begged me for food – some of them openly, others only with their eyes – but I did not respond, except once. A young German mother held a small child crying in her arms, a boy about one year old. His eyes were huge and glazed over, his arms and legs swung limply.

"Can't you help my baby?" she pleaded. "He's starving! Can't you help him?"

I thought of the broken baby in the shower room. Then I reached over and coaxed several bite-sized chunks of Spam directly into the child's mouth. He was innocent, this little boy, and I needed to do something to feel that I was still human.

It was late morning when the freight train pulled into the Schlesische Bahnhof Station in Berlin. I had no idea where I was going – the city was devastated and nothing looked familiar. Beside the shack that served as the stationmaster's office, I spied a Phoenix motorbike lying on its side. I turned the key and, to my surprise, there was enough gas in the tank to start it. That it did not belong to me meant nothing; the old order had crumbled and I had survived by just this kind of luck.

I had never driven a motorbike before and I fell a few times, but soon mastered it and began to make my way through the broken streets of Berlin. Tante Hedel's apartment was collapsed in ruins; Anne Dudacy's stood, but it was empty, its windows broken. The billiard hall still stood, but it was under different management. None of the familiar faces remained. There was no trace of my mother, no trace of anyone I knew. That night I slept out in the street. I tied myself to the bike with my jacket; it was now mine, and I would protect it.

The next morning, not far from where the Dudacys had lived, I finally got lucky. I spotted Frau Janick, the middle-aged daughter of Herr Pieck, the old boarder in our apartment on Greifswalder Strasse through whom we had met Tante Hedel and Anne Dudacy so very long ago. She did not recognize me at first, but when I repeated who I was, she rubbed her eyes in disbelief. "Lothar, Lothar Orbach, you are alive! I can't believe it, thank God! Your dear mother must be beside herself!"

My heart started to pound. "You know where she is?"

"You haven't seen her yet? They've all moved to Reinickendorf in the Weisse Stadt. There's no phone yet, but I know the address, it's Romanshorner Weg, number 26, I think." I didn't hear anything else she said.

The Weisse Stadt, the White City, how ironic. This sprawling development of attractive apartments on the outskirts of Berlin, so named because of their uniform whitewashed facades, had been built for the Nazi leadership and their families. Now it housed the bombed-out refugees of Berlin. As I drove up to the edge of the development, a serious-faced Soviet officer stopped me and asked to see my papers. It was soon obvious that I was not the legal owner of the motorbike, and my protests were no match for his automatic rifle. He gave me some meaningless receipt written in Russian, and once again I was a pedestrian.

I trudged up the Reinickendorfer Strasse, still emaciated, still weak, and sometimes feeling disassociated from my surroundings. But my brain was clear, I was utterly focused: I was going to find my mother. At Romanshorner 26, I walked up one flight, and my eyes locked onto a handprinted sign on the door that said, simply, "Orbach."

It was the most beautiful sign I had ever seen. It meant I had a name again, and a home – and a mother.

I could scarcely breathe as I rang the bell, but there was no answer. After several more tries, I knocked on the door of the apartment directly across the hall. A woman opened it, and stared at me and the number on my jacket. "Oh, good heavens, you must be the son!" she exclaimed.

"Yes. Do you know where my mother is?"

"I think she went to a town meeting of the Weisse Stadt committee. That's your mother, always involved, what a nice neighbor. Would you like to come in and wait?"

"No, thank you, I think I'll just sit out here on the stairs."

"You know, her best friends, the Dudacys, live right in the next building."

I asked her not to say anything to my mother, and flew next door. It was Anne who answered the bell. Anne, usually so gruff, so in control, was speechless. She clawed at me, touched me all over as if to make sure I was real. And then came Sylvia, and the two of them together, still without words, hugged me fiercely. Then the words flew out in a torrent. Anne was in the flush of triumph; her political dreams had finally been realized, as she and her sisters were all activists in a newly reorganized Communist party. Her husband was still in a prisoner of war camp in England, but none the worse for wear. They had news of some of our common acquaintances, but of no one with whom I was really close. Tad, Erika, Kitty, Opa, it was as though the earth had swallowed them up.

Sylvia was more beautiful and desirable than ever, yet, as we clung to each other, I knew that my initial feeling about the two of us had been correct. I belonged to another people, and we had no future together. But I would love these two extraordinary women all my life.

As thrilling as this reunion was, I could not keep my thoughts from the sign that said "Orbach" and I decided to go back and camp out on my mother's doorstep to await her return. But when I rang the doorbell once again, there she stood, Nelly Orbach, not even five feet tall, but the most welcome sight I had ever seen. We screamed and hugged each other, laughing and sobbing uncontrollably. I picked her up, she was so tiny and so light, I swung her around and then sat her down on the kitchen table.

"I knew you would make it, my Lotharchen!" she said over and over. "I prayed to God every hour of the day, I never gave up, I knew you would make it!"

My brothers had already spotted my name among the living on a Red Cross list, but it would take several weeks more for them to arrive in the Weisse Stadt. Both of them were in uniform, working for U.S. Army Intelligence somewhere in the Western part of Germany. Heinz, short but powerfully built, still had the cocky strut of the young leader I had idolized during my childhood. Manfred had inherited all of Father's smoky good looks. For two days straight, there was laughter and tears and rejoicing, and very little sleep. My brothers said that when I was ready, there was a place for me in the intelligence unit, and, later on, we would all go to America. Heinz was married and living in New Jersey. He could get me a job as a clothes cutter in the factory where he was a foreman.

I spent my last months in Germany as a member of a U.S. Army Intelligence team, MIS detachment 914, and was cited by the commanding officer for my role as an expert investigator and interrogator in the apprehension of a score of Nazi war criminals, some of them well known. I was grateful for the chance to be involved in a small way in the process of retribution. To look into the eyes of those who had committed or knew of Nazi atrocities and see the deadness and utter defeat of their insane vision for all of us was some compensation for what they had done to me, my family, and my world. Many of us, millions of us, we would learn, had been murdered but some of us had prevailed and would remember what had been, what should have been, and what instead had happened.

There was one final bit of business I needed to attend to before I left: I had to visit Siegfried Goldstein, who had pointed the finger at me and at Horst Atlass, and doubtless many others. He was among the few traitors who succeeded in surviving the war – he and the notorious Stella had managed to save themselves after all. I took with me a new acquaintance from my neighborhood, a hulking young fellow who could step in if Goldstein offered any resistance.

Goldstein's mother answered the door, and I told her I was an old schoolmate of her son's. When he saw me, his face went white, he began to tremble, and he tried to convince me that he was innocent, that he was the victim of some kind of rumor. My friend and I, after we had pushed him around a bit, dragged him to the nearest Russian compound, where we managed to persuade a Russian officer, Patkolkownik Schneidermann, who happened also to be a Jew, to arrest and book him as a Nazi informer.

Siegfried Goldstein was probably released shortly thereafter; my retaliation was only a token gesture, a small, insignificant act. But the fact that it was a score settled, no matter how trivial in the larger scheme of things, relieved me of a burden, and helped me close the book on a long nightmare. Together with my job collecting evidence against war criminals, it inoculated me against the poison of hatred and the obsession with revenge that might otherwise have dominated my thoughts and motives. In spite of everything, I now had other things to dwell on besides yesterday. Indeed, I had tomorrow, and a promising new life.

That new life began on September 1, 1946, as my mother and I boarded the *S.S. Marine Marlin* at Bremerhaven, bound for the United States.

Epilogue

During our last months in Germany, I spent a good deal of time searching for news of my friends. Berlin had been so badly damaged that many addresses no longer existed. In the eight months between my arrest on August 25, 1944, and my return in April 1945, people and places had simply vanished. My finds were few, my losses many.

In Charlottenburg, the Schelonkas cheered my return and embraced me warmly when they learned my true identity. Unfortunately, they still knew nothing of the final days or of the final resting place of the noble Hans Scheidt.

Frau Grueger, it turned out, had had a secret after all; in her little flat above the bakery, this courageous lady had been helping and harboring many Jews. One of them, Inge Deutschkron, emigrated to Israel and became a noted author and journalist. Another, a man by the name of Dr. Muentzer, she eventually married.

The building that had housed Kitty's bordello was a shambles, and no one knew anything of her whereabouts. If she were alive, she had probably found a different line of work, since women were now selling themselves on the streets for crusts of bread. If Etienne lived, he was probably back in France with his family. Frau Schreiner, who had provided us with meat, and who had hidden my mother for a time in her office, had also disappeared. But Philippe, who had been captured, had survived concentration camp, and subsequently made a life for himself in America.

I never saw Erika again but, years later, I learned that she had survived the war after all, and was living somewhere in Europe.

Nor could I ever find Tad. My best friend seemed to have vanished. Even in the billiard hall, they knew nothing of the legend of Tad Vronski. The building where he and Ilse and Trudy had all lived had been destroyed. I never saw or heard of him again, but in years to come I would often imagine that I'd spotted him whenever I saw a handsome, golden-haired young man in a magazine advertisement, in a Manhattan nightclub, on the deck of a cruise ship beneath the stars – all the kinds of places he could and should have been. After a while, I realized none of them could be him; the men I noticed were always young, beautiful and young, the way Tad had looked in his prime. If he were still alive, he would no longer look so young, but he has stayed that way forever in my mind's eye.

Sylvia, however, married happily and had children and grandchildren, her husband a senior military officer.

Before we left for America, I wanted once more to see our old apartment on the Greifswalder Strasse. The first time I went there, a frightened man refused to open the door. Then I went through the courtyard to pay my respects to Else Mueller, the angel who had hidden my mother and me from the Gestapo on that fateful Christmas eve of 1942. A young woman came to the door. She said she had heard that Frau Mueller had died in early 1943, several months after she had enabled our escape. Years later, after the fall of the Berlin Wall, I tried again. This time a different man let me come in. After nearly five decades of Nazi and Communist occupation, there was nothing there that had ever belonged to us. The apartment was filthy and seemed much smaller than I remembered. It felt alien, and I could not believe it had ever been the home of the Orbach family.

Days before we sailed for America, I learned the fate of Opa Simon. Not long after my arrest, he had been found by the police murdered in his apartment. His mouth had been sealed with surgical tape with a potato stuffed inside. I was sure that this could only be the work of Martin. I was unable to gain access to Opa's hellhole on the Lange Strasse, where I had hoped to unearth the thick wad of bills that might still have been hidden beneath the rotted floorboard of his closet, and the diary I had kept during of most of my twenty months living underground.

I was particularly dismayed over the loss of the diary, which had chronicled the events and my thoughts of some of the worst – and, dare I say, a few of the best – times of my life. "It doesn't matter, Lotharchen," said my mother, philosophically. "I'm sure you will remember everything."

And so I have. Not everything, perhaps, but certainly what was most important. And, years later, when I read the diary of another German teenager – a diary that survived while its author perished – I was grateful that I, unlike Anne Frank, had been able to bask in the forbidden sun, to roam the forbidden streets, and even to taste forbidden fruits.

Most of all, I am grateful to have lived to tell my own story, in my own voice, half a century after it all happened.

Provisional identification card
for civilian internee of Buchenwald.

Vorläufige Identitätskarte für Buchenwälder Zivilinternierte.

Current number ...1020...   Internee number ...95780...
Laufende Nr.   *Häftlings-Nr.* Auschwitz

Family name ...O r b a c h , Nr. B. 9761...
Familienname

Christian name ...Lothar...
Vorname

Born ..22.5.24.....   at ...Falkenburg...
geboren .... *in*

Nationality ..Staatenlos Jude...
Nationalität

Adress ...Berlin...
Adresse

Fingerprint:
Fingerabdruck

Signature:
Unterschrift

Arthur Orbach

Bestätigt d. Unterschrift jeder des deutsch.Komitees.

Weimar-Buchenwald, am ...17.5.1945...

Ausweis — Certification.

Herr ...O r b a c h , Lothar...
Mister

geb. am ..22.5.24.— in Falkenburg -
born   *at*

zuletzt wohnhaft. ..Berlin...
last domicile

wurde vom ...1.9.44...   bis ...11.4.1945...
in nationalsozialistischen Konzentrationslagern gefangen
gehalten und vom Konzentrationslager Buchenwald
bei Weimar in Freiheit gesetzt.

*was kept in captivity from ..1.9.44...   to ..11.4.1945..
in Nazi-German concentrationcamps and was liberated from the
concentrationcamp of Buchenwald.*

Unterschrift und Stempel:
signature and stamp:

O F F I C I A L
BUCHENWALD Camp Advisory Force
The former inmates

Lagerkomitee
Camp-Comitee

Military Camp commandant Off.

Weimar-Buchenwald, am ...17.5.1945...

Acknowledgments

My thanks must begin with the most "Righteous Gentiles," the four Richter sisters–Anne Dudacy, Hedel Pauli, Angela Ciupka, Marie Krueger–and their daughters, Sylvia, Wanda Krueger, and Femi Lindemann. They risked their own lives so that my mother and I might live, and without their protection this book could not have been written.

The only living member of this family, Sylvia, was a pillar of support at the time, and has since helped me reconstruct those underground years and restore many details I would have lost.

Katharina Ziebura of the Berlin Senate introduced me to Dr. Klaus Dettmer of the Landes Archiv, who did much research on my behalf, and to film maker Klaus Kowalke, whose interest in putting my story on the screen lent encouragement and focus to my writing. My publisher, Dean Howells, gave editorial support as well as his commitment. I thank Nat Bodian for his sage advice, and I am grateful to an old friend, the late Herman Roth, whose enthusiasm over my story gave me the confidence to continue, even though the first draft did not impress his literary son, Philip, whom he insisted should read it.

Thanks to my son, Ricky, who introduced me to the world of the computer without which I could not have undertaken such a task; my son-in-law, Richard Smith, for his assistance in my research for this book; and above all to the love and support of my wife and helpmate, Ruth Geier Orbach.

Finally, I thank my co-author, my daughter Vivien Orbach-Smith, for applying her talent as a writer, her passion for truth and justice, and the loving heart of a daughter.

– Larry Orbach

When my father asked me to help edit his manuscript, I wanted to cover my eyes and run. It wasn't an aversion to grim tales of the Holocaust for I had read a lot of them, but this time the tattooed arm would be the one that had rocked my cradle. Did I have the stomach to know what Daddy had done, what had been done to him? I was frightened of the truth, the uncensored facts; and yet—as a daughter, a writer, a Jew—I knew I had to face them. And so I did, never imagining how rewarding it would be to lift the veil that exists between so many survivors and their children.

My first acknowledgment is to my father; the extraordinarily frank manuscript he gave me was a diamond in the rough, and I am honored that he asked me to polish it.

Voices of the Holocaust survivors who surrounded me as I grew up—obsessed with life, not death—are echoed in this book. And there are images drawn from the faces of my own children—innocent, hopeful, trusting—that could be those of Lothar and his friends or any of the 1.5 million Jewish children who died in the Holocaust.

My thanks to our publisher, Dean Howells, who has helped a long-held dream become reality. Thanks to John W. Wright for his early advice, and my heartfelt gratitude to my colleague, Mary W. Quigley, the most generous of writers, and one of a circle of cherished friends who encouraged me throughout.

I am grateful to the Smith clan, for providing the support that enabled a busy mom to take on such a demanding task. Above all, I am eternally grateful to my mother, Ruth, my brother, Ricky, and my husband, Richard, each of whom sustains me and from each of whom I draw strength and inspiration.

– Vivien Orbach-Smith

DATE DUE

GAYLORD			PRINTED IN U.S.A.

BERLIN

Reinickendorf

Pankow

Weissensee

Hohenschönhausen

ENLARGED AREA

Spandau

Wedding

Prenzlauer Berg

Tiergarten

Marzahn

Charlottenburg

Mitte

Friedrichshain

Kreuzberg

Lichtenberg

Hellersdorf

Wilmersdorf

Dahlem

Zehlendorf

Steglitz

Neukölln

Treptow

Köpenick

Tempelhof

1   Ursula's and Hansi's house in Dahlem Dorf

2   Hans Scheidt's apartment, the Dietrichs' apartment, and the Schelonkas' office